RICHARD VEATCH is a member of the Department of Political Science at the University of Winnipeg.

Canada's participation in the Paris Peace Conference after the First World War and its consequent membership in the new world organization of the League of Nations were important stages in the development of Canadian autonomy. This study of Canadian international diplomacy in its first twenty years treats the subject both from a national point of view - what was Ottawa hoping to achieve? - and an international one - how did external events affect Canadian policy? The focus is mainly on political and security aspects of Canadian objectives and reactions - the framing of the Covenant, the shapers of Canadian policies particularly in regard to collective security and minorities, and Canada's role in the Manchurian and Ethiopian disputes that broke up the League - but it also includes an account of a largely forgotten episode: an appeal to the League from the Six Nation Indians against Canada.

The study is based largely on archival sources recently opened in Ottawa and Geneva, and on the personal papers of those involved, including Walter A. Riddell. The activities and influence of O.D. Skelton are also described. It is hoped that this book will serve as the standard work on the topic of Canada's first steps on the formal international stage.

RICHARD VEATCH

Canada and the League of Nations

UNIVERSITY OF TORONTO PRESS
Toronto and Buffalo

© University of Toronto Press 1975
Toronto and Buffalo
Printed in Canada

Library of Congress Cataloging in Publication Data
Veatch, Richard, 1926–
Canada and the League of Nations.
Bibliography: p.
Includes index.
1. League of Nations – Canada. I. Title.
JX1975.5.C2V43 341.22'71 75-19086
ISBN 0-8020-5331-9

To Lorraine

Contents

Preface

The decision at the Paris Peace Conference in 1919 to create an international organization, world-wide in its membership, with the primary purpose of preventing war, was a landmark in the development of relations between states. Canada's participation in the Peace Conference was likewise a landmark in the development of Canadian nationhood, as it brought Canada into its first formal diplomatic contact with the rest of the world, a contact that was to continue through Canada's membership in the new League of Nations.

The simultaneous beginnings of the world organization and of Canada's membership in the international community make particularly appropriate a study of the impact of Canada's League membership on the development of a Canadian foreign policy. Opportunity is also provided to examine the question of what impact the attitudes and policies of a smaller power, expressed through its participation in an international organization, may have on the course of international events.

The approach taken in this study has been to investigate the topic from both the national and the international standpoints. That is, Canadian policies are examined not only in terms of their domestic political origins, but also in terms of response to international pressures. The results of Canadian policies are viewed within the framework of Canadian national needs and expectations, and also in relation to their impact on the world-wide collective security system. Attention is concentrated on political and security aspects of Canadian policy, directly related to the League's primary objective of preserving the peace.

Research on Canadian foreign policy and the League of Nations would have been most difficult until recent years, because of the unavailability of the basic source materials. Now, however, the archives of the League of Nations, and of the Canadian Department of External Affairs for the period concerned, are available to researchers. Both were used extensively in preparing this work, and were invaluable sources of information. Together they provide a reasonably clear and complete account of Canadian activity at the League. Use was also made of the papers of various individuals involved in the formulation of Canadian foreign policy, the most important of which were perhaps the papers and diaries of Walter A. Riddell, head of the permanent Canadian office in Geneva from its founding in 1925 until 1937.

Published materials related to the topic are voluminous and highly informative in some cases, such as the texts of debates and minutes of committee meetings of the League, and the texts of Canadian parliamentary debates. In other instances, published materials are sketchy or nonexistent, as, for example, the absence of any adequate biography of Prime Minister R.B. Bennett or history of his government.

In general, however, the sources available, especially the unpublished materials, provided answers to the essential questions and made possible the completion, substantially along the lines originally contemplated, of a study of Canadian foreign policy and the League of Nations.

Many persons provided valuable assistance to the author in his use of unpublished materials, and through review and criticism of his manuscript. Gratitude is due in particular to Jacques Freymond, Director of the Graduate Institute of International Studies, Geneva, Switzerland; Jean Siotis and Mrs Marlis Steinert, professors at the Institute; Karl Birnbaum, professor at the University of Stockholm; Sven Welander, Chief, Historical Collections Section, United Nations Library, Geneva; Arthur E. Blanchette, Director, Historical Division, Department of External Affairs, Ottawa; Alex I. Inglis, formerly resident historian in the Division; John W. Holmes, Director General, Canadian Institute of International Affairs; and R.I.K. Davidson and Alison Adair, Editorial Department, University of Toronto Press.

Thanks are also due to Mrs Mary Craig Schuller for permission to quote from her correspondence with J.W. Dafoe; to Mrs Walter A. Riddell, for permission to quote from the diaries and papers of Walter A. Riddell; and to the following publishers for permission to quote excerpts from published works: The Macmillan Company of Canada Limited, *What's Past Is Prologue*, by Vincent Massey; Alfred A. Knopf, Inc., *Peace in Their Time*, by Emery Kelen; McGraw-Hill Ryerson Limited, *World Security by Conference*, by Walter A. Riddell; and Les Presses de l'Université Laval, *Les mémoires du Sénateur Raoul Dandurand*, edited by Marcel Hamelin.

    Research in Geneva and Ottawa was made possible by grants from the Canada Council and the University of Winnipeg. This book has been published with the help of a grant from the Social Science Research Council of Canada, using funds provided by the Canada Council, and a grant to the University of Toronto Press from the Andrew W. Mellon Foundation.

CANADA AND THE LEAGUE OF NATIONS

1
Canada's entry on
the international scene

When the League of Nations formally came into existence on 10 January 1920, with the coming into force of the Treaty of Versailles, included among its members were Canada and the other self-governing dominions of the British Empire. For Canada, as for the other dominions, membership in the League was a fact of major importance. For the first time Canada found itself in regular and continuing contact with non-British governments. For the first time it entered into international discussions and negotiations as a full and equal participant in its own right, rather than as a subordinate part of the British Empire. For the first time it was regularly called upon, in discussions and in voting, to state its position and take its stand on the international issues and controversies of the day. For Canada, the creation of the League of Nations and Canadian membership in it meant, in effect, that Canada, as a new actor on the international scene, now required a foreign policy. That foreign policy would necessarily be developed largely in the context of Canada's participation in League of Nations affairs.

Before the creation of the League, Canada had not, of course, been entirely out of contact with other governments, but, other than with Great Britain and the United States, that contact had been minimal. The Dominion of Canada had been formed in 1867, and soon included all of the British territories to the north of the United States, except Newfoundland. The Dominion, while remaining a part of the British Empire, was fully self-governing in internal matters, and controlled its own tariff and immigration policies. However, at the time of its formation it was taken for granted that the government in London had sole responsibility for the Empire's foreign policy, and no provision was made for the exercise of any responsibility in foreign affairs by the Canadian government.

In practice, however, Canadian involvement in relations with other governments grew substantially before the first world war. Beginning in 1887, Colonial Conferences, later called Imperial Conferences, were held periodically, bringing Canadian prime ministers and other officials into direct contact with government leaders of Great Britain and of the other self-governing parts of the Empire. Already in the 1880s a Canadian High Commissioner had been placed in London, and a Commissioner General's office had been opened in Paris. These two posts had no official diplomatic status, but served nevertheless as a means of contact with the British and French governments and with interested segments of the public, especially on trade and immigration matters. They were the only posts with even quasi-diplomatic functions that the Canadian government maintained outside of Canada until 1925.[1]

In addition to these continuing contacts abroad, the Canadian government with increasing frequency took part in negotiations with other governments on specific matters of common interest. Sometimes this took place because Canadian representatives were included in British delegations setting up commercial treaties, or on occasion the negotiating would be done entirely by Canadians. However, any treaties that resulted were with Great Britain, not Canada, and required the signature of British government representatives.

Outside of the British Empire Canadian contacts were most numerous and important with the United States, but no Canadian mission was established in Washington before the first world war. The first continuing official governmental contact between the two countries was through an International Joint Commission set up in 1911 for consultation primarily on questions related to the use of the Great Lakes. A wartime trade mission was established in Washington in 1918, and a Canadian trade representative remained there continuously thereafter. However, the regular channel for official communication between Ottawa and Washington was remarkably cumbersome: from the Canadian government to the Governor General in Ottawa (then the representative of the British government in Canada), from the Governor General to the Colonial Secretary in London, then to the Foreign Secretary, then to the British Ambassador in Washington, and finally from the British Ambassador to the United States Secretary of State.[2]

Notably absent from Canadian external contacts prior to the first world war, in addition to the treaty-making power and the right of legation, were involvement in decision-making on important political questions, except for sporadic consultations within the Empire. Though Canada's official contacts with governments other than that of Britain were increasingly frequent, they tended to deal only with questions of trade, tariffs, fisheries, immigration, and so on, which were of immediate but localized concern to Canada. Questions of high policy, of war and peace, were still the exclusive preserve of London. The Canadian government did not deal with 'foreign,' that is, non-British, governments on such matters, nor were its views ordinarily sought by London. It was, however, together with all other parts of the British Empire, bound by the decisions taken by London, as illustrated by Canada's entry into the first world war, which took place automatically in 1914 when Britain declared war on Germany.

The participation of Canada and the other dominions in the 1914-18 war led directly to a new international role for them. Before the war Sir Robert Borden, the Canadian prime minister, had already indicated interest in having a voice in Empire foreign policy, when pressed to contribute to Empire naval defence. Once the war had begun, Britain was anxious to obtain large-scale dominion military contributions. The dominion governments were willing, but some of them, including Canada, felt that in return they should be both informed and consulted on questions of wartime policy, to a degree much greater than had been customary before the war. This desire on the part of the dominions became stronger than ever as the war dragged on, and as the dominions became increasingly convinced that there were serious inadequacies in Britain's use of the manpower and materials that they provided. The result was the creation of the Imperial War Cabinet in 1917, on which both the dominions and the London government were represented, and which provided a means for continuing consultation with the dominions regarding the conduct of the war.[3]

As wartime planning was gradually succeeded by the drafting of the terms of the peace settlement, there was strong interest among the dominions to maintain the position they had achieved, and to be admitted as participants in the Peace Conference at Paris. In this they were successful, and Canada, Australia, New Zealand, South Africa, and India (even though the last was not self-governing, but a British colony) were given representation at the Conference. However, they were not represented as separate members in their own right, but as component parts of the British Empire.

Thus in 1919 Canada found itself for the first time a participant in a major international conference, seeking solutions to the most important international political questions of the day. It was soon apparent, however, that substantial decision-making would be almost exclusively in the hands of the major powers. The Canadian representatives, nevertheless, at least were present and able to make their views known to Britain and the other large powers, on any matters of special interest to Canada.

The Canadian delegation was headed by Sir Robert Borden, the Prime Minister and Secretary of State for External Affairs. It included three other cabinet ministers: C.J. Doherty, Minister of Justice; Sir George Foster, Minister of Trade and Commerce; and A.L. Sifton, Minister of Customs and Inland Revenue.[4] In general, the Canadian delegation's interest in the major political controversies at the Peace Conference was minimal. It was, however, very much interested in the structure and functions of the new international organization, the League of Nations, which the Peace Conference was setting up, and especially in the position which Canada would have in the organization. The specific aspects of the League in which the Canadian government took an interest and regarding which it attempted to influence the major powers' decisions were indicative of Canadian policy toward and within the League for many years to come.

In the first place, of course, the government wanted Canada to be a member of the League, thereby preserving and continuing the new international role which it had just found for itself. This proved not to be controversial at the Peace Conference (though it was to be much criticized later by opponents of the League in the United States) and Canada, the other self-governing dominions, and India were all accepted as original members of the League of Nations.

Secondly, the Canadian government wanted for Canada a position within the League in no way inferior to that of any other League member. This proved more difficult to obtain, because of the ambiguity of the dominions' relationship with Britain. The 'British Empire' was to be a permanent member of the League Council and of the Governing Body of the International Labour Organization, both key policy-making bodies with limited membership. Did the British Empire's membership automatically include the dominions as component parts of the Empire, or were they also eligible for separate membership themselves? Borden insisted that the latter must be the answer, as otherwise the status of Canada and the other dominions in the organization would be inferior to that of all its other members.

With regard to dominion eligibility for election to a non-permanent seat on the League Council, Borden pressed Canada's views on the British delegation, and on 1 May 1919 he discussed the question with President Wilson, who 'entirely agreed with the view that representatives of the Dominions [were] so eligible.'[5] Not satisfied with informal assurances to this effect, Borden succeeded in getting David Lloyd George, the British prime minister, to take the matter up officially with the United States and France. On being told that his view as to Canada's eligibility was accepted, but that no change in the language of the League Covenant was considered necessary 'as the rights of the Dominions were adequately safeguarded upon a fair construction of its terms,' Borden insisted that this view be expressed in writing.[6] He prepared a memorandum stating specifically that, under the existing language of the Covenant, the dominions were eligible for election to the Council and on 6 May 1919 he obtained the signatures to the memorandum of Clemenceau, Wilson, and Lloyd George. Certainly no more authoritative interpreters of the Covenant could have been found.[7]

Essentially the same situation existed with regard to Canadian eligibility for the ILO Governing Body. However, the problem was made more difficult by the fact that the initially proposed treaty language specifically denied Dominion eligibility: 'No member, together with its Dominions and Colonies, whether self-governing or not, shall be entitled to nominate more than one member.'[8] An interpretation would not suffice; the language itself would have to be changed. In this case also, Borden persuaded Lloyd George to take the matter up with the United States and France. It was agreed on 28 April that Borden should get in touch with the British, American, and French labour experts at the Conference, and if he could get their agreement the treaty language would be changed.[9] The next day Borden met with the American representative, but found him unwilling to agree to Canadian eligibility.[10] A.L. Sifton reported that the Japanese and Italians were opposed to dominion eligibility and he vehemently denounced their attitude, anticipating, he said, that Canadian labour representatives 'will see the Japanese and Italian delegates and their respective governments individually and collectively sizzling in the lowest depths of Hell before they will agree to accept a standing inferior to the negroes of Liberia.'[11] Sifton was also highly critical of the lack of support from Britain on 'a matter apparently of such slight interest to the Government of Great Britain as the future status of the Dominion of Canada.'[12]

Borden's reaction to the apparent impasse concerning Canadian eligibility for the ILO Governing Body was no less extreme. On 29 April he wrote Lloyd George, recounting his meeting with the American labour expert and threatening, if the situation were not remedied, to give notice immediately after ratification of the peace treaty of Canada's withdrawal from the League of Nations, 'in order that Canada ... may also withdraw from the Labour Convention and thus avoid the continuance of a condition which her people will naturally regard as humiliating.'[13] On 1 May Borden discussed this matter also with Woodrow Wilson, together with the question of Canadian eligibility for the League Council. Wilson was sympathetic, but unwilling to make the commitment Borden desired. 'So far as Canada is concerned he would have no difficulty whatever; but he explained that there was considerable difficulty with respect to some other Dominions and especially India.' Borden insisted to Lloyd George that the offending language must be removed from the treaty, urged Lloyd George to pursue the matter, and said he would otherwise make a public reservation to Canada's acceptance of the peace treaty at the plenary session of the Peace Conference.[14]

When still no action was forthcoming, Borden repeated his earlier threat to withdraw from the League and the ILO, at a meeting of the British Empire delegations on 5 May.[15] Lloyd George agreed to take up the question the next day, and after doing so informed Borden that (Borden's words), 'the obnoxious clause in the Labour Convention would be struck out.'[16] In reporting this success to his ministers in Ottawa, Borden considered Wilson's attitude to have been determining: 'President Wilson has acted extremely well in this respect as he overrode advice of his Labour experts.'[17]

In addition to questions involving Canada's status and rights as a League member, the Canadian government was interested in certain broad questions of future League policy. Here the Canadian delegation found it more difficult to make its views felt, as the British government invited the dominions to confer only with regard to their position in the League, and not with regard to substantive matters.[18] This was, of course, frustrating to the Canadians. Thus when Sifton was authorized by Britain to take part in negotiating Canadian membership in the ILO, he considered it 'the first tangible evidence of a recognition of the rights of Canadians to be alive.'[19]

A disagreement of some consequence arose when Borden learned that Britain, without consulting the Dominions, had agreed to treaty language respecting labour conditions to which the Canadian government objected.[20] The language objected to would have embodied in the peace treaty the principle of equality of rights for immigrant workers, a principle in conflict with restrictions on Oriental labour in effect in the provinces of British Columbia and Saskatchewan. (The clause read: 'In all matters concerning their status as workers and social insurance, foreign workmen lawfully admitted to any country and their families should be ensured the same treatment as the nationals of that country.'[21]) Borden's opposition was somewhat hysterical in tone. Inclusion of the clause, he said, 'might lead to great disorder, possibly rebellion on the Pacific Coast of the United States and of Canada.'[22] The question, he recorded, became 'a subject of continual and irritating discussion' between the British and Canadian representatives.[23] It was agreed, however, that Borden should negotiate the matter directly with the other interested delegations. He met with United States, Japanese, Belgian, and British representatives, and obtained their agreement to a revision in the wording of the objectionable clause which left it entirely innocuous. (The revised clause read: 'The standard set by law in each country with respect to the conditions of labour should have due regard to the equitable economic treatment of all workers lawfully resident therein.'[24])

By far the most ambitious attempt made by Canada to alter the substance of the peace treaty, however, was the effort to delete Article 10 from the proposed Covenant of the League of Nations. In this effort, Canada was challenging a major aspect of United States policy, as President Wilson was the prime author of Article 10 and considered it of crucial importance. It contained the basic guarantee by each League member, in the wording eventually agreed upon, 'to respect and preserve as against external aggression the territorial integrity and existing political independence of all Members of the League.' It embodied one of the basic ideas on which the proposed new collective security system was to be founded: a universal guarantee to all members against aggressive attack, and if such an attack nevertheless came, a universal guarantee to join in repelling the aggressor. If this principle were successfully translated into practice, the knowledge that an attack against one member would be dealt with as an attack against all should effectively accomplish the essential purpose of the League, to prevent aggressions and thereby prevent war. If an aggressor, even though faced with such overwhelming odds against success, did nevertheless attack, the system should assure the aggressor's defeat and thereby discourage such attempts in the future. When Canada, then, opposed Article 10 and sought its deletion from the League Covenant, it was seeking not a minor change in wording, but an abandonment of one of the most fundamental aspects of the new system.

The Canadian government's objections to Article 10 were emphatic from the beginning. Doherty, the Minister of Justice, in a memorandum to Lord Robert Cecil in January 1919 insisted that 'the obligation to *guarantee* boundaries ... goes far beyond what the members of the League should be called upon to undertake. It should be restricted to the agreement to respect the boundaries referred to.'[25] In February, Doherty resumed the attack, sending a detailed analysis and condemnation of the article to Borden and the other Canadian delegates. Article 10, he said, quoting the London *Times*, would make of the League 'a mutual guarantee society of unlimited liability.' It would bind all League members to preserve all existing territorial holdings, and might well involve them 'in all the horrors of wars in which they have no interest, in order to ensure respect for decisions in which they had no part.' It was exceedingly improbable that other security guarantees in the Covenant would ever become operative, because of procedural requirements most unlikely to be fulfilled, Doherty said. In contrast, the obligation in Article 10 was direct and absolute, and clearly bound League members to military action.[26]

Doherty's position was concurred in by Borden, who on 13 March 1919, in a detailed commentary on the proposed League Covenant, distributed to the members of the League of Nations Commission of the Peace Conference, recommended that Article 10 'be struck out or materially amended.' He emphasized the unreasonableness of a blanket declaration '(a) that all existing territorial delimitations are just and expedient, (b) that they will continue indefinitely to be just and expedient, (c) that the Signatories will be responsible therefor ... There may be national aspirations to which the provisions of the Peace Treaty will not do justice and which cannot be permanently repressed.'[27]

Canada was not represented on the League of Nations Commission, and Borden's views appear to have received only slight attention, though they were later cited by David Hunter Miller, the legal adviser to the United States delegation, as having constituted the most forcible argument which was presented in opposition to Article 10.[28] On 28 March Cecil, the British member of the Commission, wrote Borden that 'I am not quite happy about this Article, but I was unable to persuade my colleagues on the Commission to agree to its alteration.'[29]

The question was raised again by Doherty and Borden on 21 April at a meeting of the British Empire delegates. Both said again that they thought Article 10 should be omitted, Doherty emphasizing that it was unjust 'to throw the same obligation upon young, undeveloped countries as upon long-established and wealthy States.'[30] Cecil at this point defended Article 10, although it was Borden's understanding that he did not personally approve it, but reassured Borden that Canada could not, under the Covenant, be required to take part in any military expedition without its consent. Borden apparently considered the matter settled after this discussion, though he was still unhappy with the article, which he thought presented special difficulties for 'countries like the United States and Canada, not closely interested in territorial disputes in Central and Western Europe.'[31]

There were no other aspects of the League Covenant which Borden actively attempted to change. His record was one of substantial success on matters which were of special interest to Canada but of limited importance to the major powers. Thus he obtained for Canada full rights of election to the League Council and the ILO Governing Body, and got rid of language seeking to regulate labour standards for immigrant workers. But in the one proposal he sponsored which was of great general importance to the new League of Nations, the proposed deletion of Article 10, he was entirely unsuccessful. The attempt was by no means abandoned, however, and a new effort at deletion of the article was launched by Doherty at the first meeting of the League Assembly in 1920 (see Chapter 5).

The interests and activities of Borden and the other Canadian delegates during this first appearance of Canada on the international scene set a pattern that was to be followed for years to come, through various changes of government in Ottawa. In the first place, the government had a great interest in the League of Nations as a vehicle for establishing Canada's status as a sovereign power internationally, a status which before 1919 had in no sense existed. Secondly, there was a marked unwillingness to submit to any regulation or control by the new international organization in areas, such as labour standards or immigration, which were already within the Canadian government's jurisdiction. Third, there was an almost total lack of interest in the main purposes of the League of Nations as an agency to prevent war, as contrasted with its usefulness in promoting Canada's international status. This indifference was converted into active hostility in the case of Article 10, which was seen as involving Canada unwillingly in dangerous and undesirable commitments to other states.

This combination of attitudes confronted Canadian decision-makers with a dilemma that characterized Canadian policy regarding the League of Nations for many years to come. The Canadian government's general lack of interest in the development of a working collective security system, its opposition to any firm and specific commitments to aid a victim of aggression, and its fear of meddling by the League in what it considered its domestic affairs might ordinarily, as in the case of the United States after 1920, have led it to reject League membership and adopt a policy of isolation. Pressing it in the opposite direction, however, was the opportunity presented by League membership, and full participation in League activities, to accomplish the much desired goal of achieving for Canada a place in the international state system. The decision of the Borden government, successfully carried out, was to give first priority to the attaining of a new international status. Canada obtained the same membership and rights in the League of Nations as fully sovereign states long accustomed to conducting their own foreign relations. But along with this new international status, and inextricably tied in with it, came commitments and obligations, and regular involvement in international political crises, wherever they might arise. Attempts to accommodate a basically isolationist attitude to the international commitments and involvement which unavoidably accompanied League of Nations membership, and response to pressures generated by League membership which tended to break down Canadian isolationism, were the main themes of Canadian policy toward the League over the next two decades.

2

The formulation of policy:
cabinet ministers and civil servants

Throughout the period between the two world wars, the formulation and implementation of Canadian foreign policy was clearly dominated by the Canadian prime ministers. During these years the prime ministers were their own foreign ministers, the office of Secretary of State for External Affairs being combined by law with that of Prime Minister from 1912 to 1946. No other political official in the Canadian government had a continuing responsibility for foreign affairs, but foreign affairs were, of course, only sporadically the major centre of the prime minister's interest and attention. One notable result was a certain lack of continuity and consistency in the attention given to foreign policy, and in the effective control exercised over it. This was true with regard to foreign policy in general, as well as policy concerning the League of Nations specifically. The prime ministers dominated the scene, when interested and active; at other times other officials, for example, cabinet members representing Canada at League of Nations meetings in Geneva on a one-time basis, or the External Affairs Department's permanent representative at Geneva, spoke for Canada. To what extent they were representing a well-developed Canadian policy and to what extent their own personal views was not always clear.

The prime ministers themselves varied greatly in degree of interest, as well as in attitude, toward foreign affairs. During this period, only four men held the office of Prime Minister. These prime ministers and their political affiliations were as follows: Sir Robert Borden, Conservative, 1911-20; Arthur Meighen, Conservative, 1920-21; W.L. Mackenzie King, Liberal, 1921-26; Arthur Meighen, Conservative, 1926; W.L. Mackenzie King, Liberal, 1926-30; Richard B. Bennett, Conservative, 1930-35; W.L. Mackenzie King, Liberal, 1935-48.

As already described, the government headed by Sir Robert Borden in 1919-20 took the lead in insisting on full Canadian participation in the Peace Conference, and on full membership in the League of Nations and the International Labour Organization. Borden personally headed the Peace Conference delegation and gave most of his attention to foreign policy during 1919. His attitude toward the League of Nations at that time is clearly revealed in the published documents of the Department of External Affairs,[1] and in his memoirs, based on diaries kept at the time but not published until after his death in 1937.[2] His interest in the structure and functions of the League of Nations was high, but essentially negative, as detailed in Chapter 1. He saw the League as a useful and important vehicle for enhancing Canada's international status; he tended to view its broader purposes, and the obligations they entailed, with indifference or hostility.

Back in Ottawa as prime minister, Borden sponsored Canada's acceptance of the peace treaties and of League membership, calling a special session of parliament to which the treaties were submitted, and by which they were approved. However, because of ill health he never resumed full control of Canadian policy, domestic or foreign, and after extended periods of leave from his duties, he resigned as prime minister in July 1920, and retired from parliament in 1921.

Borden's interest in the League continued throughout his subsequent career. When a League of Nations Society was formed in Canada in 1921, he served as its first president, continuing in that post till 1925, and participating actively in speaking tours on behalf of the League. In 1930, at the age of 76, he headed the Canadian delegation to the meetings of the League Council and Assembly in Geneva. By then he was looked on, not too accurately, almost as one of the founding fathers of the organization. No other Canadian prime minister, in any case, either while in office or afterwards, was as closely identified with or as actively interested in the League and its affairs as was Borden.

Borden's successor, Arthur Meighen, also a Conservative and a member of the Borden cabinet since 1915, had not been active with regard to foreign policy matters before becoming prime minister. The delegation which his government sent to the First Assembly of the League in 1920 was unusually energetic and outspoken, but Meighen's personal interest in the League was minimal. Sir George Foster, an advocate of the League in Meighen's cabinet, has recorded, for example, that, with regard to the second League Assembly in 1921, Meighen 'seemed to think that one representative was enough, and that the agenda did not seem to be very important.' Foster found that there was among the majority of the cabinet 'little comprehension of and scant favour for the League.'[3] Meighen did find it useful, however, in opposing renewal of the Anglo-Japanese alliance at the Prime Ministers Conference of 1921, to criticize the alliance as incompatible with the aims and authority of the League.[4]

Following his retirement as prime minister and as Conservative party leader in 1926, Meighen showed some sporadic concern with Canada's policy toward collective security and the League, but his main orientation was toward maintaining diplomatic unity within the British Empire and harmonious policies between Britain and the United States.[5] At times these interests coincided in such a way as to lead him to publicly champion the League, as, for example, in a speech in Washington, DC, in November 1930, when he advocated collective security within a universal League of Nations.[6]

In the general election of 1921, Meighen and his party were defeated and the leader of the Liberal party, W.L. Mackenzie King, became prime minister. King continued in office till 1930, except for three months in 1926, and again was prime minister from 1935 until his retirement in 1948. He was the dominant Canadian political figure in the years between the two world wars, and his views, more than those of any other individual, determined the course of Canadian foreign policy in that period. His attitudes toward Canada's international role, and toward the League of Nations, were complex and often not what they at first glance seemed to be.

King was no less interested than Borden had been in establishing a separate and distinct international status for Canada and was, in addition, determined not to be bound by a common British Empire foreign policy, however that policy might be formulated. With Borden and with Meighen, there was always a certain ambiguity as to whether the ultimate goal would be a fully independent international role for Canada, or an equal role with Great Britain in determining a unified British Empire foreign policy. During King's tenure as prime minister, that particular ambiguity was resolved: a fully independent status became the goal, and it was a goal which he pursued with great skill until it had been achieved. From this it was quite often assumed, quite incorrectly, especially by advocates of a unified Empire foreign policy, that King had rejected British leadership in foreign policy and was insistent on formulating policies of his own. His position was, in fact, more subtle than that, and more complicated. What he had rejected was any obligation to follow either British policy or a unified Empire policy, while leaving open the possibility that he might, if he wished, choose to do so in specific cases. And indeed he did so choose in certain important instances, most notably in the great crises of war and peace in 1938-9, when he first gave full support to British Prime Minister Neville Chamberlain in his policy of appeasement, and then ultimately gave equally full support when Chamberlain reversed that policy. Perhaps the most illuminating illustration of the relationship which King had established with Britain was Canada's 'independent' declaration of war against Germany in September 1939. Canada declared war at that particular time only because Britain had, not because of any separate dispute or obligation of its own; but Canada followed Britain by its own choice, not because it was committed or obliged to do so.

If any one phrase could sum up Mackenzie King's foreign policy, that phrase would be 'no commitments.' Above all else he sought to avoid any advance commitments as to the position or action that Canada would take in any future political controversy. His attempt to avoid advance commitments was applied equally to commitments to Britain and the Empire, commitments to the League of Nations and its members, or commitments to the Canadian parliament and public. In so far as possible, he confined himself to platitudinous generalities, statements that his government would make its position known at the appropriate time, and warnings that any public discussion of current international problems might make their solution more difficult. What he sought, in effect, was complete freedom of action for himself as prime minister, freedom to follow any policy he might choose, subject only to the political necessities of the moment.

This approach to foreign policy was exceptionally difficult to reconcile with Canadian membership and participation in the League of Nations, as the League had been founded for the primary purpose of providing specific and firm advance commitments of assistance to victims of aggression. King was thus confronted with the same dilemma Borden had faced at the Peace Conference in 1919, but in an intensified form. He was insistent on Canadian participation in League affairs, as an indication of Canada's new international status. Moreover, a generalized support of the League, as an organization seeking to prevent war, fitted in well with his interest in being identified with commendable, but non-controversial, policy objectives. On the other hand, he not only objected to Article 10 of the Covenant, but also to any and all attempts to get League members to make new policy commitments or to consider themselves firmly bound by old ones.

In these circumstances, King's attitude toward the League of Nations was, to say the least, equivocal. His public statements were generally favourable in tone, and often also self-congratulatory about Canada's contributions, as when he told the House of Commons in 1929:

In the first place, Canada perhaps as much as any country in the world is united in its efforts to further the work of the League of Nations. It is united in that effort because this country holds strongly to the cause of peace and desires to see peace furthered not only within its own borders but amongst the nations of the world. We who are supporting so splendidly the work of the league in all its activities will wish to see that work strengthened and furthered as it will be by a treaty such as the one [the Kellogg-Briand Pact] which is now before the house.[7]

In private also, King on occasion expressed a somewhat sentimental and generalized support for the League, as, for example, in a letter to a friend in the United States in October 1919: 'I am heart and soul for a League of Nations, imperfect as the beginnings of its organization must necessarily be. Both your Federation and ours grew out of conditions which were far from perfect, but which have developed a fine unity between all the parts. Why, with this example, can't we hope for a like development between the nations of the world.'[8]

In a similar vein, King recorded in his diary in 1923 that he had said to Lord Robert Cecil: 'The great thing about the League of Nations [is that] it is teaching all countries a common language – using language in a broad sense, of like concepts & ideas.'[9]

King's attitude in practice was usually quite different, however. In his early years as prime minister he showed little interest in the League, and rarely mentioned it even in his detailed daily diaries.[10] He resisted the urgings of League supporters in Canada that he attend its sessions, though he was eventually to do so in 1928 and 1936.

In 1927 King's principal French-Canadian political lieutenant, Minister of Justice Ernest Lapointe, was urging that Canada be a candidate for a three-year term on the League Council. King disagreed, though he ultimately yielded to Lapointe, and Canada successfully sought election. During this controversy King wrote in his diary in June 1927: 'We are just as wise not to get too far into European politics (& entanglements). It wd mean French Can representation & Canada's siding on the League against England possibly, which wd raise a major political issue here. If not likely to differ with Eng. then no need for separate representation. Better avoid mistakes.'[11]

Viewing the League in retrospect in 1944, King saw its influence as essentially harmful. He recorded in his diary having told Winston Churchill that he 'did not believe there would have been a war if the League of Nations had never existed. The nations would have prepared their alliance and not depended upon a mere facade with the United States out and all looking to England.'[12]

King was defeated in the 1930 general election by the Conservatives, led by Richard B. Bennett. Bennett was then prime minister through five years of domestic and international crisis, until defeated in turn by King in the 1935 election. He came to office without any substantial background or interest in general foreign policy questions, and without any substantial disagreement with King's conduct of foreign policy. Initially, except in trade and tariff matters, there were no major policy changes. This situation was not to last, however, and before he left office Bennett became both interested and active in foreign policy decision-making. When he did so, it was with a drastically different point of view from that of King, and a major reversal of Canada's policy regarding the League of

Nations and collective security was rapidly developing when Bennett was defeated and King returned to power (see Chapter 11).

In summary, of the four prime ministers of the period between the two world wars, only Borden and King showed sustained interest in foreign policy questions. Only in 1919 did a Canadian prime minister devote his major effort and attention to international affairs. So far as the League of Nations was concerned, the only prime minister of the period who, while in office, evidenced any substantial favourable interest in its main purposes, as contrasted with its usefulness in promoting Canada's international status, was Bennett in the last months of his government. The prime ministers maintained control of foreign policy in their own hands, but for the most part treated foreign policy in general and League policy in particular, except as it related to Canada's status, as a subject of secondary importance.

The most unusual aspect of the Canadian government's organization for the conduct of foreign policy in these years was undoubtedly the fact that no cabinet minister had foreign policy as his prime responsibility. The prime minister, who was also Secretary of State for External Affairs, was fully in charge, but his main duties lay elsewhere. The cabinet, as such, appears to have given virtually no attention to foreign policy, leaving such concerns to the individual attention of the prime minister.

While Borden was leading the Canadian delegation in Paris, his cabinet did meet in Ottawa to consider the League Covenant. Its conclusions, forwarded to Borden in April 1919, were confined to a general approval of the Covenant and of Borden's proposed changes in it (including, without comment, his proposed deletion of Article 10), plus two specific recommendations originating with the cabinet: that each League member must have exclusive control of its own immigration and also of its fiscal, trade, and tariff policies. To these two recommendations Newton W. Rowell, the Acting Secretary of State for External Affairs, added a third of his own, that private manufacture of munitions should be prohibited.[13] Borden does not appear to have pursued any of these recommendations at the Paris conference. It was only, of course, in the unusual circumstances that prevailed in 1919, with the prime minister away from Canada at an international conference for an extended period, that there was any occasion for his cabinet to send formal foreign policy recommendations to him. Normally no cabinet position, separately identifiable from that of the prime minister, was formulated.

However, individual cabinet ministers with a strong interest in international affairs were at times active and influential in foreign policy decision-making, even though their regular duties were in other areas. Such influential participation in foreign policy matters based primarily on the cabinet minister's personal interest was probably possible only because Canada had no full-time foreign minister.

The two outstanding examples in the 1920s and 1930s of Canadian cabinet ministers who played an important role in foreign policy, based essentially on their personal interest, were Ernest Lapointe and Raoul Dandurand. As Dandurand himself explained it: 'Il n'y avait à vrai dire que M. King, M. Lapointe et moi qui prissions un intérêt spécial aux affaires étrangères. La plupart de nos collègues étaient absorbés par les affaires de leur ministère et les problèmes touchant spécialement leur province.'[14]*

Lapointe was a member of the cabinet, whenever the Liberal party was in power, from 1921 until his death in 1941. He was at first Minister of Marine and Fisheries, then, after 1924, Minister of Justice. More importantly, from about 1924 till his death he was in effect Prime Minister Mackenzie King's unofficial deputy, both in the Liberal party and in the government, and the most influential French Canadian in national political affairs. Lapointe had a continuing interest in foreign affairs and in the League of Nations. He was a member of the Canadian delegation to the League of Nations Assembly in 1922, and led the delegation in 1938. In 1927 he headed the Canadian delegation to the naval disarmament conference in Geneva. From 1933 to 1935, while the Liberal party was in opposition in Ottawa, he was national president of the League of Nations Society in Canada. For a time at least, copies of all League documents sent to the Canadian government were also sent to Lapointe personally.[15]

Lapointe's point of view on foreign policy and League matters was virtually identical with that of King, and no doubt tended to reinforce King's adherence to the views he already held. Both were interested in Canadian participation in the League primarily because of its effects on Canada's international status, and both were opposed to commitments to other states. Through the years the only substantial disagreement between King and Lapointe on a foreign policy question was over Canada's candidacy for a place on the League Council in 1927, which, as already noted, Lapointe favoured and King initially opposed. Even this was essentially only a disagreement over tactics. Lapointe favoured Canada's candidacy because it would 'advertise Dominion status to international world.'[16] Canada's election to the Council, he wired King, 'is natural step and crowning point of our policy. We owe it to Canadian prestige and development. Am not afraid of any dangerous aspect, quite the contrary. Let Canada again lead Dominions.'[17] King remained more impressed by the dangers of a more active Canadian involvement in international controversies, but yielded because, he recorded in his diary, 'a cleavage with Lapointe on a matter on which he feels deeply would be more unfortunate in the long run.'[18]

---

* 'There were in fact only Mr King, Mr Lapointe and I who took a special interest in foreign affairs. Most of our colleagues were absorbed with the affairs of their ministry and the problems specially affecting their province.'

In general, however, Lapointe was no less apprehensive than King of excessive foreign involvements, and was uncomfortable and evasive about the obligations which Canada had already undertaken as a League member. Thus in 1928, in a parliamentary discussion of the Locarno treaties, Lapointe said:

... as a Canadian citizen I do not see that Canada should assume obligations in connection with the boundaries between France and Germany ... I do not believe it would have been good policy for us to assume any obligation which might result in a war to guarantee any boundaries in central Europe or elsewhere outside our own country ...

I am free to admit that as a member of the League of Nations Canada has certain obligations, and if she is ever called upon to fulfil them, if there is a war with regard to any of these boundaries, Canada will have to consider what are her obligations as a member of the league.[19]

Except for King and Lapointe, the only member of the Liberal cabinets of the 1920s and 1930s who played an important role in foreign policy was Raoul Dandurand. Dandurand, who was Minister without Portfolio and Leader of the Senate in each of the Mackenzie King governments from 1921 till his death in 1942, became more nearly a specialist in League of Nations affairs than any other Canadian political figure. He was a member of the Canadian delegation to the League Assembly each year from 1924 through 1929, and again in 1936 and 1937, heading the delegation except on the two occasions when Prime Minister King attended. During Canada's term of membership on the League Council, 1927-30, he was the regular Canadian representative at Council meetings. In 1925 he was elected President of the Assembly, the highest recognition given to a Canadian at the League.

Dandurand's role in the formation of Canadian foreign policy appears, however, to have been less important than might have been expected. He had been an inveterate traveller to Europe long before becoming a delegate to League meetings. He enjoyed his stays in Geneva and his association with the leading international political personalities gathered together there, and was both well known and respected. However, he appears only occasionally to have made any significant attempt to influence foreign policy decisions, either in Geneva or in Ottawa.

Probably Dandurand's best known statement on foreign policy was made in a speech to the League Assembly in Geneva in 1924, the first year that he represented Canada there. He gave a classic definition of the North American isolationist position with regard to the League of Nations, saying that 'in this association of Mutual Insurance against fire, the risks assumed by the different States are not equal. We live in a fire-proof house, far from inflammable materials.'[20] This statement was later the subject of much adverse comment, and when Dandurand wrote his memoirs in the 1930s, he omitted any mention of it.

In fact, however, while Dandurand's 'fire-proof house' speech was an accurate enough expression of the attitudes then prevailing in the Canadian government, it was by no means typical of the views which he himself represented during his long association with the League. Dandurand was far more world-minded than most Canadian political leaders of his time, and when he did attempt to influence policy, it was generally in a more internationalist direction. He was an early advocate of Canadian acceptance of the compulsory jurisdiction of the Permanent Court of International Justice; he privately, though unsuccessfully, urged Canadian acceptance of the Geneva Protocol of 1924, a major attempt to strengthen the collective security commitments of League members; he was the author, in 1929, of a Canadian effort to make more effective the protection given by the League Council to the rights of minorities in eastern Europe. He was also active, and entirely in harmony with the views of Prime Minister King, in insisting, as the leader of successive Canadian delegations to Geneva, that Canada at no time accept there a position in any way subordinate to Great Britain.

Even cabinet ministers like Lapointe and Dandurand, who played an important foreign policy role, had no responsibility for the Department of External Affairs itself, or for its staff of career officials. The Department was headed by the prime minister, in his capacity as Secretary of State for External Affairs, and there were no other political officials attached to it. The top career official, responsible directly to the prime minister, was the Undersecretary of State for External Affairs. Only two men held this office in the first thirty-three years of its existence: Sir Joseph Pope, from the foundation of the Department in 1909 till his retirement in 1925, and O.D. Skelton, from 1925 till his death in 1941.

The remarkable continuity in office of the undersecretaries, in combination with the absence of any full-time political official in the Department, made it possible for the undersecretaries to be extremely influential in foreign policy formulation. This was not actually the case, so far as Pope was concerned. In 1909, when the External Affairs Department was created, it was viewed primarily as a record-keeping office. Even after Canada had begun to play an active role internationally, Pope's interests appear to have continued to centre on keeping the departmental files in order, and on his editing of the papers of Sir John A. Macdonald, Canada's first prime minister. (He had been one of Macdonald's secretaries.) He was entirely out of sympathy with any tendency to loosen Canada's ties with England, and with such new inventions as the League of Nations. In December 1920 he recorded in his diary the following observations: 'Our reps are making a great stir at the League of Nations, advertizing Canada and incidentally themselves. I think it all absurd, and am convinced that Canada's true policy right now is to develop her resources and to leave European questions such as the Bessarabian frontier etc to our Imperial statesmen and the trained experts of Downing Street.'[21] With such an approach, Pope was not in a position to be influential with either the Conservative or the Liberal prime ministers of the years 1919-25.

This situation changed completely after Pope was succeeded by Skelton in 1925. Skelton, formerly a professor of political science and Dean of Arts at Queen's University, had a close identification with the Liberal party. He was the author of a distinguished and laudatory biography of Sir Wilfrid Laurier, Liberal prime minister from 1896 to 1911. Mackenzie King, who had begun his political career as a protégé of Laurier, named Skelton chief of his advisory staff for the Imperial Conference of 1923, brought him into the Department of External Affairs in 1924, and made him undersecretary on Pope's retirement the next year. Skelton quickly became exceptionally influential. J.W. Pickersgill, one of King's secretaries in the late 1930s, records that Skelton was by then 'Mackenzie King's closest adviser on all public affairs, domestic as well as external,' with an influence greater even than that of Lapointe.[22] Besides being discreet, competent and unobtrusive, Skelton held views on foreign policy that were remarkably similar to King's own. Their views on policy toward the League of Nations were so close, throughout the 1920s and 1930s, as to be virtually identical.

Skelton's close identification with King's views and policies, and his earlier associations with the Liberal party, naturally posed a problem when the Conservative party government of R.B. Bennett held office in 1930-35. Skelton was retained in his post, and although Bennett initially distrusted him, he soon became very influential with Bennett too. However, as an advisor to Bennett he never approached the degree of influence he had had with King, and toward the end of Bennett's government a major conflict in their foreign policy attitudes had developed (see Chapter 11).

Throughout the years before world war II, the Department of External Affairs had only a very small professional staff, in addition to the undersecretary, an indication both of the small volume of Canadian international transactions and the secondary role given by the Canadian government to foreign affairs. As late as 1925, the Department had only two administrative officers in addition to the undersecretary.[23] Following Skelton's appointment as undersecretary in that year, a modest expansion in staff began. By 1930 the number of officers at the Department's Ottawa headquarters had grown to seven, with the gradual addition of promising young university graduates, 'Dr Skelton's young men.'[24] The quality of these new appointees brought in by Skelton was exceptional, and a number of them, such as Lester B. Pearson, Norman A. Robertson, and H. Hume Wrong, were to play key roles in the development of Canada's foreign policy.

Simultaneously with the beginning of an expansion of staff in the Department of External Affairs in Ottawa, the Department began an equally modest expansion of overseas offices and staff. Prior to 1925, the only Canadian governmental offices abroad were the High Commissioner's office in London and the Commissioner General's office in Paris. Neither had official diplomatic functions or status. British diplomatic and consular offices still represented the interests of all of the Empire, including Canada. On an *ad hoc* basis, however, treaty negotiations with foreign governments had been conducted by Canada, and in 1923, for the first time, a treaty had been both negotiated and signed by Canada, without participation by British government representatives. (The treaty was a fisheries treaty with the United States, signed in Washington by Ernest Lapointe as Minister of Marine and Fisheries.) Later in 1923, the Imperial Conference of that year accepted the procedure which had been followed by Canada, recognizing, in effect, that the self-governing dominions possessed treaty-making power.

The first step in the expansion of Canadian representation abroad came, appropriately enough, at Geneva. Beginning in 1920, Canada was regularly represented at the annual League Assemblies and at other conferences and meetings sponsored by the League, but it had no permanent representation at Geneva. This situation was changed by the appointment, effective 1 January 1925, of a 'permanent Dominion of Canada Advisory Officer for League of Nations purposes,' resident in Geneva.[25] The unusual title adopted reflected the fact that Canada did not yet have any official representatives abroad with diplomatic status or titles. The functions of the Canadian Advisory Officer were to represent Canada in its relations with the Secretariats of the League and of the International Labour Organization, and to provide information and advice to the government in Ottawa and to Canadian delegations to League and ILO meetings.

As the first Canadian Advisory Officer, Prime Minister King appointed Walter A. Riddell, who continued to hold the position until 1937, thus representing Canada at the League during its years of greatest strength and vitality, and also in its years of crisis and decline. Riddell had not previously been associated with the Department of External Affairs, under which the new office was placed. While Deputy Minister of Labour for the Province of Ontario, he had been included among the advisers to the Canadian delegation to the first conference of the ILO at Washington in 1919, as had Mackenzie King, a former federal Minister of Labour.[26] In 1920 Riddell had joined the permanent staff of the ILO in Geneva, and had remained there until appointed Canadian Advisory Officer. The staffing of the Advisory Office was small, in keeping with all Department of External Affairs staffing in the 1920s and 1930s. At its largest, there were only three officers assigned to it, in addition to Riddell.

In 1926, the Imperial Conference of that year adopted a formula describing the relations of Great Britain and the self-governing dominions which gave formal recognition for the first time to a fully independent role for the dominions in international affairs: 'They are autonomous communities within the British Empire, equal in status, and in no way subordinate one to another in any aspect of their domestic or external affairs.'[27] This was followed by the first exercise of the right of legation by Canada, though initially on a very small scale. The first Canadian legation was opened in Washington in 1927, followed by Paris in 1928 (replacing the Commissioner General's office), and Tokyo in 1929. No other Canadian diplomatic offices were opened until 1939, Canadian interests continuing to be represented elsewhere by Great Britain. In accordance with another decision of the 1926 Imperial Conference, the Governors General ceased to be British government representatives in the dominions, British High Commissioners being named instead for that purpose. The effect was to establish a system for official contacts within the Empire essentially the same as that between a dominion and a 'foreign' state, with the respective High Commissioners exercising the same functions as Ministers.

The new Canadian diplomatic posts were filled almost exclusively, during the 1920s and 1930s, with appointees whose principal qualifications were political. Not until 1939 was the post of Minister or High Commissioner given to a career External Affairs officer, although a career man, Hume Wrong, was named Riddell's successor as Advisory Officer in Geneva in 1937. When Bennett succeeded King as prime minister in 1930, Conservative party figures were named to replace Liberals as head of mission in London and in Washington, and were themselves both replaced after King's return to office in 1935. Lower level positions in the foreign missions were, however, filled with career External Affairs officers from the beginning. These offices, too, all remained small. The total number of officers in the Department, both in Ottawa and abroad, was only 18 in 1930, 21 in 1935, and 30 in 1940.[28]

The small size of the Department's staff, in combination with the sources of its officer personnel, led to some unusual patterns of activity and influence. In Ottawa, even a very junior member of the Department's staff, far from being submerged in a vast bureaucracy, was in close and immediate contact with the undersecretary, who in turn was, after 1925, an unusually influential adviser of the prime minister. On the other hand, all of the offices outside of Canada, including Geneva, were headed by officials who had never worked in the External Affairs Department, who might well have different views on policy from those prevailing within the Department, and who might also have direct access to the prime minister on a political basis. In either case, there were great opportunities for individual External Affairs officials to make their views felt.

Of particular importance in carrying out, and sometimes in formulating, Canadian policy toward the League of Nations were the delegations to League meetings. Canada was represented at all twenty-five regular and special sessions of the League Assembly held from 1920 to 1939, and at the fourteen sessions of the League Council held during the period of Canadian membership from 1927 to 1930, as well as at a variety of special meetings and conferences organized by the League. At the Assemblies each League member was entitled to three full delegates, plus an unlimited number of substitute delegates and advisers. At the Council meetings, each Council member was entitled to one representative only.

As might be expected, the individuals who were active in foreign policy matters as cabinet ministers or External Affairs officials also frequently appeared as delegates to League meetings. On occasion the prime minister was available to head a delegation, as King did to the Assemblies of 1928 and 1936, and Bennett to the Assembly of 1934. King also represented Canada at two Council sessions in 1928. Dandurand, as the cabinet's specialist in League affairs, was a member of eight Assembly delegations in 1924-9 and 1936-7, and took part in ten Council sessions in 1927-30. No other cabinet member approached this record, even Lapointe who attended only two Assembly sessions.

In the External Affairs Department, Riddell was of course the specialist in League affairs, and he was regularly included in the Canadian delegations throughout his almost thirteen years as Canadian Advisory Officer. Skelton was a member of the Assembly delegation on five occasions between 1924 and 1936. Others frequently included were the heads of the London and Paris missions.

The most striking feature of the Assembly delegations, however, was the very large number of delegates who never attended more than a single session. Of fifty-two individuals who served as Assembly delegate in 1920-39, there were thirty-six who did so once only. In other words, there was a remarkable lack of continuity in delegation membership, in spite of such important exceptions as Riddell and Dandurand.

Critics of the League and of Canada's participation in it often criticized the trips to League meetings as nothing more than useless vacations in Europe at the taxpayers' expense. Senator J.P.B. Casgrain (Liberal, Quebec), a persistent critic of the League, was eloquent on the subject:

Sitting in a comfortable rattan arm-chair on the terrace of a luxurious 'Palace,' inhaling the balmy breezes from Lake Leman, and sipping the choicest vintages of France's sparkling wine ... listening to the harmonious voice of the azure billows breaking gently on the white sands of those enchanting shores, admiring the beautiful nymphs, the stenographers of the League of Nations, in diminutive one-piece bathing attire to show their charms and shapely forms to the best advantage, a delegate would say: 'Oh boy! What a fine life is the life of a delegate!'[29]

Walter Riddell, the permanent Canadian representative in Geneva, also had reason to doubt the seriousness of some of the delegates. He has recounted his difficulties with Maurice Dupré,* Solicitor General in Bennett's cabinet and a delegate in 1932, in part as follows:

This man appeared to have looked upon an appointment as delegate as a means to strengthen his hold on his home constituency; for him a conference was an electioneering stunt. From the day he arrived he looked upon the use of the delegation stationery, which had been specially embossed for the occasion, as his private advertising prerogative, and at once decided to send letters to the doubtful voters in his constituency for this purpose, and for almost a week monopolized the full time of a secretary, sometimes far into the night, in order that these letters should catch the first westbound mail.[30]

It would indeed appear that many of the delegates had only the briefest and most superficial connection with the work of the League. Altogether, twenty-one different cabinet ministers served as Assembly delegates, fourteen of them one time only. Judging from their participation in parliamentary debates and their general reputation, most of them showed little or no interest in League affairs, either before or after their trip to Geneva as a delegate.

In a different category, except as to the briefness of their service, were another sizeable group of Assembly delegates, those delegates appointed from outside both the cabinet and the Department of External Affairs. Through the two decades of the Assembly's meetings, twenty such delegates were appointed, nineteen of them representing Canada at one session only. The individuals selected were often persons well known for their interest in the League of Nations as individual members of parliament, or in the League of Nations Society or other private organizations. Beginning in 1929, a woman was usually included in the delegation, and on occasion a member of the political opposition was named, though never an important figure in the opposition leadership. In short, appointments to the Assembly delegations were used for public relations purposes, to encourage support for or good will toward the government by giving interested individuals an opportunity to participate in an Assembly session.

The amateurism and lack of continuity which characterized the Canadian Assembly delegations was most important, however, with regard to the delegation leaders. A total of eighteen different individuals served as First Delegate, and therefore as spokesman and leader of the delegation. Of these, twelve were First Delegate one time only. Only Dandurand, who was First Delegate at six

---

* Riddell discreetly omits Dupré's name from his narrative, but from the information given, the unnamed delegate is readily identifiable.

Assembly sessions, headed delegations with any frequency. Usually the First Delegate was a cabinet minister, and therefore was relatively free to act independently of the advice and instructions of the Department of External Affairs, if he saw fit. More often than not he was a cabinet minister with no continuing responsibility for foreign affairs and no substantial experience in international negotiations. Thus, for example, at the two critical Assemblies which dealt with the Lytton Commission report on the Manchurian crisis (1932) and with the Italian invasion of Ethiopia (1935), the Canadian delegations were headed by political figures who had never previously attended an Assembly session, and who had quite different ideas regarding the crises from those contained in the instructions sent them from the Department of External Affairs.

Canadian policy toward the League of Nations was formulated and carried out, then, by a combination of busy prime ministers, influential civil servants, interested cabinet members, and amateur diplomats. In the circumstances, it is perhaps more surprising that there was by and large a substantial consistency and continuity in policy, than that there were also some major breakdowns and confusions.

3
The formulation of policy:
parliament, parties, and pressure groups

The Canadian parliament was, throughout the 1920s and 1930s, the scene of debates and questions on foreign policy subjects. It served as a principal forum for major foreign policy statements by the government and by the leaders of opposition parties, as well as for challenges to official policy by individual questioners and critics.

The Canadian House of Commons, like its British counterpart, serves primarily as such a forum for discussion of governmental policies and as a means of bringing pressure to bear on the government to change its policies. It does not itself defeat governments or reverse their policies, except in the unusual circumstance of a minority government, though formally it has such power. Voting is normally by disciplined party blocs, assuring a virtually automatic victory to any majority government, on any measure. In 1926, after the 1925 elections had failed to produce a majority party in the House of Commons, first a Liberal government headed by W.L. Mackenzie King and then a Conservative one headed by Arthur Meighen was forced out of office by lack of majority support in the House. In neither case was any foreign policy issue involved. At all other times in the period concerned the government in office routinely received House support for whatever policies it ultimately adopted, foreign as well as domestic. While House of Commons debate often served to clarify government policy, and to make clear conflicting views on policy questions, in no case does any major change in foreign policy appear to have resulted from such debate.

The role of the Senate in Canadian political life is usually a peripheral one. Senators are appointed for life by the government in office. The legislative powers of the Senate are formally similar to those of the House of Commons, except that a defeat in the Senate does not require a government to resign. Senate debate is usually brief, followed by approval of whatever the House of Commons has approved. On occasion, however, when a party out of power in the House of Commons has control of the Senate, this control has been used to defeat major government legislation. No such use of the Senate's powers took place, however, during the period concerned, with regard to any foreign policy question. The membership in the Senate of two prominent political figures closely identified with League of Nations affairs, Sir George Foster and Raoul Dandurand, led to more Senate discussion of League policy than might otherwise have been the case, but the marginal political importance of the Senate reduced the significance which the discussion might otherwise have had.

Only one parliamentary session during the League period, a special session called by the Borden government in 1919 to approve the Versailles treaty (including the League of Nations Covenant), devoted its attention primarily to foreign policy. This session had a strikingly unreal quality to it. As the treaty provisions could not be changed in any respect through unilateral action of the Canadian government, the usual discussion and criticism function of the parliament could not operate effectively, since the government was unable to make any concessions, small or large, to critics. Moreover, parliament was not informed by the government of its objections to Article 10 of the League Covenant, or of its attempts at the Peace Conference to have the article deleted. Sir Robert Borden, the prime minister, in presenting the treaty to the House of Commons for approval, made only the following limited reference to the government's earlier criticisms of the Covenant:

The Canadian delegates took exception both in form and in substance to certain of its original provisions. Our views were set forth in a confidential memorandum which I circulated to the members of the Commission who drafted the Covenant and to the representatives of the five great Allied Powers. Many of our objections were met in the revised draft; and as to the others we felt that important as we regarded them, they ought not to be accounted of moment in comparison with the supreme purpose embodied in the Covenant.[1]

As the treaty was a government measure, and the government had a large parliamentary majority, approval of the treaty without change was a foregone conclusion, and duly took place after about a week's debate in the House of Commons, and one day's debate in the Senate. The debates did serve to clarify government and opposition attitudes toward the treaty and the League, though even that function was served in only a limited way owing to the failure of the Borden government to present to parliament a full or frank statement of its real views on the League Covenant.

During these debates on the peace treaty in September 1919, spokesmen for the Liberal opposition concentrated their criticism on the Covenant without, for the most part, going so far as to advocate rejection of membership in the League. Much of what they said was clearly isolationist in tone. For example, D.D. McKenzie (Liberal, Nova Scotia), the acting party leader in the House of Commons, said with reference to Article 10 and the League Council:

But I do not think it is consistent with the feeling of the Canadian people that they should be called upon, for instance, to enter into some petty quarrel between any of the new kingdoms or republics that are being formed in Europe, or to intervene in some troubles that may exist between Mexico and any of the minor republics of South America. Under this Article, when this Council, in which we have no representation, calls upon us to do so, we are bound to take a part in such quarrels as I have mentioned.[2]

Various other opposition members voiced similar suspicions of the effects of League membership, for example, Lucien Cannon (Liberal, Quebec), who said: '... I am not in favour of England ruling this country, but I would rather be ruled by England than by Geneva ... I have very poor confidence in Brazil and in Spain, very little also in Greece, and not very much in the Kingdom of The Hedjaz.'[3] Charles G. Power (Liberal, Quebec) opposed the Covenant in stridently isolationist terms:

There is one more reason for rejecting the Covenant which I cannot pass over ... We as Canadians have our destiny before us not in continental Europe but here on the free soil of America. Our policy for the next hundred years should be ... absolute renunciation of interference in European affairs – and ... 'freedom from the vortex of European militarism.' I believe this policy to be the true expression of a Greater Canadianism. I believe the people of Canada will approve of this policy, namely, to let Europe be the arbiter of its own destiny while we in Canada, turning our energies to our own affairs, undertake our own peaceful development strong in the faith that we have within our national boundaries and within ourselves the material to become a great and powerful nation.[4]

The position of the Liberal leadership, however, was much more restrained. One of the party's principal parliamentary spokesmen, W.S. Fielding (Liberal, Nova Scotia), a former Minister of Finance, moved on 11 September 1919 the following addition to Prime Minister Borden's resolution approving the peace treaty: 'That in giving such approval this House in no way assents to any impairment of the existing autonomous authority of the Dominion, but declares that the question of what part, if any, the forces of Canada shall take in any war, actual or threatened, is one to be determined at all times as occasion may require by the people of Canada through their representatives in Parliament.'[5]

The Fielding amendment in no way rejected Canadian participation in the League of Nations, nor was it in direct conflict with the language of the League Covenant, which by Article 10 required all members to 'preserve as against external aggression' each other's territory and independence, but did not specifically make mandatory the use of a country's armed forces. Nevertheless, the intent of the amendment was clearly to minimize any commitment on the part of Canada to take action in opposition to aggression, as well as to make the Liberal party appear a stronger defender of Canadian autonomy than was the government.

This line of attack by the parliamentary opposition must have been something of an embarrassment to the government. The Liberal proposal was in fact consistent with the attitude which the government had privately taken at the peace conference, though Borden had gone even further, by proposing the deletion of Article 10. However, the government had not revealed its actual views to either parliament or the public, and was not about to do so now, when under attack by the Liberals. The main reply of government spokesmen during the September 1919 debates was, therefore, not to deny the validity of an essentially isolationist position, but rather to deny that the League Covenant effectively committed member states to any course of action. C.J. Doherty, the Minister of Justice, explained Article 10 in these terms: 'There it is stated in words as clear as the English language affords that the Council is to exercise an advisory function, not that it is to order any of the nations to do anything ... it will only be if the Parliament of Canada decides to accept and act upon that advice that it will proceed to send soldiers and to raise money.'[6]

Doherty also insisted, as did Newton W. Rowell, President of the Privy Council and Minister of Health, that in any case, if the League Council were considering a recommendation for a Canadian military contribution, Canada would be entitled to a voting representative on the Council during such consideration and, since unanimity was required, could prevent any unacceptable recommendation being made.[7]

The general tone of the debate, then, from both government and opposition, was one of reluctance to accept any commitments to military action, the main argument being over whether any such commitments were in fact included in the League Covenant. The idea of collective security was not, however, entirely lacking in support. Its most forthright advocate in the parliamentary debate was Herbert M. Mowat (Liberal Unionist, Ontario):

If there is an invasion of the integrity or the territory of one of the nations composing it [the League of Nations], we must go to her rescue – we bind ourselves to it. Such a thing was never incorporated in any previous treaty, but we are bound to do that because we are turning ourselves for the good of the world into international policemen ... So by this treaty, the most important in the history of the world, the civilized nations have agreed to do the policing of the world, and it would ill become Canada churlishly or shrinkingly or fearingly to excuse herself from participating in a work which must, it seems to me, redound to the good of the world ... My hon. friend, the leader of the Opposition [D.D. McKenzie], asked: Does the approving of the Treaty take away our liberty of choice as to entering into a European war? Yes, it does. And I thank Heaven that it does, because ... if, owing to the politics of the times, any nation could divorce itself from the general action of the associated nations, then the League of Nations would not be worth the paper it is written on.[8]

Nevertheless, the leadership of both government and opposition were as unwilling to give full support to collective security as they were to reject Canadian membership in the League. Instead, both sought, on slightly different terms, to accept League membership while minimizing Canadian obligations. On 11 Sept. 1919, Fielding's amendment, which the government insisted was unnecessary, reserving to Canada the right to decide what part, if any, its armed forces would take in any war, was brought to a vote. The vote followed party lines, in accordance with the normal working of the parliamentary system, and the amendment was defeated, 70-102. The resolution moved by Sir Robert Borden approving the Treaty of Versailles, including the Covenant of the League of Nations, was then agreed to by the House of Commons without a recorded vote.[9] The Senate had already given its approval a week earlier.[10]

Parliamentary discussion of League affairs, and of foreign policy generally, during the succeeding two decades was usually brief, and limited to only a handful of members. Government spokesmen rarely initiated such discussions, for the most part confining themselves to answering questions at the time of the annual vote to cover Canada's contribution to the League's expenses.

A rather different approach to parliament's role in foreign policy decision-making might perhaps have been expected of Prime Minister W.L. Mackenzie King, the dominant political figure of the period. He repeatedly and emphatically stated his government's policy that, on vital questions of foreign policy, 'Parliament will decide.' The extent of parliament's responsibility, as he saw it, was spelled out by King on various occasions. Thus, on 1 February 1923, after having the previous September refused a British request for troops in an impending conflict with Turkey, King explained to the House of Commons: 'It is for parliament to decide whether or not we should participate in wars in different parts of the world, and it is neither right nor proper for any individual nor for any group of individuals to take any step which in any way might limit the rights of parliament in a matter which is of such great concern to all the people of our country.'[11] In 1926 King announced that parliamentary approval would be asked, prior to ratification, of 'important treaties such as involve military and economic sanctions.'[12] In 1928 he indicated a still broader application of his formula: 'I would not confine parliamentary approval only to those matters which involve military sanctions and the like. I feel parliamentary approval should apply where there are involved matters of large expenditure or political considerations of a far-reaching character.'[13]

The reality behind the 'Parliament will decide' formula was, however, quite different from what the words appeared to mean. At first glance the formula might seem to imply that a free vote would be allowed in parliament on major foreign policy issues, thereby permitting the members of parliament to directly 'decide' the question at issue, in accordance with their own best judgment. Any such procedure on major policy matters, however, would have been entirely out of keeping with the prime responsibility of the government for determining policy which characterized the Canadian political system, and no such modification of the Canadian system was intended or practised by King. If decision-making, then, was to remain in the government's hands, with parliament routinely giving approval through disciplined party bloc voting, the 'Parliament will decide' formula could have real substance only if, through extended analysis, criticism, and debate of government proposals, parliament was able to exercise its normal functions in an exceptionally effective way. Nothing could have been further, however, from King's practice regarding parliamentary debate.

In general, he avoided as completely as possible any meaningful foreign policy discussion in parliament. Not until June 1936, after the Italo-Ethiopian and Rhineland crises and the collapse of the League collective security system, did he give any over-all foreign policy statement to the House of Commons. He would answer specific questions in the House about past policy, but would typically refuse to comment in specific terms on future policy or on his government's attitude toward current controversies, often pleading that any public discussion would only make resolution of existing problems more difficult. The net result of this practice by King, which was also followed by Prime Minister Bennett in 1930-35, was to limit the role of members of parliament to stating their own views on policy and to getting answers to some questions, without being able to engage the government in general discussion or debate of its policy. Parliament, then, not only did not 'decide' major foreign policy questions, but found little opportunity given it to exert real influence on the decisions of the government.

What reality was there, then, in the frequently enunciated formula that 'Parliament will decide'? In a purely formal way, it meant that important international agreements would be submitted to parliament for its approval before being ratified by the government, but with parliamentary approval a foregone conclusion, as in the case of Borden's submission of the peace treaties. More significantly, it meant that the prime minister could, when he chose to do so, plead an inability to make international commitments without first obtaining parliamentary approval. In other words, rather paradoxically, King's insistence that 'Parliament will decide' became little more than another way of enunciating the 'no commitments' policy which characterized his conduct of foreign affairs, and which left him an almost completely free hand in their conduct.

This approach toward parliament's role was not without its critics. Most persistent in his attempts to get some substantial and meaningful discussion of foreign policy and of League of Nations affairs in parliament was J.S. Woodsworth, Labour member from Winnipeg. In the House of Commons in 1923, for example, he criticized the failure of the government to make any policy statement regarding League activities:

There are a number of very important matters concerning the league, which is regarded as the nearest approach we have to a central body for negotiating world relationships, and it seems to me that we ought not to pass over these items as a matter of form, but rather that we should consider very carefully the work of the league. If this is the proper place to do it, I for one should like to hear some report and to offer some observations regarding the league.'[14]

The government's reaction was revealing. Prime Minister King said that, if Woodsworth wished to make some observations, 'Now is the time, then.' W.S. Fielding, the Finance Minister, added, 'There is no objection at all to my hon. friend's discussing it.'[15] Woodsworth then proceeded to give a detailed critique of League of Nations activities and of Canadian policy toward it, and to call again for a full discussion by the government in the House. There was no further discussion or response of any kind from the government.[16]

Seven years later, Woodsworth was still voicing the same complaint. The only foreign policy matter which had been submitted to the 1930 session of parliament was the proposed contribution to League of Nations expenses. 'It does seem to me,' Woodsworth said, 'that not merely should these items of expenditure in connection with the league be brought before the house but also the various policies that are being discussed in the league should come under review ... I wish to ask if we will have an opportunity at this session of the house to discuss Canada's foreign policies.' King, after denying that there was inadequate opportunity for discussion of foreign policy, concluded: 'As to fixing a specific time I confess I find it somewhat difficult to undertake anything of that nature.'[17]

In 1932 Woodsworth criticized the same lack of interest in parliamentary discussion of foreign policy under the Conservative party government of R.B. Bennett:

... it is unfortunate that questions relative to our imperial or external relations are so often left until the last days of the session, a time when most members are tired and impatient to get away. In the dying hours of the session we have a very inadequate opportunity of entering into full discussion ... He [Bennett] seems to take for granted that the League of Nations is something apart from ourselves, something that has a more or less independent existence, and that we must stand aside and wait until the league takes action.[18]

Woodsworth's complaints were without avail, however, and Bennett, like King, studiously avoided any general presentation to parliament of his government's foreign policy views.

Still another indication of the real role of parliament in foreign policy decisions was the failure to utilize parliamentary committees for review of policy in this area. In 1924, a House of Commons Standing Committee on Industrial and International Relations was established, reflecting a favourite idea of Mackenzie King's, that the techniques of mediation and conciliation used in resolving labour disputes were equally applicable as the prime means of resolving international disputes. Although the committee continued to function until 1936, no real foreign policy question was ever referred to it. Its nearest approach to a discussion of international affairs was in connection with the reference to it in 1931 of a private member's proposal 'to promote peace by instituting international professorships and scholarships in leading Canadian universities.'[19]

With all these limitations, the Canadian parliament nevertheless was not without importance as a forum for foreign policy discussion. Individual members had substantial opportunity to present and publicize their own foreign policy views, if not necessarily to engage the government in debate. Prime ministers could be prodded into answering some questions about, and presenting some justification of, their policies. And on occasion time was set aside for debate and discussion of a proposed international agreement, or even of a private member's legislative proposal.

So far as League of Nations affairs were concerned, the most prominent participants in parliamentary discussion, other than government spokesmen, were Sir George Foster and J.S. Woodsworth. Foster was a veteran Conservative party political figure, who had first been elected to the House of Commons in 1882, and had received his first cabinet appointment in 1885 from Sir John A. Macdonald. While Minister of Trade and Commerce in the Borden and Meighen governments of 1911-21, he had been a member of the Canadian delegation to the Paris Peace Conference in 1919, and had headed the delegation to the first League of Nations Assembly in 1920.

Beginning with his attendance at the 1920 Assembly, Foster became strongly identified with the support and promotion of the League of Nations. He was active in the League of Nations Society in Canada from its founding in 1921, was its president in 1925-9, and made regular speaking tours on its behalf. He headed the Canadian delegation to Geneva in 1926 and, at the age of 82, was once more an active member of the delegation in 1929.

As a member of the Canadian Senate from 1921 till his death in 1931, Foster made an annual review in the Senate of League of Nations affairs, which was often the only systematic review of League activities in the parliament. While a certain amount of debate and discussion regarding the League was stimulated by his statements, they tended not to deal with controversial questions of current policy, but rather to consist of explanations of how the League operated and what it was doing, in combination with flowery praise. An excerpt from Foster's 1923 Senate speech on the League is all too typical:

And so I turn ... to the League of Nations, which stands like a beacon tower in a lone and weary land; which points the way, and which guides the wayfarer. It is a friend sitting constantly, watchfully, with a heart that feels and a sympathy which acts, and a fairness of judgment which cannot be swayed even by the strongest members that belong to the League of Nations. It is the helpful counsellor that goes to the different nationalities, bruised and bleeding and torn with their credal, racial and national animosities, and says: 'Be reasonable men; sit down around a common table; we are your friends; tell us your grievances; let us help you to accommodate them; let us together come to a solution which will be human, and which will be just as well.'[20]

On occasion, however, Foster, in his role as principal parliamentary advocate of the League, did champion specific strengthening moves, as when he spoke in favour of the Geneva Protocol in 1925,[21] and urged acceptance of the compulsory jurisdiction of the Permanent Court of International Justice in 1927.[22]

By far the most persistent and acute foreign policy critic in the House of Commons during these years was J.S. Woodsworth. Woodsworth was first elected to the House as a Labour candidate in 1921, and remained a member until his death in 1942. In 1932 he became the first leader of the Cooperative Commonwealth Federation, Canada's first democratic socialist party organized on a national basis. Woodsworth was also a convinced pacifist. Unlike many with pacifist convictions in peacetime, he adhered just as strongly to pacifism in time of war.

In 1918 he had resigned from the ministry of the Methodist Church because of the church's backing for the first world war;[23] in 1939 he spoke and voted against Canadian participation in the second world war.[24]

What attitude to take toward the League of Nations was a difficult problem for Woodsworth to resolve, both as a socialist and as a pacifist. He saw it initially as a league of victors in the war, and as likely to represent nothing more than 'the old game of imperialistic groups pitted against rival imperialistic groups.'[25] In 1925 he saw great danger that the League would become 'little more than a tool of the great international financiers,' and was pleased that the government had rejected the additional commitments embodied in the Geneva Protocol.[26]

However, as the League's membership expanded and as it appeared to be functioning successfully as an agency for international reconciliation, Woodsworth's attitude toward it changed. By 1930, he had concluded that 'within somewhat narrow limits ... the league has done very good work ... I think any thoughtful student of world affairs must come to the conclusion that to-day we cannot go along just within our own national limits; we must have some form of world organization if we are to prevent world wars in the future. Therefore I urge that we should support the League of Nations.'[27]

In 1931 Woodsworth accepted an invitation to spend several weeks at the League headquarters in Geneva during the fall Assembly and Council meetings, and came away guardedly optimistic. While he thought the League seemed 'almost impotent' in dealing with the major powers, he also thought that 'an enormous amount of good work is being done' in lesser matters, and that 'one could not be there even for a month without realizing that there were wonderful possibilities in this organization. The very fact that men gathered around a common table to discuss matters instead of immediately flying to arms is a very great advance.'[28]

The crises of the 1930s posed a new dilemma for Woodsworth in his attitude toward the League of Nations, as they did for pacifists elsewhere. He had become an advocate and supporter of the organization, and was a member of the National Council of the League of Nations Society in Canada. His support, however, was for the League as an instrument for preventing war, and not as an instrument for waging war. So long as non-violent measures, including economic sanctions, seemed to him likely to be useful in forcing a would-be aggressor to give up its plans for conquest, he was prepared to support collective security action through the League. But if League action seemed to him likely, instead, to simply enlarge an existing war, he was opposed to it, and he was of course opposed to military sanctions in any case.

Throughout these shifts in his reactions to the League, Woodsworth was persistent in the House of Commons in calling for government explanation and justification of its policies, in asking pertinent and often embarrassing questions about government attitudes, and in presenting his own analyses of League activities and of desirable Canadian policy. Such serious and informed discussion of League affairs as took place in the House during the 1920s and 1930s was more the result of Woodsworth's efforts than those of any other individual.

Except among a few, such as Foster and Woodsworth and the top leadership of the two major parties, discussion of League of Nations affairs in parliament was minimal. During the thirteen parliamentary sessions in the years 1925 through 1936, the period of the League's greatest activity and vitality, a total of only 34 members of the House of Commons and 30 senators spoke in parliament on the subject of the League or on Canadian policy toward it. These numbers are exceptionally low when it is considered that, at any one time, the total membership of the House was 245 and of the Senate 96. If discussion of the League was infrequent, the submission of private members' resolutions regarding it was even more so. This was the case, of course, primarily because of the futility of such action. Under the normal working of the parliamentary system, only government measures would be adopted, and very little time was allotted by the government even for discussion of private members' proposals.

Nevertheless, on two occasions private members initiated proposals for Canadian withdrawal from the League. The first was a motion for withdrawal introduced in the House of Commons in 1923 by Charles G. Power (Liberal, Quebec), who had previously opposed Canadian membership in the League during the special parliamentary session of 1919. The motion came up for discussion by the House at a time when only one day was left for consideration of all private members' resolutions. Power withdrew it, and it was never discussed.

In 1934 a similar motion for withdrawal from the League was introduced in the Senate by A.D. McRae (Conservative, British Columbia). The proposal was promptly disavowed by Prime Minister Bennett,[29] but was nevertheless scheduled for debate in the Senate. An extended discussion followed, over a period of some six weeks, and produced the most thorough parliamentary review of the activities of the League of Nations, and of Canada's League policy, of the entire period (see Chapter 10).

If the role of parliament in influencing the course of Canadian foreign policy was at best a secondary one, the role of the political parties, except through the party leadership and members in parliament, appears virtually negligible. During the 1920s and 1930s only two political parties, the Liberals and the Conservatives, led the voting in any national election or participated in any national cabinet. The party which formed the government after each of the elections was as follows: 1917, Conservatives and Liberal Unionists; 1921, Liberals; 1925, Liberals, then Conservatives; 1926, Liberals; 1930, Conservatives; 1935, Liberals.

The Conservatives, in power since 1911, had won the war-time election of 1917 in alliance with 'Liberal Unionists' who had left the Liberal party and joined with the Conservatives in support of military conscription. By 1920, the Liberal Unionists had either been absorbed into the Conservative party or had returned to their former Liberal affiliation. The election of 1925 was unique in that it failed to produce a stable government. First a Liberal minority government held office, then a Conservative minority government; when both proved unable to maintain a voting majority in the House of Commons, a new election was held in 1926.

In none of the elections of the period was foreign policy a dominant, or even significant, issue, except for the question of Canada's relationship to Britain. Mackenzie King's identification with a policy of Canadian assertion of full independence was a factor of some importance in his victory in the 1926 election. However, the centre of controversy was the role of the Governor General, who at the time was always British rather than Canadian, in Canada's internal political system, rather than a question of external policy.

Political party positions tended always to be dominated by the national party leaders, who were as follows: leaders of the Liberal party – 1919-48, W.L. Mackenzie King; leaders of the Conservative party – 1901-20, Sir Robert Borden; 1920-26, Arthur Meighen; 1927-38, Richard B. Bennett; 1938-40, Robert J. Manion.

All of these men, except Manion, also held the office of prime minister. Their attitudes toward the League of Nations, as already discussed, did not indicate any major differences on a party basis. The same is true, for the most part, of foreign policy in general. Party lines were not drawn to any substantial degree on the basis of foreign policy issues, with the exception of the Canadian attitude toward the British connection, and at times the attitude toward protective tariffs. The Liberal party in general was ready to move further at any given time toward a fully independent status for Canada than was the Conservative party. The Conservatives in general were prepared to support a higher level of tariff protection than were the Liberals. Otherwise, foreign policy attitudes appear to have had more of a personal than a party basis. Nevertheless, the system of voting in disciplined party blocs regularly assured full party voting support in parliament for the policies, foreign as well as domestic, decided on by the party leaders.

Outside of parliament, party organization at the national level was minimal in both the Liberal and the Conservative parties. After Mackenzie King's election as party leader in 1919 a Liberal party national committee had been appointed, but for a decade after 1921 it never met. A central party office had also been established to publish and distribute literature during election campaigns. In practice, provincial party organizations dealt with federal cabinet ministers as representatives of the national party.[30] In 1932, while the party was out of power, a permanently staffed national party organization, the National Liberal Federation, was established for the first time. It was active in publicity and fund raising, but it did not become a forum for the discussion of party policy.[31]

The situation was essentially the same in the Conservative party, so far as national party organization was concerned. In 1924 a permanent national organization, the Liberal-Conservative Association of Canada, was established. (The official party name was 'Liberal-Conservative.') It did little more than exist in name, though it was involved in calling national party conventions in 1927 and 1938 to select a new party leader.[32] Publicity and fund raising for national elections were handled not by this organization, but by a national organizer chosen by the party leader. The headquarters office set up by the national organizer usually ceased to function altogether between elections.[33]

In short, the determination of national party policy, whether on foreign or domestic issues, was, in both parties, kept firmly in the hands of the parliamentary leadership, and was not shared with such rudimentary national party organizations as existed. In a potentially more influential position were the major providers of party campaign funds. Both the Liberal and Conservative parties were financed primarily by contributions from wealthy individuals and from corporations. Moreover, important contributors to party funds were often rewarded with political appointments, especially to the Senate and to diplomatic posts, which brought them directly into the policy-making process. Among the Liberals, for example, Peter C. Larkin (High Commissioner in London, 1922-9) and Vincent Massey (Minister in Washington, 1927-30, and High Commissioner in London, 1935-46) had been prominent contributors of party funds. Senator Raoul Dandurand was one of many senators who was a substantial contributor to the party.[34] Among the Conservatives, Prime Minister R.B. Bennett was himself a major provider of party funds, as were such senators as A.D. McRae.[35]

The precise influence of important contributors of funds on the formation of party policy is, at best, very difficult to determine. In Canada in the 1920s and 1930s, however, as already noted, the Liberal and Conservative parties were, in any case, not sharply divided on issues related to the League of Nations. Questions of Canadian policy toward the League bore little direct relationship to the immediate private interests of either wealthy individuals or corporations. There would appear to be no reason to assume that party funds were either given or withheld based on that area of policy. Once again, the party leaders in both major parties would appear to have had a virtually free hand in determining policy toward the League.

During these years, three other political parties met with some success in Canadian national elections, though never reaching the point of cabinet representation. These were the Progressive party, which won important support in the 1921 and 1925 elections, and the Cooperative Commonwealth Federation and Social Credit parties, both of which contested the 1935 election with some success. Only the Progressives ever held a balance of power position in the House of Commons between the two major parties, and thus had the opportunity to exercise a major influence on policy decisions. However, with the exception of the Progressives' advocacy of tariff reduction, the three smaller parties were formed and sought support almost exclusively on the basis of demands for internal social and economic reform. Individuals within the parliamentary ranks of the minor parties, as within the major parties, did, largely as a matter of personal interest, take an active part in foreign policy criticism and discussion. The most notable figure in this category was, of course, the CCF party leader, J.S. Woodsworth. Woodsworth's foreign policy views had essentially a personal rather than a party basis, however, as evidenced, for example, by the refusal of any of the other CCF members of the House of Commons to follow him when in September 1939, he opposed Canada's entry into the second world war.

Another measure of the relationship between policy attitudes and party affiliation is the parliamentary record of voting and debate. Throughout the years of the League of Nations' existence, there were no roll call votes in either the House of Commons or the Senate on League matters, except for the 1919 House vote, already discussed, on the Fielding amendment to the resolution approving the Versailles Treaty. Participation in debate on League affairs did not reveal major differences either in interest or in attitudes, based on party membership. The thirty-four members of the House of Commons taking part in such debates in the years 1925-36 consisted of ten Liberals, fourteen Conservatives, and ten minor party members. Favourable attitudes toward the League predominated among the participants: seven of the Liberals, nine of the Conservatives, and five of the minor party members. In the Senate the pattern was much the same. Participating in debate regarding the League in 1925-36 were thirteen Liberals and seventeen Conservatives. Predominantly favourable attitudes were expressed by ten Liberals and twelve Conservatives. While the numbers involved are too small to justify any conclusion as to prevailing party attitudes, they at least demonstrate the absence of any division along party lines among those members of parliament giving public expression to their views.

The same figures permit examination also of the assertion frequently made that Quebecers, or at least French Canadians from Quebec, were strongly isolationist in their views in this period. It has already been noted that, next only to the prime ministers, the cabinet members most active in foreign policy and League matters were both French Canadians from Quebec, Ernest Lapointe and

Raoul Dandurand. Of the thirty-four participants in House of Commons debate on the League in 1925-36, nine were from Quebec, of whom seven were French Canadians. Predominantly favourable attitudes were expressed by five of these Quebec members, including four French Canadians. In the Senate during the same years, seven members from Quebec, all French Canadians, took part in debate on the League, five of them expressing predominantly favourable views. Here again, the numbers are too small to justify any sweeping conclusions. However, neither the extent of interest in nor the attitudes expressed toward the League of Nations were strikingly different for Quebec members of parliament, as compared with the membership in general.

Opportunity to influence government policy regarding the League, and interest in doing so, also existed, of course, outside of parliament and the political party organizations. The most prominent individual in this category, and a major advocate of the League of Nations in the 1930s, was John W. Dafoe, editor of the *Manitoba Free Press* (after 1931 the *Winnipeg Free Press*). Dafoe edited the newspaper from 1901 till his death in 1944, and by the 1920s had built a national reputation for it, and for himself as editor. The *Free Press* was owned by Clifford Sifton, a minister in the Liberal government of Sir Wilfrid Laurier. Dafoe was also strongly identified with the Liberal party, and the *Free Press* became a principal Liberal party organ. In 1917, however, Dafoe took a Liberal Unionist position, supporting military conscription and the Borden government; after the war, he gradually found his way back into the regular Liberal ranks.

Dafoe's interest and involvement in foreign policy questions was always strong. In 1919 Borden took him to the Paris Peace Conference as a press officer for the Canadian delegation, and Mackenzie King took him to London to the Imperial Conference of 1923 in the same capacity. Dafoe's interest in the League of Nations was initially, like that prevailing in the Canadian governments of the 1920s, almost exclusively based on its usefulness in establishing full Canadian independence of Britain, in external as well as domestic affairs. To his publisher, Sir Clifford Sifton, who considered the League 'a preposterous and expensive farce ... designed to involve us in European and Imperialistic complications,'[36] Dafoe wrote in May 1921:

Meanwhile the Canadian government should be careful to protect itself against being involved in any European or Asiatic adventures under the auspices of the League and this can be readily done if the government at Ottawa is on guard. Meanwhile membership in the League is a simply invaluable argument at the disposal of those who urge the opinion that the Dominions have obtained sovereign power. The centralists have only realized how fatal the implications of Dominion membership in the League are to the conception of the Empire as a diplomatic unit and there is no way out for them excepting a demand that the Dominions renounce their connection with the League ...[37]

In keeping with these views, Dafoe opposed such attempts to strengthen collective security arrangements as the Draft Treaty of Mutual Assistance of 1923, and the Geneva Protocol of 1924.[38] At the same time he supported Canadian membership in the League, and was a speaker for the League of Nations Society.[39] By the time the crises of the 1930s arrived, Dafoe's views had substantially changed, and Sifton's death in 1929 had removed any necessity to defer to the latter's strongly isolationist point of view. Dafoe now championed the League and collective security as a means of preventing another world war, and waged a vigorous and continuing editorial campaign in support of effective League action in opposition to aggression. He was also now an active member of the National Council of the League of Nations Society, and was in general the country's most influential and vocal advocate of full support for the League system.

In 1921 organized support for the League from outside of governmental circles was launched with the formation of the League of Nations Society in Canada. The Society was modelled after counterpart organizations in Great Britain and the United States. Unlike those organizations, however, which were formed to promote the idea of establishing a League of Nations, the Canadian Society was not organized until after the League had already been established, with Canada as a member. Thus the Canadian Society, in backing the League and Canadian membership in it, was, from the beginning, promoting an idea which had been officially accepted by the Canadian government, however superficially, and which was essentially non-controversial as long as it did not imply backing for specific policies. Throughout its existence the League of Nations Society tended to emphasize a generalized support for international co-operation and for the League as an institution, and to concentrate on promoting interest in the League and on spreading information about its activities. It avoided subjects of controversy regarding Canadian policy toward the League, such as the question of Canada's commitment to economic or military sanctions, as much as possible. By taking this approach the Society was able to obtain at least nominal support from persons primarily interested in the development of a working collective security system, from persons whose main interest was the promotion of Canada's international status and who were indifferent or opposed to collective security obligations, and from those concerned only with such political or public relations benefits as might be obtained from associating their names with a worthy, but non-controversial, cause.

As a result, formal public support for the League of Nations Society was at first glance most impressive. Until the late 1930s, the Society was always able to obtain the affiliation of the prime minister and the leader of the opposition as honorary presidents. The list of officers, and of members of the Society's National Council, was a roster of leading political and academic personalities and, to a lesser extent, of business and labour leaders. Beginning with a grant of $2250 in 1928,[40] the Society received a small annual subsidy from the Canadian government to assist in the distribution of League publications. Well-known national figures from political life or the universities were obtained as President of the Society, including Sir Robert Borden (1921-5), Sir George Foster (1925-9), and Ernest Lapointe (1933-5).

Behind this façade of widespread and influential support for the League, the reality was, of course, more modest, but not without substance. In the 1920s, Borden, Foster, and Newton W. Rowell were among those actively involved in speaking tours for the Society. By 1923, there were twenty-seven branches in operation, and during that year the Society sponsored visits and speeches by Lord Robert Cecil and Fridtjof Nansen.[41] Individual memberships by January 1924 numbered 8000, and the cities in western Canada were especially active in League work, according to H.G. Richardson, the Society's general secretary.[42] In the fall of 1924 Richardson attended the League Assembly meeting in Geneva, and worked briefly on the staff of the Information Section, writing articles on the sessions for the Canadian Press.[43]

By 1929 the Society's membership had increased to 19,500,[44] and its news bulletin had been succeeded in 1928 by a monthly publication, *Interdependence*. According to a Canadian official at the League who had recently returned from a visit home, the Society's educational campaign had been highly successful. 'In fact,' he reported, 'at least in the large cities, the saturation point has almost been reached and only very special speakers could draw crowds on a purely League subject.' Sir Herbert Ames, the former League financial director, was now an active lecturer for the Society, and for the first time Catholic church officials, as well as Protestant, were becoming active in support of the League.[45]

As the League entered the period of crises of the 1930s, the League of Nations Society in Canada had developed into an organization of considerable vitality. This proved deceptive, however, as major controversy over League activities and Canadian policy toward the League developed. The orientation which the Society had adopted, emphasizing a generalized institutional support for the League, and avoiding divisive policy questions, had not equipped it to take any effective stand when controversy arose. In the crisis over League and Canadian policy regarding the Italo-Ethiopian War in 1935, the Society was immobilized by dissesions within its own ranks. Ernest Lapointe, who had left the presidency of the Society only the preceding February, in November of that year played a key role in Canada's refusal to support effective League sanctions. By the late 1930s, the widespread affiliation of influential persons with the Society had evaporated as quickly as it had arisen.

In 1928 another national organization with a prime interest in foreign policy, the Canadian Institute of International Affairs, was founded. The CIIA, unlike the League of Nations Society, was not established to promote any particular idea or point of view, but rather to encourage study and discussion of the full range of contemporary international relations questions. It took no official stand on issues. Nevertheless, through an overlap in membership of many key officials in the League of Nations Society and the CIIA, opportunity was at least provided for influential proponents of the League to establish contact with the wider community of persons interested in foreign affairs. Among the presidents of the CIIA were Sir Robert Borden (1928-32), Newton W. Rowell (1932-4), and John W. Dafoe (1936-7), all of whom were prominent also in the affairs of the League of Nations Society. The activities of the CIIA, then, provided an additional opportunity for publicizing the League, without becoming involved in controversy over policy.

Still another source of active promotion in Canada of favourable attitudes toward the League was the Secretariat of the League itself, and more particularly the Canadian members of the Secretariat. When the initial staffing of the new international organization was done, the secretary-general, Sir Eric Drummond, established the principle that members of the Secretariat would be appointed by the League and serve as part of a new international civil service, rather than being appointed by and serving their home governments. Officially, then, there was no special relationship between an official of the Secretariat and his home state. In practice, however, this was by no means the case. Careers in a national civil service sometimes were only interrupted, not terminated, by an appointment to the Secretariat. Drummond himself provides a prime example. After serving as Secretary-General from 1919 to 1933, he promptly resumed his previous career as an official of the British Foreign Office, and was named British Ambassador to Italy.

It was also common practice for a key official, while serving in the Secretariat, to act as an informal liaison representative for the League with both the government and private organizations in his home country, even though the subject of the contact was unrelated to his official position at Geneva. This was very much the case with the only Canadian who served in a top administrative position in the Secretariat, Sir Herbert Ames, who was financial director of the League from 1919 to 1926.

Ames was a Montreal businessman and Conservative party member of parliament. He was appointed the League's first financial director in August 1919, but did not resign his seat in the House of Commons until February 1921, an early indication of the possibility of combining national and international careers. In June 1920, during a trip home to Canada, he spoke in the House of Commons as a member, explaining the current state of the League's activities and answering questions from other members.[46]

Throughout his years as financial director, Ames was also actively in contact with the League of Nations Society in Canada. Indeed, he and Walter A. Riddell, then the ranking Canadian on the staff of the International Labour Organization, were apparently instrumental in getting the Society established in the first place. In November 1920, shortly before the First Assembly of the League met, Riddell contacted Ames and F.P. Walters, assistant to Sir Eric Drummond, suggesting conversations with Newton W. Rowell and Sir George Foster while they were in Geneva, 'to discuss with them plans for setting on foot a Canadian League of Nations Union.' Ames agreed that such discussions would be desirable, and Walters wished them success with the project.[47] The following April Ames wrote Rowell in Canada, again advocating the setting up of a Canadian Society.[48] The League of Nations Society in Canada was founded at about the same time, and held its first public meeting in Toronto in October. Ames promptly sent a congratulatory letter to Rowell.[49] In the succeeding years Ames was involved in such activities as helping Society officials get information they desired, urging his former political associates to join and support the Society, and going on speaking tours for the Society while on home leave in Canada.

In addition, Ames was also in direct contact with Canadian government officials, attempting to encourage support for the League. For example, when Arthur Meighen reorganized his cabinet in September 1921, in preparation for the general election of that year, Ames wrote six of the new ministers, congratulating them on their appointments, wishing them success in the election, and commenting on the advantage to Canada of its membership in the League. To those who replied indicating interest, he offered to provide any specific information they could use whenever it might be needed. The same offer was sent to Meighen.[50]

Ames was better acquainted with Conservative party figures than with the Liberals, who came into power in Ottawa in December 1921. In February he wrote a cordial letter to the new prime minister, Mackenzie King, urging that a strong Canadian delegation be sent to the 1922 Assembly, and suggesting that King head it himself if possible.[51] He also made inquiries, of Sir Robert Borden among others, as to King's attitude toward the League,[52] and reported to Sir Eric Drummond in March that the new government was favourably disposed.[53]

In the following years Ames' Canadian government contacts included such activities as providing information to an official of the Department of Labour, hosting a visiting senator, and writing Raoul Dandurand to urge promotion of a pro-League attitude at a meeting of United States and Canadian legislators.[54] On vacation in Canada, he met with King, Meighen, and Borden, among others, to discuss League affairs.

The public relations work done by Ames while Financial Director of the League was revealing as to the type of support which the Secretariat sought. In effect, what was sought was a generalized support for the League of Nations as an organization doing important and useful work in the cause of world peace. Any reference to controversial policy questions was studiously avoided. From the Secretariat's standpoint, this prevented generating pressures on itself to follow this or that policy. Virtually no demands were placed on the Secretariat as a result of Canadian contacts which it initiated, except demands for information. The demands in the other direction were for precisely what both the Canadian government and such groups as the League of Nations Society in Canada were prepared to give, a generalized endorsement and support not involving commitments on any policy question. Thus, for example, while the Canadian government was, from 1920 to 1923, actively attempting to get Article 10 of the League Covenant deleted or modified, a question of considerable importance to the League's ability to function successfully as a collective security organization (see Chapters 5 and 6), Ames in his contacts with government officials and private individuals in Canada seems never to have broached the question. The support that was sought was essentially superficial, and that was exactly what was obtained.

More fundamentally, the apparent lack of interest on the part of the Secretariat in generating effective support for the main purposes of the League, may have reflected a widespread lack of commitment to those purposes within the Secretariat itself. The main impression obtained from the internal memoranda of the top Secretariat officials is of an interest in carrying out the Secretariat's responsibilities competently, in avoiding unnecessary controversy, and in being responsive to the expectations of the most influential member states. Except for actions likely to result in criticism of or pressures on the Secretariat itself, its top officials appear to have been as neutral in private as in public. Sir Eric Drummond's career provides, again, a prime example. After fourteen years as the League's Secretary-General, he was so little identified personally with the principal objectives of the League that he continued to be acceptable to Mussolini as British Ambassador throughout the period of League economic sanctions against Italy during the Italian invasion of Ethiopia.

Of course, many Secretariat officials were undoubtedly devoted to the cause of a strong and effective collective security function for the League, whatever the limitations may have been on their seeking more than a generalized and non-controversial backing for the organization in their external contacts. Sir Herbert Ames' own identification with the League remained strong after he left the Secretariat in 1926. Later that same year he was one of the delegates appointed by the Meighen government to represent Canada at the League Assembly. Back in Canada, he was an active speaker for the League of Nations Society,[55] and was an outspoken critic of Japan's occupation of Manchuria in violation of the League Covenant.[56]

Various other Canadians besides Ames were employed by the League Secretariat, but none in a position of comparable importance. In addition to appointments to the permanent Secretariat staff, occasional appointments were made as 'temporary collaborators' in the Information Section. These appointments were essentially a part of the Secretariat's public relations activities. Prominent individuals known to be interested in the League were invited to accept a temporary appointment, without salary but with expenses paid, during the annual fall meetings of the League Assembly and Council. They were able to attend the meetings of those bodies, as well as to observe the operations of the Secretariat, and to obtain a good deal of behind-the-scenes information. It was hoped that they would leave Geneva both better informed and favourably impressed. The most notable such appointment of a Canadian was that of J.S. Woodsworth in 1931. Woodsworth had been found 'an interested and cooperative temporary collaborator' by the Information Section, which attributed in part to this first-hand experience of the League the fact that he was friendly toward it and active in the League of Nations Society in Canada in the following years.[57]

In the 1930s, the most active member of the Secretariat's staff in public relations contacts with Canada was Miss Mary Craig McGeachy. Miss McGeachy was a young woman from Sarnia, Ontario, who, after graduating from the University of Toronto, teaching history in high school, and working as an editor for an international students' organization, had been employed by the Information Section in 1928. As the only Canadian in the Information Section she soon became responsible for the Section's contacts with Canada, even though she was only a junior staff member. In 1930, 1932, and 1933, she went on speaking tours of Canada on behalf of the League. Her tours were a great success, a reflection largely of her own energy and enthusiasm, and she quickly made herself known to the key Canadian figures involved in League affairs. The General Secretary of the League of Nations Society wrote the Information Section in 1930, at the time of her first tour, that Miss McGeachy had 'started on a whirlwind campaign,' had given ten talks about the League in three days, and was 'helping us tremendously by delivering addresses before teachers and students.'[58] He wrote Sir Eric Drummond at the conclusion of the tour, sending a resolution of appreciation for Miss McGeachy's work adopted by the national executive committee of the Society, and adding that 'from Montreal to Victoria word has been received from Educationalists expressing their appreciation.'[59] Edgar Tarr of the Winnipeg branch of the Canadian Institute of International Affairs (later national CIIA president) wrote that he and John W. Dafoe had decided to call a special branch meeting to hear 'this unknown representative of womankind,' and that there had been general agreement afterwards 'that it was the most constructively interesting and informative Institute meeting that we have had in connection with League affairs.'[60] Later Dafoe wrote that he considered Miss McGeachy 'one of the ablest young Canadians of the day.'[61]

During her visit in 1932, Miss McGeachy had an interview with Prime Minister Bennett and met with O.D. Skelton, Lester Pearson, Hume Wrong, and Hugh Keenleyside of the External Affairs staff.[62] In 1933 she saw Bennett again, spoke on Canadian foreign policy at Liberal and Conservative party study conferences, and discussed with CCF party leaders the chapter on foreign policy in a party booklet that was being prepared.[63]

The contacts which Miss McGeachy made during these visits were put to good use. She was a regular contributor to *Interdependence*, the League of Nations Society publication. She kept up a correspondence on League affairs with John W. Dafoe and maintained contact with the External Affairs officers she had met, both providing and obtaining confidential information about developments related to the League. The views she expressed were at times clearly personal, rather than official; her own position on policy questions was by no means neutral. She was enthusiastic about the League of Nations, anxious to see it strong and successful, and not at all hesitant in urging action which she thought might be useful. The breadth of her contacts in Canada enabled her to report in detail to the Secretary-General and other League officials on the current attitudes of key governmental and private individuals and groups; her interest in encouraging effective backing for the League also led to a significant flow of information to League supporters in Canada.

In general, then, demands made on the Canadian government regarding its attitude toward the League of Nations came from two principal sources: from individuals, both within and outside of parliament, with a strong personal interest in the League, and from the League of Nations Society in Canada. Parliament itself had no substantial role to play, except as a forum where interested individual members could make themselves heard. The political parties, and private organizations other than the League of Nations Society, were not active in any significant way in attempting to influence policy toward the League.

The desires of those who did attempt to influence Canadian policy differed greatly. The League of Nations Society sought only a generalized, non-controversial endorsement of and co-operation with the League, rather than urging specific policies on either Ottawa or Geneva. The Secretariat of the League itself also sought to obtain essentially that type of support. This was rather easily accomplished, but was superficial and of little value in time of crisis. Various influential individuals in parliament and in the League of Nations Society were prepared to offer a more meaningful support for the League's essential objective of preventing or defeating aggression through a system of collective security, but the absence of any organizational base for promoting their views, as well as many differences in approach from one individual to another, tended to minimize their effective influence. The over-all effect was to leave the government of the day a remarkably free hand in formulating and carrying out whatever specific policies it might choose.

4
The main themes of
Canadian policy at Geneva

The main themes of Canadian policy within the League of Nations, and the attitudes and objectives which they reflected, had been foreshadowed by the positions taken by Canada at the Peace Conference. One recurrent theme was a feeling of detachment from, and a reluctance to become involved in, what were viewed as essentially European problems. This in turn was based to a large extent on feelings of superiority, both moral superiority and superiority in conducting the practical business of international relations. These feelings were, of course, common in the United States as well as in Canada in the period between the two great wars, and were an important ingredient in each country's version of isolationism. Canadians, however, as regular participants in League meetings, frequently presented their view of the relative merits of the New World and the Old to the assembled delegates, and can hardly have had a very favourable reception.

An early example of this attitude is contained in an address by Newton W. Rowell at the First Assembly in 1920:

You may say that we should have confidence in European statesmen and leaders. Perhaps we should, but it was European policy, European statesmanship, European ambition, that drenched this world with blood and from which we are still suffering and will suffer for generations. Fifty thousand Canadians under the soil of France and Flanders is what Canada has paid for European statesmanship trying to settle European problems. I place responsibility on a few: I would not distribute it over many; but nevertheless it is European.[1]

Four years later Raoul Dandurand, also in a speech to the League Assembly, sounded the same theme: 'The three chief pillars upon which this structure has been erected – arbitration, security and disarmament – have long been accepted and applied in my country ... Not only have we had a hundred years of peace on our borders, but we think in terms of peace, while Europe, an armed camp, thinks in terms of war.'[2]

This underlying distrust, even among such internationally-minded Canadians as Rowell and Dandurand, of Europe's ability to settle its own disputes led also to frequent lecturing of the League delegates on how their countries' conduct might be improved, usually citing Canadian-United States relations as an example. Prime Minister King, in his address to the League Assembly in 1928 stressed this theme. Describing Canada's peaceful relations with the United States, as illustrated by the unfortified border and the creation of the International Joint Commission to deal with boundary water problems, King urged on his listeners the importance of developing a public opinion opposed to war, and of establishing procedures for arbitration, conciliation, and investigation, in international as in industrial disputes.[3] The International Joint Commission, which had had considerable success in resolving relatively minor disputes between two friendly neighbours, was repeatedly cited by Canadian spokesmen at the League as an example to be followed elsewhere in the world. Thus at the height of the Assembly's consideration in 1932 of the Japanese invasion and occupation of Manchuria, C.H. Cahan, a senior cabinet minister who was the Canadian First Delegate, was advised by the Department of External Affairs that possibly a 'permanent body on lines of our International Joint Commission might be considered' as a means of resolving Sino-Japanese difficulties,[4] and he duly made the suggestion in his Assembly speech.[5]

Combined with the feeling that Canadian experience in its international relations provided a useful guide to European and Asiatic powers was, however, the greatest reluctance to become involved in the settling of their disputes, beyond a platitudinous exhortation to better behaviour. While verbal endorsement of the conciliatory as opposed to the coercive role of the League was frequently given, Canadian initiatives within the League to aid in finding solutions to other countries' problems or disputes were notably absent. The only example of any consequence of such an initiative by Canada was the proposal by Raoul Dandurand in 1929 for a revised procedure in the review of minorities complaints by the League Council, and this proposal, though it had Ottawa's acquiescence, was essentially an initiative of Dandurand himself (see Chapter 8).

Initially, the Canadian government appears to have considered a more active role. At the 1920 Assembly, Newton W. Rowell in particular was much involved in the discussion of a wide range of political problems. He was emphatic, for example, in urging the League Council to impose a solution of the Polish-Lithuanian dispute over Vilna: 'I wish to point out ... that unless the Council is prepared to back up its own decisions by invoking the powers of the League, the economic and other powers, if necessary ... it will cease to hold the respect of the nations. The Council is on trial before the Assembly and the nations to-day, which are waiting to see if it has the courage to implement its own decisions ...'[6]

Similarly, Rowell gave support in committee and in the full Assembly to the admission of Albania to the League, over the initial objections of Britain and France.[7] As he explained it later in the House of Commons, a majority of the Assembly feared partition of Albania by the powers, 'and they determined to put it out of the hands of the powers to carve up Albania in the future by admitting her to the League, and by article ten all the States became guarantors of her territorial integrity.'[8]

Neither Rowell's activism nor his favourable view of the effects of Article 10 were, however, in keeping with the attitude prevailing in the government at Ottawa. This attitude was more accurately indicated when the League Council inquired whether Canada would be willing, either by itself or jointly with other states, to attempt to negotiate a cessation of the hostilities then taking place between Armenia and Turkish nationalist forces, which threatened the existence of the new Armenian state. Prime Minister Meighen's reply on 1 December 1920, was, quite simply, that the Canadian government 'could not undertake the responsibility therein referred to,'[9] although later the same month Canada was one of only eight states to vote in the Assembly for admission of Armenia to the League.[10]

In subsequent League meetings prior to the great international crises of the 1930s, the Canadian delegates were usually silent when specific political problems between other states were discussed. Occasionally some positive suggestion was made, but statements or actions which might in any way embroil Canada in controversy were carefully avoided. Thus in 1921 and again in 1922 the Assembly adopted, without discussion, Canadian resolutions urging the settlement by the Allied Supreme Council at an early date of the status of Eastern Galicia,[11] a territory with a predominantly Ukrainian population which was under Polish control, but had not yet been officially recognized as part of Poland. The resolutions gave no hint as to what status would be considered satisfactory for the territory. They may have provided some satisfaction to the substantial Ukrainian minority in Canada, but stopped well short of involving the Canadian government in any attempt to settle the matter.

When, in 1926, agreement had been reached among the major powers on admission of Germany to the League with a permanent seat on the Council, as a major step in the reconciliation of Germany with its opponents in the recent war, Canada favoured the course of action which had been agreed upon. A deadlock ensued within the League because of demands by Brazil and Spain that they also be given permanent Council seats. Walter A. Riddell, the Canadian Advisory Officer in Geneva, proposed to Lord Cecil, the British representative on the committee attempting to resolve the impasse, that an enlarged Council be created with a number of semi-permanent members, eligible for re-election, in addition to the permanent and non-permanent members. Cecil was favourably impressed by Riddell's suggestion; Riddell discussed it also with the Secretariat's Legal Section, and it was in fact the solution adopted and successfully put into effect.[12] The suggestion had originated with Riddell himself, not with the government in Ottawa, and was not an official Canadian government proposal. It was nevertheless a good example of the opportunities for constructive accomplishment available to smaller powers at the League. In September 1926, when a German delegation headed by Foreign Minister Gustav Stresemann took its place in the Assembly, and was welcomed by a stirring speech from French Foreign Minister Aristide Briand, the Canadian delegation abandoned its usual reserve. The First Delegate, 79-year old Sir George Foster, wrote in his diary about Briand's speech: 'The applause at its conclusion was overwhelming – the compact of Peace sealing the book of War. I was led by my enthusiasm to raise the British *Hip-Hip-Hurray*, to which delegates and galleries responded.'[13]

In contrast was Canada's complete lack of activity with regard to political developments in the Far East in the mid-1920s. In the House of Commons, J.S. Woodsworth repeatedly challenged the government to initiate some action at the League to protect China from the interventions of stronger powers. In 1925, at a time of British military intervention in China and Chinese boycott of British goods, Woodsworth, citing 'the exploitation and shooting of Chinese workers by British soldiers,' asked Prime Minister King, 'Has our government, as a member of the League of Nations, taken any action at all, and if so what?' King, as usual, refused to discuss the matter: 'As a member of the league the government has not taken any action such as my hon. friend suggests. It is rather a large subject and at the moment I can only promise to see that the matter will be taken into consideration.'[14]

When similar events occurred in 1927, Woodsworth reviewed the situation and asked again, '... has the government of Canada made any representations to the assembly or to the council of the League of Nations with regard to the despatch of British troops to China?' King's only comment was, 'No representations of the character my hon. friend mentions have been made by the government.'[15]

In 1928, with Canada now a member of the Council as well as the Assembly, Woodsworth raised the same question again, this time in the context of civil warfare and Japanese military intervention in China. King first denied having any first-hand information regarding what was taking place. Then, when Woodsworth persisted, he pointed out that China itself had not submitted the matter to the League, and said that 'certainly this government has not felt that Canada has any special responsibility to take action while all other nations refrain from so doing ...'[16]

If Canada was typically unwilling to become involved in the details of settling other countries' disputes, it was greatly interested in the general structure of international organization and the nature of the commitments undertaken by member states. As already discussed, Canada at the Peace Conference had been most uneasy about accepting the collective security obligations of the League Covenant, and had made an unsuccessful attempt to get Article 10, with its guarantee of each member's territory and independence, deleted. This effort was continued by Canada within the League at the first three Assemblies, and was the only important Canadian initiative at Geneva in the League's early years (see Chapters 5 and 6).

While opposed from the beginning to Article 10 and to any commitment to use military forces against an aggressor, the Canadian government did not initially show the same concern about the possibility of economic sanctions. At the 1921 Assembly proposed amendments to Article 16 of the Covenant were adopted, intended to make possible the gradual or partial application of economic sanctions when recommended by the Council, in place of the immediate and universal application by League members required by the original text of the Article. (Though adopted unanimously, the amendments never received the necessary ratifications to come into force.[17]) Canada, along with all other members voting, supported the amendments, but took no active part in drafting or discussing them. The Department of External Affairs' analysis of the amendments, prepared in 1922 by Loring C. Christie, the Department's legal adviser, expressed the view that it was 'important that Article 16 ... should be made as effective as possible' in order to be able 'to bring a recalcitrant State to its senses through the use of the economic weapon alone and without recourse to the extreme step of war,' and considered that the amendments would help achieve that goal.[18] They were subsequently ratified by Canada.[19]

By 1925, however, the Canadian government had extended its opposition to sanctions to include the economic as well as the military variety, and Prime Minister King, in recommending approval of a non-controversial amendment to the Covenant, noted that 'from Canada's point of view ... the whole Article XVI is open to objection ...'[20]

King's view of economic sanctions was spelled out in some detail in instructions to Walter Riddell in 1928:

Emphasize view security not synonymous with sanctions ... Undertakings of military and economic pressure against state violating Covenant have place but on whole this is least distinctive and least profitable course for League to develop.

Most effective sanction whether in international or in industrial disputes is force of informed and focussed public opinion ... Regarding Article Sixteen any increase or elaboration of obligations of League members should await progress in solving problem of possible attitude of neutral states outside League.[21]

The change from the King government to the Bennett government in 1930 produced no immediate change in this general hostility toward sanctions of whatever variety, and especially toward any strengthening of the system. Sir Robert Borden, Canada's First Delegate at the 1930 Assembly, expressed it this way:

... I am not enthusiastic, and I do not think my country ever has been enthusiastic, to increase the measure of sanctions. If I have a right conception of the value of the League of Nations to the world, its significance rests on something that transcends any effort to provide sanctions ... In short, Mr Chairman, I do not think that Canada would desire to become subject to any contractual or moral obligation not already set forth in the existing Covenant to undertake the enforcement of sanctions. Therefore, so far as the extension of sanctions is proposed ... I am not authorised, nor indeed would I desire, to give my assent to any such proposal.[22]

Given the firm opposition by the Canadian government to advance commitments to military action, and eventually also to economic action, it is not surprising that it was consistently opposed to the efforts at Geneva in the 1920s to expand and strengthen the collective security provisions of the Covenant. The first important move in this direction was the adoption by the 1922 Assembly of a resolution asking League members to state their views on a proposed Treaty of Mutual Guarantee, whereby specific guarantees of military assistance in case of attack would be given on a regional basis, to make possible a general reduction of armaments, and to take effect only after such a reduction had been carried out.[23]

Sir Joseph Pope, the Undersecretary of State for External Affairs, replied, not very helpfully, 'that the views expressed in the Assembly Resolution ... commend themselves to the Canadian Government, which has every sympathy with the object sought to be attained.'[24] The League Secretariat was unhappy with so vague a statement, and through Sir Herbert Ames, the League's financial director and its top Canadian official, suggested informally to the Canadian government that the reply be withdrawn and a more specific one substituted. Ernest Lapointe, the Minister of Marine and Fisheries, reviewed the matter and agreed that a new reply should be sent. He recommended to Prime Minister King that strong support should be expressed for disarmament, but not for new military guarantees. 'I do not think,' he said, 'that our people would be prepared to ratify any agreement binding Canada to help other nations, under our present circumstances.'[25] Lapointe's recommendations were accepted by King. The new reply sent by Pope to the League Secretariat repeated, essentially, the language recommended by Lapointe, and concluded that 'the Government, therefore, does not see its way to a participation in the Treaty of Mutual Guarantee.'[26]

At the 1923 Assembly a draft treaty was prepared, now titled the Treaty of Mutual Assistance, along the lines of the previous year's proposal. It was not endorsed by the Assembly, but was instead sent to governments for comment. Canada took no part in the discussions leading to its preparation, either in committee or in the full Assembly. When the draft treaty was submitted for comment, the reply sent by Mackenzie King rejected it, as was to be expected.[27] It was also rejected by various other governments, including the new Labour government of Great Britain headed by Ramsay MacDonald, and the proposal was dropped.

Attempts to strengthen the security system of the Covenant were by no means at an end, however, and the MacDonald government joined in sponsoring at the 1924 Assembly a 'Protocol for the Pacific Settlement of International Disputes,' or Geneva Protocol, which was accepted by the Assembly and opened for signature. The Protocol provided for compulsory arbitration of all disputes not settled peacefully by other means, for military measures on a regional basis against any state resorting to war rather than arbitration, and for the convening of a general disarmament conference; it was to come into force only when a general plan for reduction of armaments had been agreed to. At the Assembly the opinions expressed by the delegates were almost entirely favourable. Only Canada, whose spokesman was Raoul Dandurand, took a somewhat negative position,[28] and even he did not oppose the Protocol, but only reserved judgment on it: 'Our Government and our Parliament will have to consider in what measure this Protocol will meet the conditions of our country, and decide whether it can undertake to subscribe to its obligations.'[29]

The public reactions at Geneva were highly misleading, however. The Geneva Protocol, in fact, suffered the same fate as the Treaty of Mutual Assistance, and never came into effect. Once again, Great Britain played a key role: the Conservative government which came into office late in 1924 rejected the Protocol which its predecessor had helped to sponsor. In Canada, Dandurand was privately an advocate of the Protocol, but the prevailing opinion in the government was decidedly to the contrary. Dandurand wrote later: 'A mon retour au pays, M. King invita quelques collègues à "Laurier House" [King's residence] et quelques techniciens qui avait déjà étudié le Protocole. La discussion fut fort vive et se continua tard dans la nuit ... Je défendis le Protocole sur tous ses points, mais il me fallut me rendre à l'évidence et constater que la majorité était d'un autre avis.'[30]*

The Protocol was referred for review to an interdepartmental committee which included, among others, O.D. Skelton of the Department of External Affairs. The committee's recommendation to King was that 'it would not be in the interests of Canada, of the British Empire, or of the League itself, to adhere to the Protocol, and particularly to its rigid provisions for the application of economic and military sanctions in every future war.' The committee also recommended that the Canadian statement rejecting the Protocol, in order not to appear entirely negative, should include an expression of willingness to consider acceptance of the compulsory jurisdiction of the Permanent Court of International Justice.[31] King accepted these recommendations, and a letter embodying them was prepared by Skelton,[32] and sent on 9 March 1925, to the League Secretariat.[33]

The question of ratification of the Geneva Protocol received a certain amount of attention in the Canadian parliament. The government made no presentation to the parliament on the subject of the Protocol prior to formally rejecting it on 9 March, although parliament had then been in session for over a month. This omission was criticized by Arthur Meighen, the Leader of the Opposition, who also indicated his own doubts as to the advisability of accepting the Protocol. In reply, King in effect refused to discuss it, saying that 'up to the present, the matter has not been disposed of in any final way ... The government will make its position known at the right time ...'[34] No explanation was offered to parliament following 9 March either, until after the government's failure to advise or consult parliament, as well as its decision to reject the Protocol, had been strongly criticized in the Senate by Sir George Foster:

... Canada may be involved this very day in weakening, maybe in striking down, that which so many peoples of the world after long strivings have come to consider as high record-mark along the line of assured peace and of freedom from war ...

I say that it [the Geneva Protocol] struck high-water mark in the history of the world, and that no more forward and no more courageous statement was ever made by the community of nations in the history of the wide world than was made there ... No wars of aggression – Arbitration for all Disputes – these were the high notes struck ...

* 'On my return to the country, Mr King invited some colleagues to "Laurier House" [King's residence] and some technicians who had already studied the Protocol. The discussion was very lively and continued late in the night ... I defended the Protocol in all its aspects, but it was necessary for me to yield to the evidence and admit that the majority was of another opinion.'

Anyway I do not think Canada should ... declare that she will assume no sanctions, because she is afraid that she will be called upon to do her reasonable part in carrying out the obligations of the League of Nations.[35]

Dandurand, the government leader in the Senate, finally in April gave an explanation and defence of the government's rejection of the Protocol, without, of course, revealing his own personal views on the subject.[36] Some years later, when the King government was no longer in office, he reviewed the history of the Geneva Protocol again in the Senate and, without criticizing the decision which the Canadian government had taken, made clear where his sentiments lay. The Protocol, he said, had 'clearly provided for determining which country was the aggressor in any dispute.' It had 'affirmed the principle of one for all and all for one. There was great disappointment when the protocol was dispensed with.'[37]

If supporters of the League were unable to move the government on questions involving military or economic sanctions, such was not the case when non-coercive measures were being considered. The Canadian government, though not ordinarily willing to involve itself in attempts at mediating specific disputes, was quite willing to consider strengthening the international machinery for peaceful settlement.

One area in which Canada took some direct initiative was with regard to acceptance of the compulsory jurisdiction of the Permanent Court of International Justice. The Court, made up of judges chosen jointly by the League Council and Assembly, was established in 1922, and all League members were entitled to bring cases before it, with the consent of the other state or states involved in the case. It was also possible to accept an 'optional clause,' whereby a state agreed in advance to the jurisdiction of the Court, either in all cases or with specified exceptions. From the beginning there had been substantial interest in Canada in acceptance of the Court's jurisdiction. One early advocate of acceptance was Raoul Dandurand, who in May 1921, at the time the Court was being organized, criticized the Conservative government then in office for not accepting its jurisdiction in all cases from the outset.[38] In 1924 Dandurand, in the discussions of the Geneva Protocol, urged acceptance at least of the principle of compulsory arbitration.[39] King's other advisers agreed and, as already noted, a statement to that effect was included in the letter rejecting the Protocol. Action along these lines was not favoured, however, by the Conservative government which had come to power in London in 1924, and it was also anxious to maintain a common British Empire policy on the question. Canada acquiesced, and at the Imperial Conference of 1926 the following policy statement was unanimously agreed to: '... the feeling was that it was at present premature to accept the obligations under the Article in question [the optional clause]. A general understanding was reached that none of the Governments represented at the Imperial Conference would take any action in the direction of the acceptance of the compulsory jurisdiction of the Permanent Court, without bringing up the matter for further discussion.'[40]

The 'further discussion' referred to was generally taken to mean the next Imperial Conference, not likely to be held for several years, with the result that any action was indefinitely postponed. This placed the Mackenzie King government in the somewhat embarrassing position of seeming to have abandoned its earlier announced policy because of British objections, a position which King, with his strong interest in Canadian independence in foreign policy matters, could hardly have found comfortable. Criticism of this decision from supporters of the League and of the Court continued. In 1927 Sir George Foster urged acceptance of the optional clause,[41] as did J.S. Woodsworth in 1928, advocating the immediate initiation of discussions with Britain in accordance with the 1926 agreement.[42]

In 1927 Dandurand had replied to Foster that the question was not pressing, and that Canada could well afford to wait three or four years, when the next Imperial Conference would meet.[43] By 1928, however, the government was changing its mind, and King announced his general agreement with the course advocated by Woodsworth.[44] Meanwhile Dandurand had been contacted by Lord Cecil, recently resigned from the British cabinet because of dissatisfaction with Britain's policy toward the League, who told him that Canada could give a very effective lead to Great Britain by acting on its expressed intention of accepting the optional clause. Cecil was told by Dandurand that Canada was moving in that direction. In the fall of 1928 Dandurand informed Sir Cecil Hurst, the British Foreign Office legal expert, that Canada was about to accept the optional clause. As Dandurand later recalled the conversation, Hurst 'expressed surprise ... for he thought we were bound to await another conference. I told him in a bantering tone that he had drafted the 1926 resolution badly, and that we were conferring through the circularizing of the sister-nations, without waiting for an Imperial Conference.'[45] Finally, in January 1929 Prime Minister King made this policy change official, advising both the British and the other Dominion governments that Canada had concluded that it would be desirable for it to accept the optional clause, and inviting their comments.[46] In February, in response to a question from Woodsworth, King made this initiative public in a statement to the House of Commons.[47]

The British government had promptly replied that it favoured postponement of any action until various problems, including the attitude of the United States, had been worked out.[48] New Zealand and South Africa had also favoured postponement. King, proceeding with his usual caution, backed off a bit from his announced intention. In March he agreed to postpone consideration of accepting the optional clause, as requested, until there had been opportunity 'for considering the United States phases of the general question of arbitration and conciliation.'[49] In May, in answer to a question in parliament, he said he did not think Canada necessarily had to wait until all parts of the Empire were in agreement, but that the government would decide its course of action after further conference with other British Empire governments.[50]

Over four years had passed since, in March 1925, the Canadian government had announced its willingness to consider accepting the compulsory jurisdiction of the Permanent Court of International Justice, and the matter was still entirely unresolved, and the Canadian action undetermined. The impasse was broken shortly afterwards, not by Canadian action, but by the defeat in the 1929 general elections of the British Conservative government, and the return to office in June 1929 of Ramsay MacDonald and the Labour party. MacDonald, shortly after resuming office as prime minister, advised the dominions of his interest in working out a joint acceptance of the optional clause.[51] Deciding on the details presented no major problems, so far as Canada was concerned, and at the meeting of the 1929 Assembly in September, Dandurand joined the British and the other Dominion representatives in formally signing the optional clause. The only reservation of importance was the exclusion from the Court's jurisdiction of disputes between component parts of the Empire.

Canada's willingness to take the initiative in pressing for acceptance of the optional clause was quite striking, in comparison with the negativism or inactivity which characterized so much of Canadian participation in League of Nations affairs. The difference, however, was somewhat deceptive. The optional clause could obtain Canada's sponsorship largely because, while promoting the image of Canada and of the King government as strong advocates of the peaceful settlement of disputes, it was unlikely to get Canada into any international difficulties. No commitment to coercive measures was involved, nor was any interference in disputes between third parties. No dispute between Canada and another state could go before the Court unless that other state had also given its consent. Indeed, the chances of Canada being brought before the Court because of its acceptance of the optional clause were obviously quite slim. Disputes with Great Britain were excluded by the British and Canadian reservations. While the United States was giving some serious consideration to adhering to the statute of the Court, thus entitling itself to bring cases before it, United States acceptance of the optional clause was not under consideration. The result was that, even if the United States did adhere to the statute of the Court, it would be able to bring a case against Canada only with Canada's consent in each individual case. With the compulsory jurisdiction of the Court thus not applicable to disputes between Canada and either Great Britain or the United States, its acceptance by Canada was virtually risk free. (And, in fact, Canada was never a party to a case before the Permanent Court of International Justice, either through operation of the optional clause or otherwise, at any time during the Court's existence.) Even then, the Canadian initiative was somewhat hesitant, and it is not clear how far the Canadian government would have pressed it if Britain had not reversed its policy in 1929. Nevertheless, Canada could still quite properly accept a certain credit for acting to strengthen the international system for the peaceful settlement of disputes and for, most unusually, bringing pressure to bear on Great Britain to do the same.

In the other main area in which efforts were made through the League of Nations to restructure international relations in ways more conducive to peace, the attempt at a general reduction of armaments, Canada's role was of minor importance. Canada's own armaments had, after the war, been reduced to their customarily low level. Its relations with Great Britain and the United States, the only countries from which, for geographical reasons, it might conceivably be the object of hostile action, were excellent, it had no aggressive ambitions itself, and it had therefore little or no need for arms. The danger to Canada from a high level of armaments in other states lay not in the possibility of a direct attack on itself, but in the danger of a new outbreak of general war. Canada was quite prepared to give its support to proposals for reduction of armaments, but was not in a position to provide much itself except exhortation. It might have used its position within the British Empire to encourage Britain to reduce its arms; however, to Canadian leaders the British navy seemed a protection and not a threat, and they were inclined instead to support Britain's view that the potential threats to world peace came primarily from large land armies, such as Britain itself did not maintain.

At the 1930 Assembly, dissatisfied as were many other members with the long delays in doing anything to carry out the long-promised general reduction of armaments, Canada took the lead in criticizing what the major powers had so far agreed on as entirely inadequate. Sir Robert Borden, the Canadian First Delegate, gave a forceful presentation of the Canadian position:

So far as I understand the present situation, it is proposed ... that, for the limitation of armaments, there shall be merely publicity of budgetary appropriations, and that the number of trained reserves shall not be taken into account. I confess that that to me seems no limitation at all. With all respect, I express my profound conviction that it does not, in any measure, fulfil the supreme purpose expressed in the Covenant.

The report speaks of mutual confidence. We have renounced war, have we not, by solemn engagement? To what end does the maintenance of enormous armaments still continue? Our engagement was solemn and sincere, was it not? Shall it not find expression in something more enduring than words, something more effective than what has been proposed up to the present?

I must say with all respect that, in this regard, the League of Nations stands to-day at the bar of public opinion. The burden of armaments is intolerable; their continuance is a perpetual menace to world peace.[52]

Aristide Briand replied eloquently for France, referring to the striking gains made by the Nazis in the recent German general elections and chiding Canada for views which merely reflected its remoteness from danger:

Yet not so long ago, just when I was uttering none but words of concord, words for which I am sometimes bitterly blamed, words of conciliation and co-operation – at that very moment clamours from the polling-booths penetrated to my ears, and cries of hatred and of death were the response that reached me ...

In such a case, I say, are not those who may be threatened at some future date entitled to reflect, and in a gathering such as this, have they not a right to turn to the nations with nothing to fear, who live in a state of blissful well-being remote from danger, and to say to them: 'We are brothers, all of us here in this Assembly. Leave your heights of security, come down into the valley, come nearer, listen to what is going on and say if we are not justified in showing caution'?[53]

The gulf separating Canadian and French views on disarmament was also fully applicable, of course, to questions of security, and the instructions to the Canadian delegation to the Disarmament Conference which finally convened in February 1932 emphasized Canada's disagreement with the French 'security thesis' and with any new 'political proposals designed to protect nations faced with invasion or aggression.'[54]

Prime Minister Bennett, speaking in the House of Commons at about the time the Disarmament Conference opened, found the key to disarmament to be in the abolition of military conscription (a system not in use by either Canada or Britain).[55] The same opinion was presented at the Conference in July by Maurice Dupré, Solicitor General in the Bennett cabinet.[56] However, in general Canada was content at the Conference to support the principal initiatives taken by others.

The approach of the Disarmament Conference had been the occasion in Canada of a massive campaign, sponsored by the League of Nations Society and various civic and religious organizations, to obtain signatures on petitions supporting its objective of reducing armaments. The campaign was a great success, and early in the Conference petitions with over half a million signatures, out of a total

Canadian population of ten million, were laid before the Conference.[57] Intensity of interest was certainly demonstrated, but not in a way designed to help resolve any of the conflicting points of view which led the Conference eventually to end in 1934 in complete failure.

Another major theme of Canada's policy regarding the League of Nations was an objection to any League involvement in what Canada regarded as its internal affairs. This had already been evident at the Peace Conference, in Canadian objections to any League jurisdiction in questions of labour standards for immigrant workers.

League involvement in Canadian internal affairs never became a serious issue at Geneva. The nearest approach was the attempt in 1923 of the Six Nations Indians to get their complaints against the Canadian government before the League for discussion. The attempt came close to succeeding, but was eventually successfully headed off by Canadian and British objections (see Chapter 7).

Otherwise, this Canadian attitude led primarily to a reluctance to have the League take an active role in economic questions, other than sponsoring conferences or preparing factual studies. The first problem arising in this area was the Italian sponsorship in 1919-20 of League action to bring about a more equitable distribution of raw materials among industrial countries, at a time of post-war economic depression. At the initial conference of the International Labour Organization in 1919, Canada joined in defeating an Italian resolution recommending that the League Council take up the question, with Newton W. Rowell insisting, on behalf of the Canadian government, that the ILO and the League had no jurisdiction.[58] The same view was repeated by Rowell at the First Assembly of the League in 1920: '... I think it is unfortunate to throw out to this Assembly and to the public any proposal to the effect that the Covenant of the League covers the question of raw materials. I submit, with respect, it is clear beyond peradventure that it does not.'[59] To this the Italian First Delegate responded that 'if all the representatives of countries ... were to adopt such an uncompromising attitude and refuse to discuss or accept any compromise, what would become of the League of Nations? Its task would be impossible.'[60]

Sir George Foster at the same Assembly opposed in committee an Italian proposal for an inquiry by the Council into problems of raw material distribution which, he said, appeared 'to introduce a new economic doctrine, which permitted interference in the free disposal of the natural wealth of the various nations.'[61] While Italy was successful in getting some study and discussion of the question, ultimately nothing was done,[62] and the problem itself largely disappeared with reviving prosperity.

With the onset of the great depression in 1929, international economic problems again came to the fore, centring on tariff questions and on proposals for

League-organized international economic action. The Bennett government which came to power in Canada in 1930 was especially sensitive about the tariff, since it proposed to end the economic depression in Canada through a policy of high protective tariffs combined with preferential access to the markets of Great Britain and the rest of the Empire, while keeping other world markets open to Canadian exports as much as possible. It was especially anxious that the League not take any action which might interfere with these plans, and was, of course, entirely unwilling to participate in any League-sponsored activity inconsistent with them. At the 1930 Assembly, therefore, Walter A. Riddell objected strongly to a proposed League endorsement of preferential tariff treatment in Europe for European-grown cereals, although he was unable to object to preferential tariffs in general.[63] At the same Assembly, Sir Robert Borden refused to give Canada's endorsement to a proposal for concerted economic action to prevent competitive tariff increases.[64]

At the 1931 Assembly, the question of League endorsement of preferential tariffs in Europe for European grain reappeared, and was again opposed by the Canadian representatives.[65] Because of its own interest in preferential tariffs, the Canadian position was technically not to oppose them, even for Europe, at League meetings, but rather to oppose the League's taking any position with regard to them. Therefore when a League-published brochure in 1933 included statements made at an international conference which were highly critical of the system of preferential tariffs within the British Empire which had been sponsored by Bennett, the prime minister complained vigorously to Secretary-General Joseph Avenol. Avenol assured him that the League was only reporting, not endorsing, the conference statements.[66]

As already noted, the greatest interest of the Canadian government in the League of Nations at the time of its formation was centred not on the expected functions and activities of the League, but on its usefulness as a means of achieving an independent international status for Canada. This theme of Canadian policy continued, of course, to characterize Canada's participation in League affairs. It was manifested both in seeking specific recognition of Canada's status, and in great insistence on avoiding any subordination, or appearance of subordination, to Great Britain at the League.

Formal questions of status at Geneva in general posed no problems, as Canada was from the beginning a full member of the League, in the same way as was 'the British Empire.' The British Empire membership was interpreted in practice as meaning Great Britain, plus those other parts of the Empire which did not hold separate membership in their own name.

Nevertheless, specific recognition of Canada's status was welcomed, and sometimes sought after. In April 1925, for example, O.D. Skelton wrote Walter A.

Riddell requesting that he discuss with Sir Eric Drummond, the League Secretary-General, the possibility of Raoul Dandurand being elected President of the 1925 Assembly. 'The choice of a Dominion's representative as President of the Assembly,' Skelton wrote, 'would be a very notable recognition of the distinct status of the Dominions in the League.'[67] The selection of Dandurand was agreed to by Austen Chamberlain and Aristide Briand, the British and French foreign ministers,[68] and he was elected. Reporting to Skelton on Dandurand's inaugural speech in September, Riddell again put the emphasis on status: 'His speech of acceptance was well received, and his reference to the six nations under one king no doubt helped to clear up in the minds of some delegates the status of the Dominions within the British Commonwealth of Nations.'[69]

The other main accomplishment of Canada in achieving recognition by the League members was its election in 1927 to a three-year term on the Council. It was the first dominion to be so elected, which at least made it clear that Canada was accepted in practice by the international community as a separate and distinct entity from Great Britain, with its permanent Council membership. The initial disagreement between Mackenzie King, who was apprehensive about too much Canadian involvement in international controversies if elected to the Council, and Ernest Lapointe, who urged Canada's candidacy for status reasons, has already been described.

Considerably more bothersome was the continuing question of Canada's relations with Britain at Geneva. A working arrangement soon developed whereby Canadian delegates met with the other Empire delegations for discussion and exchange of views, but did not bind themselves to support a common policy, nor advocate a common policy even on matters of concern to Canada. Policy decisions made in London or Ottawa in advance of League meetings were sometimes, but not always, communicated privately prior to being publicly announced. While public disagreements at Geneva between Britain and Canada were almost always avoided, Canada was insistent on its right to formulate and carry out its own policies, and was usually suspicious that Britain was not really reconciled to its doing so.

One of the first questions to arise regarding British-Canadian relations with the League had to do with the channels for communication between the Secretariat and Canada, which had no permanent representation at Geneva till 1925. The British government suggested to the Dominions in January 1920 that, to 'ensure that on doubtful and controversial issues, we should present a united front,' the British and Dominion governments all use the British Cabinet Secretariat as their channel of communication with the League and that, 'in order to facilitate arrival at agreement on common policy,' each Dominion appoint a representative in London for League of Nations purposes.[70] Neither this procedure nor the rationale on which it was based was acceptable to Canada, which insisted instead that correspondence be sent directly between the Secretary-General and the prime minister in Ottawa, and that telegrams be sent through the Canadian High Commissioner's Office in London.[71] As of November 1920, Canada was the only dominion which had rejected the British proposal and was communicating directly with the League.[72] This arrangement continued until the Canadian Advisory Office was established in Geneva in 1925, after which it served as the sole channel of communication between Ottawa and the League.

In the early days of the League, however, the Canadian governments of Borden and Meighen had not clearly chosen between an entirely independent Canadian role internationally, and Canadian participation in formulating a common British Empire policy. The uncertainty existing in this regard was brought out by the question of whether Canada should attempt to have some part in the naming of the British Empire representative on the League Council. Loring Christie of the Department of External Affairs recommended in February 1920 that Canada seek no part in the selection process. He urged that the British Empire representation on the Council be treated, in effect, as United Kingdom representation only, in order to maintain Canada's freedom in policy matters. 'If we demand the right to join in the selection of the representative,' he wrote, 'we admit that he represents Canada, and we become responsible to that extent for any action he may take.'[73] C.J. Doherty, the Minister of Justice, disagreed entirely, insisting in a rebuttal to Christie's memorandum that Canada, as a part of the Empire, would be bound by the actions of the Empire's representatives in any case, and that 'if we waive our right to share in the selection of the Empire's representative then we fall back to the status of voiceless dependency from which we have so loudly boasted we had emerged.'[74] In the short run Doherty's views prevailed in Ottawa, and when the British government proceeded to name the British Empire representative on the Council without any consultation with Canada, the Canadian government protested.[75] No change in British policy resulted, however, and the question was apparently not pursued by Canada. Instead, the position which Christie had advocated, which was required if Canada was to assert an independent policy role, was accepted in Ottawa.

The London government, however, if it was not inclined to consult Canada before appointing a Council representative, was quite willing at times to assume that its appointee represented all the Empire. In December 1924 this again became an issue when Austen Chamberlain, the British Foreign Secretary, explained his role as follows at a meeting of the League Council: 'I must add that in the case of the British Empire there is the additional difficulty, which will be present to your minds, that their representative here speaks the mind not of one Government only but of five or six Governments widely divided by oceans and seas, and with whom communication is necessarily slower than if the Government of the British Empire were wholly centralised in our capital city of London.'[76]

The Mackenzie King government of course rejected any such interpretation of Chamberlain's responsibilities.[77] Chamberlain was not easily dissuaded, however, and at a meeting of the British delegations during the March 1926 Assembly session, referred again to his responsibilities as representative of the dominions on the Council. He was promptly contradicted by Dandurand, who said that Canada was represented only by the non-permanent Council members which it took part in electing as a member of the Assembly. Chamberlain, Dandurand reported, 'showed some humor when he remarked somewhat curtly that he had nothing to say if Canada preferred to be represented in the Council by the six Assembly Delegates than by Great Britain ...'[78] Again in May 1927 the Canadian government protested another similar statement by Chamberlain at a Council meeting, and was informed this time by the Dominions Office that the Foreign Secretary had been misquoted.[79]

The question was finally settled by Canada's election as a non-permanent member in 1927, since clearly the British representative could then no longer claim to speak for all the Empire. According to Dandurand, Chamberlain had until then not been convinced: '"J'en suis très heureux," fit-il, "seulement je dois reconnaître que je ne pourrai plus parler au Conseil au nom de l'Empire."'[80]*

During these same years there were also continuing difficulties regarding the type of consultation which was appropriate among the British Empire delegations. Dandurand has described one such meeting during the 1924 Assembly, at which British Prime Minister Ramsay MacDonald presided:

[MacDonald] entra en séance publique sans avoir causé avec nous ... Il était à peine à son siège depuis quelques minutes, lorsqu'il se leva avec sa délégation et nous envoya son secrétaire, convoquant tous les Britanniques dans la salle voisine ... Je vins m'asseoir a cette conférence, à l'autre extrémité de la table où présidait MacDonald, sans lui avoir été presenté. Il nous dit le programme qu'il allait suivre: arbitrage obligatoire et désarmement. Je lui dis, sur un ton assez ferme, que cette formule ne serait pas accepté par les voisins de l'Allemagne, que la seule signature de cette dernière ne serait pas une garantie suffisante. Il demanda a son secrétaire qui j'étais, et il maintint son attitude.[81]†

* '"I am very happy about it," he said, "but I must recognize that I can no longer speak in the Council in the name of the Empire."'
† 'MacDonald entered the public session without having spoken to us ... He had been in his seat only a few minutes, when he rose with his delegation and sent us his secretary, calling a meeting of all the British in the adjoining room ... I seated myself at that conference at the other end of the table where MacDonald presided, without having been

Dandurand, representing the King government, objected not only to any attempts at formulating a common Empire policy, but also to conferring on matters not of vital importance to the Empire in general.[82] He expressed the same unwillingness to discuss nonessential matters in 1925 to Austen Chamberlain,[83] and in 1929 objected when Ramsay MacDonald proposed to take a vote in the Empire delegations meeting, insisting that any voting there would be inappropriate since each delegation remained free to vote in the Assembly as it saw fit.[84] At that same Assembly session Dandurand also broke with precedent by calling a meeting of the Empire delegations himself, where previously all meetings had been called by Great Britain.[85]

In these various moves to assert an independent dominion role at the League, Canada, though it played a prominent part, was not alone. In general, South Africa and, after its formation in 1922, the Irish Free State, took the same position as Canada, while Australia and New Zealand tended to follow the British lead.

In contrast with the continuing procedural difficulties over British-Canadian relationships at Geneva, policy differences were comparatively few, though not without significance. From the First Assembly in 1920, Canada carried out in practice the right which it asserted to pursue its own policies. The first important Canadian initiative at the League, the attempt to delete or amend Article 10 of the Covenant, was a Canadian and not a British proposal. Only in 1923, when it had been greatly modified and put into the form of an interpretative resolution, did it receive any open British support. The other principal Canadian initiative of the 1920s, a proposal presented by Dandurand in 1929 to reform the League Council's procedures for dealing with minorities problems, was presented without prior consultation with Britain and did not receive British support.

Roll call votes were very infrequent in the Assembly. The unanimity rule which applied to most votes led, instead, to a procedure which sought to achieve consensus, and to persuade dissidents to abstain from voting. Nevertheless, at the 1920 Assembly the Canadian delegation exercised its right to vote in a way contrary to the British. The issue was the admission of Armenia to the League, which failed by a vote of 8 to 21, with Canada voting for and Britain, as well as the other Empire delegations which participated in the vote, voting against.[86] The issue was, of course, one which was hardly of vital importance to either Canada or Britain, and the outcome of the vote was presumably not in doubt, since a

introduced to him. He told us the program he was going to follow: compulsory arbitration and disarmament. I told him, in a rather firm tone, that that formula would not be accepted by the neighbours of Germany, that the sole signature of the latter would not be a sufficient guarantee. He asked his secretary who I was, and maintained his position.'

two-thirds majority in favour of admission was required. The roll call did serve to demonstrate, however, that Canada's vote was not simply an additional vote for Britain. The action was not repeated; no other conflicting votes by Britain and Canada in the full Assembly are recorded.

Nevertheless, the occasions on which Britain and Canada took different positions on questions before the League were fairly numerous. In 1920 they differed on the Italian proposal for a Council study of inequities in the distribution of raw materials, which Canada opposed, and initially on the admission of Albania to the League, which Canada favoured. In 1924, they differed on the Geneva Protocol, on which Canada reserved judgment while Britain supported it. Beginning in 1925, Canada supported the principle of compulsory arbitration, which Britain did not do until 1929. In 1930 Britain opposed preferential tariffs in general, while Canada opposed the League's taking any position on the question.

However, on most important issues at the League in the 1920s the policies of the Canadian and British governments were much the same, even if not always well co-ordinated. Both eventually supported the modification of Article 10 by an interpretative resolution, both rejected the Treaty of Mutual Assistance and the Geneva Protocol, both supported Germany's entry into the League, and both eventually accepted the compulsory jurisdiction of the Permanent Court of International Justice. In the case of both the Treaty of Mutual Assistance and the Geneva Protocol controversy arose over whether the proposals had been rejected by Britain in large part because of opposition from Canada and the other dominions. The Canadian government resented British statements which implied that this was the case, and pointed out that in both instances Canada had been advised of the proposed rejection by Britain before notifying Britain of its own position.[87] On the other hand, Canadian opposition in each case was entirely predictable without waiting for an official statement.

Perhaps the most important result, so far as Canadian policy was concerned, of the pattern of British-Canadian relations at the League was that Canada effectively deprived itself of important support that might otherwise have been available to it. Throughout the League's active existence, Britain and France were the most influential powers in its affairs. Canada, as a part of the British Empire, an Empire which Britain was extremely anxious to hold together, was in a position to exert substantial influence on Britain in behalf of policies which it favoured. However, Canada's insistence on having no policy commitments to Britain, on not negotiating a common Empire policy, on not necessarily even consulting on significant policy moves, meant in effect that it chose to do without British support. Canada was quite successful in establishing its independent policy role, but in doing so also reduced itself to much the same position as the other small powers.

Besides Great Britain, the other power whose views were of the greatest concern to Canada was, of course, the United States. There was little opportunity to co-ordinate Canadian policy on League of Nations matters with the United States, since it was never a League member. The only substantial exception was with regard to the Manchurian crisis of 1931-2, when the United States was co-operating fairly actively with the League, and there were at that time American-Canadian discussions of policy both in Washington and Geneva. In general, however, there seems to have been virtually no direct attempt at harmonizing policies.

Nevertheless, in formulating and presenting its own policies, the Canadian government was always keenly aware of United States attitudes and frequently cited them. This is not to say that Canadian positions were identical with, or were determined by, American positions. The first important Canadian initiative regarding the League of Nations, the proposed deletion of Article 10, was proposed by Sir Robert Borden in 1919 when the prime sponsor of the article was the United States. After 1920, however, it was entirely accurate to say that in opposing Article 10 Canada was acting consistently with the prevailing opinion in the United States, and Canadian spokesmen regularly said so.

The Canadian government was always concerned about the possibility of becoming involved in some League-sponsored economic or military action which was opposed by the United States, and which would therefore inject controversy into Canadian-American relations. The most promising way to avoid this appeared to be eventual American membership in the League, and Canada from time to time attempted to encourage such a development. In November 1919, for example, Borden agreed to a British proposal to try to mollify American criticism of the British Empire's six votes in the League, by announcing that no portion of the Empire would take part in Assembly voting on a dispute involving any other portion of the Empire.[88] The plan was dropped because of opposition from other dominions.

In 1926, when the United States was negotiating with the League members on adherence, with reservations, to the statute of the Permanent Court of International Justice, the Canadian government disliked the proposed reservations, but considered achieving American adherence more important, especially as it might be a step toward eventual League membership.[89] Nevertheless, at the conference at which the American reservations were considered, Canada eventually joined with the other powers in rejecting one of the reservations, even though it meant, at least temporarily, rejection of United States adherence to the Court.[90] In 1928, Prime Minister King, in accepting the American government's invitation to be a signatory of the Briand-Kellogg Pact outlawing war, took advantage of the opportunity to expound upon the reasons why Canada considered the League of Nations 'an indispensable and continuing agency of international understanding.'[91]

More frequently, however, the strong similarity between American isolationist views and the Canadian government's own version of isolationism led to the citing of American anti-League attitudes in support of Canadian positions within the League. Thus, for example, in 1920 Rowell and Foster gave American objections to interference in domestic affairs as one of the main reasons for not undertaking an investigation of the distribution of raw materials;[92] in 1925 Dandurand explained Canada's rejection of the Geneva Protocol to a large extent in terms of American refusal to support sanctions, and American non-participation in the League.[93] The use of these arguments, however, meant, not that Canada was following United States policy, but rather that the policies of the two countries on such matters were as nearly identical as Canadian membership and American non-membership in the League would permit.

The main themes of Canadian policy at Geneva, then, were opposition to any attempts to give strength to the collective security commitments which League membership entailed, and to any League activity viewed as infringing on Canada's domestic affairs; support for international machinery for the peaceful settlement of disputes and for disarmament; reluctance to become involved in attempts to settle specific disputes between other powers; and insistence on maintaining an independent foreign policy role. It was in this policy context that the principal Canadian initiatives at the League were undertaken.

5

Article 10: the attempt to delete

On 4 December 1920, the President of the First Assembly of the League of Nations gave notice to the Assembly of a motion by C.J. Doherty, Minister of Justice in the Canadian cabinet and a member of the Canadian delegation to the Assembly, 'That Article 10 of the Covenant of the League of Nations be and is hereby struck out.'[1]*

The campaign thus launched by Canada was to continue for three years before being resolved. It constituted the first important initiative by Canada in the new international organization, and gave expression to a major continuing theme of Canadian foreign policy in the 1920s and 1930s: a desire somehow to find a way not to be bound by the more onerous obligations which League membership entailed.

Canadian objections to Article 10 were, of course, not new. As already noted, Sir Robert Borden had privately urged deletion of Article 10 from the draft Covenant of the League at the Peace Conference in 1919. His recommendation had apparently received no serious attention at that time, but by December 1920, the world situation had drastically changed. The United States Senate had rejected membership in the League in March 1920, and that decision had in effect been confirmed by the electorate in the November elections. Dissatisfaction with

---

*   The full text of Article 10 was as follows: 'The Members of the League undertake to respect and preserve as against external aggression the territorial integrity and existing political independence of all Members of the League. In case of any such aggression or in case of any threat or danger of such aggression the Council shall advise upon the means by which this obligation shall be fulfilled.'

the obligations contained in Article 10 had been one of the key factors in United States rejection of the League. Thus, whereas at Paris in 1919 the principal advocate of Article 10 had been President Wilson, and American and Canadian policies were diametrically opposed, at Geneva in 1920 the United States was absent from the discussions and eventual American entry into the League could perhaps be facilitated by removal of the objectionable article. Canada, in publicly attacking Article 10, was now acting in harmony with American policy, and might well expect a sympathetic hearing from other League members who had accepted Article 10 only at American insistence in the first place, or who might be ready to make major changes in the Covenant to accommodate the now prevailing American views.

In other ways, however, the task which Canada had set for itself was a most difficult one. The League Covenant, including Article 10, was now officially in effect and legally binding on all member states, including Canada. All member states, in ratifying the Covenant, had voluntarily accepted its provisions, including Article 10, and indeed had just finished giving their acceptances. Under the voting procedures established, unanimous agreement by the member states taking part in the Assembly vote would be required in order for a change in the Covenant to be proposed. The chances of obtaining such unanimity could hardly have looked bright. In addition to a normal reluctance to make major changes in the Covenant before any experience had been obtained with it, certain states had much to gain if the guarantees of Article 10 could be given a real vitality. These included France and various other European states which had gained territory in the 1919 settlement, as well as small states in general which, without the advantages of Canada's geography, were realistically fearful of the designs of more powerful neighbours on their territory.

It was in this context that Doherty's proposal came up for consideration by the Assembly on 6 December 1920. It was not discussed at that time, but on motion of Hjalmar Branting of Sweden was referred to a committee to be named by the League Council to review various proposed amendments to the Covenant. Doherty said he would have much preferred consideration of the proposal at the First Assembly, but would yield to the inevitable and agree to referral to the committee.[2]

The first official discussions of the Canadian proposal thus took place in a Committee on Amendments to the Covenant, appointed by the Council on 21 February 1921. Arthur J. Balfour, former British prime minister and foreign secretary, was the committee's chairman. The other members represented the other major powers in the League (France, Italy, and Japan) and a selection of smaller powers from Europe (Belgium, Czechoslovakia, Denmark, and Spain), Latin America (Colombia and Uruguay), and Asia (China).[3]

The Council had invited Sir Robert Borden, who had retired as Canadian prime minister in July 1920, to serve on the committee, but he had declined. The Secretary General of the League, Sir Eric Drummond, was interested in finding another Canadian for the committee. Both he and Sir Herbert Ames, a Canadian who was the League's financial director, considered Newton W. Rowell a good choice, but from previous conversations with him Drummond was convinced that he would not consent. After an unsuccessful attempt to get Borden to reconsider, the search for a Canadian member was abandoned.[4]

The interest shown by the Secretariat in the possible selection of Rowell as a committee member would seem to indicate a desire to have a forceful and competent Canadian representative, but not necessarily representation of the views of the Canadian government. As a member of the Canadian delegation to the 1920 Assembly, Rowell had expressed views on Article 10 rather different from those previously presented by Borden and Doherty. In advocating the admission of Albania to the League, he had spoken in favourable terms of the territorial guarantee given to all League members: 'On the question of Article 10 ... the net result would be to protect all parties concerned. [If Albania] is admitted, then the other States are bound to preserve her territorial integrity as against external aggression, and her admission should prevent any conflict between Albania and the adjoining States.'[5]

The Amendments Committee, at its first meeting in April, decided, on Balfour's proposal, to defer consideration of Article 10 until after some informal attempt had been made to sound out current United States opinion on the subject.[6] A presentation of Canada's views was invited and Doherty responded on 1 June 1921, by sending Balfour copies of the 1919 memoranda by Borden and himself criticizing Article 10 and recommending its deletion from the draft Covenant. This was, at least, a clear indication of the continuity in Canadian policy, regardless of the shifts in the United States' views. Doherty noted, however, in his accompanying letter that Article 10 'has played a very large part in depriving the League of the great advantage of counting among its Members one of the greatest States of the world.'[7] The Canadian case against Article 10 was thus based on Canada's initial objections to a blanket territorial guarantee, supplemented by the new argument that it was an obstacle to United States membership.

Meanwhile in Ottawa the revelation that Borden and Doherty had opposed Article 10 at the Peace Conference of 1919 had come as a surprise, and created a certain confusion among the government's opponents in the House of Commons. Henri S. Béland, a former Liberal cabinet minister, interpreted the new information as fully vindicating the Liberal opposition's earlier criticisms of the Covenant, and added the criticism that Article 10 had 'prevented an important nation from joining' the League.[8] On the other hand, W.S. Fielding, a senior member of the Liberal leadership, and a leading critic of automatic commitments in 1919, now attacked the government's stand, perhaps feeling that the job of the opposition was to oppose:

Article X and the whole treaty constituted a solemn compact to which this House became a party, and I deny the right of the Minister of Justice or anybody else, without the authority of this House, to go to Geneva and undertake, in the name of Canada, to move to amend that contract ... [He] should have come to this House for instructions, and he should not have tampered with that Covenant in a single line.[9]

Another prominent Liberal, Ernest Lapointe, strongly criticized the government for its secrecy, while, like Béland, interpreting its policy as in accord with the views which the Liberals had been expressing.[10]

For the government, Doherty defended the proposed deletion of Article 10, expressed optimism about its eventual acceptance, and denied that he had acted primarily from the hope that the United States might be induced to join the League, though American membership would be welcomed.[11]

Members of parliament who had previously supported the government's public stand in favour of the Covenant and of Article 10 were no doubt embarrassed by the new revelations. Only one member, John A. Currie (Conservative, Ontario) undertook to defend the article against both government and opposition. Article 10, he said, 'means, not aggression, but protection. It means that every nation that signed the covenant of the League, when its territory is threatened by any other nation, will have behind it all the other members of the League.' Such a guarantee might well be important to Canada, he said, if, for example, in some future conflict with the United States, Japan should attempt to occupy Canadian territory. 'That Article is the backbone of the whole thing; ... it is the enacting clause of the Covenant.'[12]

In general, nevertheless, the government could proceed with its attack on Article 10 with the knowledge that that policy was acceptable to both political parties at home.

When the Committee on Amendments to the Covenant met for its second session in June 1921, Canada's comments on its proposal had been sent, but not yet received. Balfour again recommended deferring consideration of Article 10, and in addition proposed that a committee of jurists already examining Article 18 for the committee be asked to 'give a legal opinion regarding the additional obligations, if any, which Article X imposed upon the members of the League.' According to Balfour, there had been much dispute about the meaning of the Article, especially in America. His proposal was accepted by the committee.[13]

With this referral to the committee of jurists, there began a long legal controversy within the League as to alleged ambiguities in the wording of Article 10. The claims as to a need for interpretation are somewhat difficult to evaluate. While any legal text is likely to give rise to some uncertainties, the two sentences which constituted Article 10 seem relatively clear and uncomplicated. Each League member undertook 'to respect and preserve as against external aggression' the territory and independence of each other member. In case of such aggression, or the threat or danger of it, 'the Council shall advise upon the means by which this obligation shall be fulfilled.' The Canadian opposition to the article was, at this time, centred not on any contention that the words were unclear, but rather on the assertion that they clearly spelled out a guarantee of existing territory against aggression, a guarantee to which Canada objected. By claiming that the language of Article 10 was unclear, however, it became possible for states unwilling to admit hostility to the main intent of the article to seek, nevertheless, to 'clarify' it in ways that would substantially change its apparent meaning.

When the Amendments Committee met again on 3 September 1921, two days before the opening of the Second Assembly, it had before it the report of the committee of jurists. The committee, made up of legal experts from Italy, Britain, France, Belgium, and the Netherlands, had concluded that 'Article 10 contains the governing principle to which all Members of the League subscribe.' All members were obligated to maintain the status quo against a wrongful act of violence. However, the members were not obliged by the article to take part in any military action; the Council was given advisory powers only. Although Article 10, in the jurists' view, contained 'no obligation which cannot be found elsewhere in the Covenant, it nevertheless possesses a certain value of its own. It enunciates one of the legal principles upon which the League of Nations is based ...'[14]

The jurists' report gave but slight comfort to those seeking to delete or substantially modify Article 10. It endorsed the article as an important statement of principle, gave no support to claims of ambiguity, and said in effect that even if the article were deleted the member states' legal obligations would remain essentially unchanged. It did provide ground for substantial controversy, however, in its contention that the guarantees of Article 10 did not go beyond those of the other articles in the Covenant. Whereas Articles 12 and 15 left available the possibility of a legal resort to war if the prescribed procedures for peaceful settlement of disputes had failed (the so-called 'gap in the Covenant'), Article 10, read alone, gave an unqualified guarantee of territorial integrity. Any attempt to interpret Article 10 as meaning that territorial changes could, in certain circumstances, be legally brought about by external aggression, was bound to encounter sharp resistance.

The problem of the 'gap in the Covenant' was, in reality, a largely theoretical one. The possibility of a would-be aggressor first exhausting the prescribed procedures for peaceful settlement, and then waiting the additional three months required by Article 12, was unlikely in the extreme. Nevertheless, the contention that the 'gap' also applied to Article 10 and that this should be made clear appealed to certain jurists. It also, no doubt, appealed to some parties inclined to favour any language which might appear to undercut the guarantees of Article 10. It had, however, played no part in the Canadian case against Article 10, which was based not on procedural considerations, but on objections to the main purpose and intent of the article.

On 3 September 1921, then, the Committee on Amendments to the Covenant finally began its discussion of the Canadian proposal. It quickly became apparent that the unanimity necessary in the Assembly for any decision to be taken would be most difficult to achieve. No member of the committee supported the Canadian proposal to simply strike out Article 10. Only the Colombian member spoke in opposition to any modification of the article. Balfour, the chairman, favoured a clarifying amendment, and submitted a proposed text: 'No change of territorial integrity, or existing political independence of Members of the League could be tolerated as a result of external aggression until all the proper methods of conciliation set out in Articles 11-17 of the Covenant have been tried under the auspices of the League.' This proposed amendment in effect accepted the interpretation by the committee of jurists that Article 10 was no more comprehensive in its coverage than other articles, and modified its wording accordingly. Vittorio Scialoja (Italy) suggested that Article 10 be clarified by an interpretative resolution of the League Assembly, rather than by amendment. He was supported in this by the French and Belgian committee members, who also made clear their disagreement with the jurists' interpretation limiting the scope of Article 10.

The committee concluded its first day's deliberations on the subject by unanimously deciding to retain the principle of Article 10 and by agreeing, by a vote of seven to three, to appoint a drafting committee to prepare both an amendment and an interpretative resolution for its further consideration.[15]

On 8 September 1921, with the Second Assembly of the League already in session, the Committee on Amendments to the Covenant met again. Scialoja presented three alternative texts of an amendment to Article 10 and the text of a proposed interpretative resolution, all prepared by the drafting committee. Balfour again favoured amendment of the article, and was supported by the Japanese and Uruguayan committee members. However, when the French, Italian, Czechoslovak, Belgian, and Danish members of the committee indicated their preference for an interpretation, the point was yielded, and the principle of an interpretative resolution agreed upon unanimously. The interpretative text proposed by the drafting committee was then considered and adopted, after discussion and deletion of language which would have stated specifically that war might in certain cases be a legal means of bringing about changes in 'territorial and political organisation.'[16]

The outcome of the controversy within the Committee on Amendments to the Covenant was a striking victory for the proponents of Article 10. While the need for an official interpretation had been conceded, the proposed text of that interpretation added strength to the article, rather than undercutting it. It read as follows:

Article 10 was not intended to perpetuate the territorial and political organisation as established and as existing at the time of the recent treaties of peace. Changes may be effected in that organisation by various legitimate means. The Covenant admits of this possibility.

The intention of Article 10 is to enunciate the principle that hereafter the civilised world cannot tolerate acts of aggression as a means of modifying the territorial *status quo* and the political independence of the States.

To this end, the Members of the League have pledged themselves, first, to respect the territorial integrity and the existing political independence of all the States Members of the League, and, secondly, to maintain this integrity and this independence against any external aggression, whether on the part of a State Member or a State not Member of the League. With a view to assuring the fulfilment of this second obligation, the Council shall advise upon the means; it must do so not merely in the case of actual aggression, but also in the case of any danger or threat of such aggression. The Council will perform this function by addressing to the Members such recommendations as are deemed proper in regard thereto, taking into account Articles 11, 12, 13, 15, 16, 17 and 19 of the Covenant.[17]

In its accompanying report to the League Council on 9 September, the committee discussed and rejected the Canadian contention that Article 10 served to freeze the territorial status quo, saying that Canada had failed to recognize the availability of peaceful means for change. Canada had also misinterpreted the role of the Council, which was limited to making 'simple recommendations,' the nature of which would naturally be influenced by political and geographical considerations. Furthermore, the committee in effect rejected the advice given it by its committee of jurists, and found specifically that Article 10 was not merely a duplication of other articles in the Covenant.[18]

The Assembly was thus asked by the committee to reaffirm the importance and the basic intent of Article 10, rejecting claims as to implicit qualifications in its coverage and as to ambiguity in its language. However, even though a unanimous report was presented, the discussions in the committee had revealed great divergence in attitudes toward the article. They had also revealed a total lack of support for Canada's desire to strike out Article 10, and that British and Canadian policies differed significantly on this question. Balfour had rejected from the initial discussions the idea of striking out the article; he had taken the lead in proposing a restrictive amendment to it, but had soon acquiesced in a non-restrictive interpretation.

The recommendation of the Committee on Amendments to the Covenant was referred by the Second Assembly, already in session, to its First Committee (Constitutional Questions), and by that committee to a sub-committee. On 30 September, Professor A.A.H. Struycken (the Netherlands) presented the sub-committee's report. In general, it accepted the recommendation of the Amendments Committee, favouring a slightly reworded interpretative resolution which rejected the Canadian arguments and strongly endorsed Article 10. However, the sub-committee also drew on the report of the committee of jurists, of which Struycken had been a member, and made one major change in the language recommended by the Amendments Committee: it added wording that territorial and political organization may be changed 'even by war, provided that the peaceful measures laid down in the Covenant have been exhausted.'[19] The proposed interpretation thus became the vehicle, once again, of an attempt to widen the 'gap in the Covenant,' as Balfour had proposed earlier and the Amendments Committee had rejected.

C.J. Doherty, Canadian First Delegate to the 1921 Assembly and a member of the Assembly's First Committee, tried to get the discussion back to Canada's more fundamental objections. The real question at issue, he said, was 'whether the obligation laid down in Article 10 should be maintained.' He was sceptical of any attempt by the Assembly to interpret the article. A direct change in the wording would be preferable. The main purpose of Article 10 he still found unsatisfactory. The League of Nations would not maintain peace between the nations 'if it forbade them to secure justice for themselves' and if it did not provide an alternative means of obtaining justice.[20]

The ensuing discussion in the committee again revealed widely divergent opinions. Scialoja, the Committee chairman, supported the sub-committee's report. The Portuguese and Belgian members disagreed with the sub-committee's interpretation that war could be a legitimate means of modifying the territorial status quo. The Portuguese and Colombian members favoured postponing the whole question till the next Assembly, and Doherty, whose views were clearly not about to prevail in any case, agreed to consider postponement.[21]

On the following day, 1 October, the First Committee decided, with Doherty's concurrence, to recommend postponement of any further consideration of the Canadian proposal till the next Assembly, on the condition that a decision be taken on it then ahead of any other proposed amendment.[22]

The full Assembly unanimously accepted the committee's recommendation on 4 October, after a presentation by Struycken emphasizing the lack of any general agreement, and some final words by Doherty stressing once again Canada's fundamental objections to Article 10. 'By its wording it seems to lay down the principle that possession can take precedence over justice. If this opinion is justified, Article 10 must disappear.'[23]

The question of deleting Article 10 was thus held over for a full year, and was not to be dealt with again at the League by spokesmen for the Canadian Conservative party. The Conservatives had been the dominant political party in Canada since 1911. But long before the election of 6 December 1921, it appeared probable that the government's political fortunes had run out. Prior to the election, there was a substantial exodus of key figures from the government, and even from political life. Of the main figures involved in foreign policy questions in 1919-21, only Arthur Meighen, who had succeeded Borden as prime minister in 1920, was a candidate in 1921. Newton W. Rowell had left the cabinet with Borden in July 1920, and neither of them sought re-election to the Commons the next year. Sir George Foster and C.J. Doherty both left the cabinet in September 1921, when it was generally overhauled by Meighen in preparation for the elections. Neither sought re-election in December, though Foster was appointed to the Senate and continued his parliamentary career there.

On 6 December the expected débâcle arrived. The Conservatives won only 50 of 235 Commons seats, placing third, after the Liberals and the new Progressive party.[24] Meighen himself was defeated, though he promptly found a safe Conservative constituency in which he ran again and won. The Liberals, though lacking a clear majority, were able to obtain and hold enough Progressive support to form a stable government under Prime Minister W.L. Mackenzie King. For the next nine years, except for one short interval in 1926, King and the Liberals continued in power. So far as policy toward the League of Nations was concerned, the first important test of the new government's attitude was provided by the Article 10 controversy, inherited from the Conservatives and still totally unresolved.

6

Article 10: the attempt to amend

A clear indication of the attitude of the new Liberal government toward Article 10 of the League Covenant was provided in the House of Commons on 19 June 1922, by Ernest Lapointe, Minister of Marine and Fisheries in King's cabinet. At the last Assembly meeting, he said, 'the representatives of Canada moved that Article x be stricken from the Covenant of the League. I am pleased that they did so. No action was taken on that motion, which was postponed; but I hope that whoever represents Canada at the next meeting of the assembly will see that the motion ... is proceeded with and that Article x shall be eliminated from the covenant.'[1] When the Assembly convened in September, the Canadian delegation included Lapointe himself. As a member of the First Committee (Constitutional Questions), he made the initial Canadian presentation on the subject of Article 10.

What Lapointe called for, however, was not the deletion of the article, but its amendment, in effect adopting the arguments presented by delegates of other states in 1921 claiming that its meaning was unclear. On 14 September 1922, he offered the text of a proposed amendment, which would add certain language to the article, as follows [new wording in italics]:

The Members of the League undertake to respect and preserve as against external aggression the territorial integrity and existing political independence of all Members of the League. In case of any such aggression or in case of any threat or danger of such aggression the Council shall advise upon the means by which this obligation shall be fulfilled, *taking into account the political and geographical circumstances of each state.*

The opinion given by the Council in such cases shall be regarded as a matter of the highest importance, and shall be taken into consideration by all the Members of the League, which shall use their utmost endeavours to conform to the conclusions of the Council; but no Member shall be under the obligation to engage in any act of war without the consent of its Parliament, Legislature or other representative body.[2]

Lapointe made it clear to the First Committee that the new Canadian proposal represented more a shift in tactics than a change in views. Following 'conversations which he had held since his arrival in Geneva, he was convinced that it would be impossible at the present moment to secure the deletion of Article 10 ... But this article had given rise to different and contradictory interpretations.' The Committee, 'if it was unwilling to propose its deletion, should at least make suggestions with regard to its modification, so as to remove the misunderstandings to which its present wording gave rise.' Moreover, Lapointe asserted, the maintenance of Article 10 had prevented 'several states' [i.e., the United States] from adhering to the League of Nations, and thus, by implication, modification of the article might encourage their participation.[3]

Canada had, then, abandoned, at least for the moment, its position that Article 10 should be deleted, a position which had failed to win the public support of any state at the 1921 League meetings. It now sought an amendment which would emphasize the voluntary nature of the action, if any, to be taken by states in carrying out their obligations. This had been the position which had obtained the most support among the critics of Article 10 in the 1921 Committee on Amendments, though it too had eventually failed to win the endorsement of either that committee or of the League Assembly.

Even before Lapointe spoke, it had become apparent that the unanimity needed for a change in Article 10 would still be extremely difficult to obtain. On 11 September Prince Arfa-ad-Dovleh, the First Delegate of Persia, had told the First Committee that 'the abrogation of Article 10 of the Covenant, as proposed by the Canadian Delegation, would be a fatal blow to the prestige of the League of Nations in the East. The League ought not to become a charitable and public health organisation only. Persia could not accept an amendment to Article 10, which would jeopardise the security of States Members of the League.'[4] Thus the opponents of the Canadian amendment refused from the start to treat it as merely technical or clarifying, but insisted that it involved an attempt to undermine the security system of the Covenant.

Initial comment following Lapointe's presentation of the Canadian proposal showed the now familiar lack of consensus. Belgium offered full support to Canada. Romania and Poland opposed any change in Article 10. France was opposed to deletion of the article, and considered unrealistic the suggestion of possible United States entry into the League if Article 10 were sacrificed. Switzerland was prepared to sacrifice the article only if United States membership could thereby be obtained.[5]

Faced with this obvious inability to reach unanimous agreement, the First Committee decided again in favour of postponement of the Canadian proposal, and so recommended to the Assembly on 19 September without opposition from Canada. It also recommended that the League Council provide for a detailed study of the proposal before the meeting of the 1923 Assembly.[6]

On 23 September the Committee recommendation for postponement was discussed in the full Assembly. Only the French and the Canadian delegations spoke. The jurist Joseph Barthélemy, speaking for France, made clear his country's opposition to the Canadian amendment, denied that there was ambiguity in the language of Article 10, and gave an eloquent defence of the article as the 'pediment of the great temple of our international organisation; ... our standard, our crest, the declaration of the new international law.' It was already clear, he said, that no state was obliged to furnish military forces against an aggressor. 'We have not the general obligation of rushing with our whole forces to the assistance of any Member which is the victim of unjust aggression; we have the option of witnessing, as mute and inactive observers, the accomplishment of injustice.' Nor did Article 10 seek to preserve unchanged the territorial status quo. It merely barred changes of frontiers by force. Deletion of Article 10 'would create consternation among the young, adolescent, or convalescent countries which had joined [the League] in order to place themselves under the protection of this article.' It did not require interpretation; it should be kept unchanged.[7]

The Canadian reply was delivered by W.S. Fielding, Minister of Finance and Canada's First Delegate to the Assembly. He defined the Canadian position in rather different terms from those used by Lapointe. First he denied any interest in eliminating Article 10 entirely, and dissociated the new Canadian government from the views expressed by C.J. Doherty at the first two Assemblies. 'I frankly say, I quite admit that you cannot reasonably strike out Article 10 entirely. I think the objections which have been raised to the motion of my illustrious predecessor were well founded.' While favouring action that might encourage United States membership in the League, Fielding denied that that was the reason for the Canadian proposal, which, he said, was 'merely giving expression to a motion made in the Canadian Parliament at the moment when the Peace Treaty was presented for approval.' (He did not mention that the motion, which he had presented, had been defeated by the parliament; see p. 31.)

Fielding then gave full endorsement to the contention that Article 10 was unclear, and that Canada wanted only to have it clarified:

If it means the right to put nations into war by the mere vote of the Council, let us have the courage to say so; but, speaking as a Canadian, as a member of a democratic Parliament, representing a democratic people, I say that we object to the idea that the Council should by its own action set the nations at war ...

Let us know what Article 10 means, and then Article 10 will be worth something in the present system. We shall not have one set of lawyers telling us that it means one thing, and another set of lawyers telling us that it means something else. We plead with you not to strike it out, but to make it clear. Let us know what it means.[8]

The Assembly then adopted, without further discussion, the First Committee's proposal to adjourn the whole matter for another year.[9] The division of opinion was, at least, more clearly drawn than previously. As summarized by the Canadian delegation in its report on the Third Assembly, it

did not appear that the proposal [to delete Article 10] had found favour in any quarter of the Assembly. It had, on the contrary, aroused marked hostility. The French representatives were particularly strong in their objections to the elimination of the Article. Many of the smaller nations too were disposed to regard the Article as a protection against aggression and naturally did not look with approval on the proposal to strike it out.

In view of these reactions, the delegation had proposed that Article 10 'be allowed to stand with the addition of a few explanatory words.'[10]

In short, Canada had abandoned a position that was clearly unacceptable to the international community. Not only was it no longer seeking deletion of Article 10, but it was insisting, not too accurately, that that proposal represented, after all, only the views of the defeated Conservative government. What was now sought was an amendment to Article 10 which might have the effect of minimizing the obligations of states in general, and of states geographically removed from the scene of potential conflict, in particular.

The chances for success in obtaining unanimous agreement on such an amendment must have seemed bleak after the 1922 Assembly, and bleaker still after the League Council in 1923 sent the Canadian proposal to the governments of all member states for comment. Twenty-five replies were received. Of these only five – those from Austria, Bulgaria, Hungary, Uruguay, and Canada itself – favoured the amendment. Not only was the number of favourable responses negligible, but the source of those responses must have been something of an embarrassment. Austria, Bulgaria, and Hungary were all ex-enemy states which had lost territory following their defeat in the first world war, and were now championing revision of the peace treaties in their own interest. Only Uruguay, among all the League members, might be assumed to favour revision of Article 10 for essentially the same reasons as Canada.

Of the other twenty states replying to the Council's inquiry, fifteen indicated opposition to the Canadian amendment, three advocated a further postponement of the question, one (Belgium) favoured an interpretative resolution, and one simply said it had no comments to offer. Of the major powers, France was opposed to the amendment, and Italy and Japan favoured postponement. The British, Australian, New Zealand, Irish, and Indian governments did not reply to the Council, demonstrating at least that no overt support for the Canadian initiative was available from within the Empire.[11]

With the evidence thus clear that achieving unanimous support for amending Article 10 was an impossible task, the Canadian government made a further tactical retreat, and supported the adoption by the Fourth Assembly of an interpretative resolution. On 12 September 1923, Sir Lomer Gouin, Minister of Justice in the King government and Canada's First Delegate to the Assembly, explained once again to the First Committee the background of the Canadian proposal. As W.S. Fielding had done at the preceding Assembly, Gouin based Canada's position on Fielding's House of Commons resolution of 1919, which, he said, 'was an exact reflection of the opinion of the country' (although it had, in fact, been defeated by the Commons).[12] He did not pursue the proposal for an amendment, but accepted membership on a sub-committee charged specifically with drawing up an interpretative resolution dealing with the questions raised by the Canadian proposal.

On 17 September the sub-committee reported the text of a proposed resolution. The proposed interpretation of Article 10 was essentially the same in content as the amendment sponsored by Lapointe in 1922. The League Council should take account of geographical situation and other special conditions in recommending measures to be taken against an aggressor. The Council's recommendations should be given serious attention by League members, but they retained full discretion in deciding whether Article 10 had been violated and what military measures, if any, should be taken. Though very similar in language to the earlier Canadian proposal, the effect of such a resolution being adopted would be less far-reaching. It would, if adopted, represent the opinion of the Assembly, or rather of a particular Assembly, regarding the meaning of Article 10. The language of the article would remain unchanged, and those members who wished to interpret it otherwise could continue to do so. To the extent that the adoption of such a resolution would have any effect, however, the effect could only be to weaken the League security system. While presenting a defensible legal interpretation of the article, the intent of the interpretation was clearly to emphasize the absence of any obligation on the part of League members to follow Council recommendations. It at least implied that member states could choose to ignore their legal obligation to resist aggression, if they wished. Thus the proposed interpretative resolution, though a weaker attack on Article 10 than the now abandoned attempts to delete or amend the article, raised once again the same basic conflict between those seeking to maintain, and those seeking to weaken, the collective security system.

On 17 and 19 September 1923, the sub-committee's resolution was discussed in the First Committee. For the first time the Canadian proposal had reached the stage of First Committee debate, backed by a favourable sub-committee resolution. While only a majority of those states voting was needed for action by the First Committee, any negative votes in the committee would indicate that difficulty lay ahead in obtaining the unanimity required for action by the full Assembly.

In the initial committee discussions on 17 September Canada's chances for success looked as bleak as ever. Only Chile and Switzerland joined Canada in supporting the interpretative resolution. France, Finland, Persia, and Romania were opposed, Prince Arfa-ad-Dovleh of Persia going furthest in his opposition and insisting that his government would accept no amendment or interpretation of Article 10. A number of other states, including Britain, Australia, and Italy, again favoured delaying the matter. Gouin at this point retreated another step, saying that Canada would be satisfied with a majority vote for the resolution, as this would serve to indicate how the other League members interpreted Article 10. In other words, Canada was now prepared to settle for the 'moral victory' which could be claimed if majority support were obtained in the Assembly, even though the resolution would have been defeated.[13]

When discussion was resumed by the committee on 19 September, it was apparent that a move was under way to reach a compromise solution acceptable to both sides. The British delegate proposed a revision in wording giving emphasis to the obligation to preserve the independence and territorial integrity of all League members, as well as to the voluntary nature of any military action. This wording, he said, would avoid any appearance of weakening the moral or legal effect of Article 10. Canada had accepted the proposed change, and Barthélemy announced that France would now support the interpretative resolution. In other words, Canada, by accepting a further weakening of its assault on Article 10, had for the first time obtained the backing of Britain and France, the League's most powerful and influential members. For the first time adoption by the Assembly of an interpretative resolution seemed possible.

A number of smaller states then indicated their readiness to support the revised resolution. Only Persia and Finland restated their opposition. The committee chairman, Giuseppe Motta of Switzerland, urged them to abstain in the full Assembly, rather than prevent unanimous action. The committee vote was then taken by a show of hands, and the revised Canadian resolution was adopted, by a vote of 26 to 4.[14]

As a result of this vote, the Canadian proposal, as amended, was favourably reported on 24 September 1923, to the full Assembly. The text was as follows:

It is in conformity with the spirit of Article 10 that, in the event of the Council considering it to be its duty to recommend the application of military measures in consequence of an aggression or danger or threat of aggression, the Council shall be bound to take account, more particularly, of the geographical situation and of the special conditions of each State.

It is for the constitutional authorities of each Member to decide, in reference to the obligation of preserving the independence and the integrity of the territory of Members, in what degree the Member is bound to assure the execution of this obligation by employment of its military forces.

The recommendation made by the Council shall be regarded as being of the highest importance, and shall be taken into consideration by all the Members of the League with the desire to execute their engagements in good faith.[15]

Obviously anticipating that something less than unanimity might be obtained when the Assembly voted, Henri Rolin of Belgium, the rapporteur for the First Committee, in presenting the resolution claimed, in effect, that even if it were defeated it might be considered as having been accepted. 'Once an interpretation has been accepted unanimously, or by a large majority of delegates,' he said, 'as being the sense in which we, in all good faith, read the Articles of the Covenant, it is certain that Canada will no longer have reason to fear any discussion on the subject, either in Canada or abroad. If this article were ever to be put into execution, Canada would, without fear of danger, be right in complying with the interpretation which we give to-day.'[16]

At the Assembly session on 25 September Sir Lomer Gouin opened the discussion with a defence of the Canadian proposal. With victory almost, but not quite, in hand, his comments were conciliatory. The interpretation contained in the resolution made no fundamental change in Article 10, he said, and was accepted by all authorities.[17] Gouin was followed by Prince Arfa, who restated Persia's opposition to 'any proposed amendments to or interpretation of Article 10 of the Covenant which would have the effect of lessening the force of that article.'

Several other delegates, including the British and the French, spoke in favour of the resolution, and one other, the delegate of Panama, spoke in opposition.

The delegate of Estonia was not in favour of the resolution, but would abstain in the voting. Giuseppe Motta of Switzerland, as he had done in the First Committee, urged all opponents to abstain rather than prevent unanimity. He also repeated Rolin's contention that the resolution could be regarded as having been approved in any case, and 'should occasion ever arise for the application of Article 10, the Council will, without a shadow of doubt, consider the proposed interpretation as the one by which they must abide.'[18]

At the last minute the Persian delegation wavered, and asked an adjournment of the vote while it wired Teheran recommending a change in instructions. Gouin, however, opposed any further delay, perhaps feeling that the Assembly was closer then to unanimity than it was likely to be at a later date.[19]

The vote was therefore taken on 25 September 1923, and resulted in twenty-nine votes for the Canadian resolution, one vote against (that of Persia), and twenty-two absences or abstentions. Among those voting for the resolution were all of the component parts of the British Empire and all the major powers who were League members. Finland and Panama, the states which, along with Persia, had most recently opposed the resolution in debate, did not vote. The Assembly President declared the resolution 'not adopted,' for lack of unanimity.[20]

After four years of discussion, the Canadian attempt to delete, amend, or interpret Article 10, in such a way as to lessen its impact, had ended on a note of ambiguity. According to the opponents of Canada's proposal, and according to the Assembly's official procedures, the resolution had been defeated. R.W. Erich, the Finnish delegate who had opposed the Canadian resolution in the First Committee, viewed the Persian vote in retrospect as having accomplished its purpose. Speaking several years later, he recalled that 'very insistent attempts were made' to persuade delegates not to oppose the Canadian proposal. All had acquiesced, 'though unwillingly,' except Persia. 'I think that to-day we are all glad to have avoided the fatal act which we were then about to accomplish.'[21]

Canada's position was, however, that its resolution had been effectively approved, using the arguments which Rolin and Motta had presented at the Assembly. In London at the Imperial Conference of 1923, Gouin thanked Lord Robert Cecil for the great help he had given Canada at the Assembly with regard to the Article 10 resolution, and said that 'in effect we have obtained the interpretative declaration which we were seeking.'[22]

Likewise, in their official report on the work of the 1923 Assembly, Gouin and George P. Graham, the other Canadian delegate, found that their efforts had met with success:

While it is true that unanimity is necessary under the constitution of the League to give legal effect to a declaration of this nature, it nevertheless remains that should occasion arise, the Council would be expected to give to Article 10 the interpretation which by its vote the Assembly has expressed. An additional guarantee is to be found in the fact that all the powers represented on the Council are amongst those States who voted in favour of the interpretative declaration.

Your delegates feel that, under the circumstances, a satisfactory answer has been given to the question ...[23]

As time went on, Canadian insistence that its interpretation had been accepted continued. Thus in 1928 Prime Minister King, in a letter to the United States Minister to Canada, said that 'the Fourth Assembly, with a single negative vote, accepted [sic] the interpretative resolution.'[24] F.P. Walters, then a top assistant to the League's Secretary-General, tended to agree. 'The Canadian proposal,' he wrote in later years, 'had none the less received such authoritative support that its essential purpose had been in practice achieved.'[25]

Although it could be argued, with some semblance of logic, either that the Canadian proposal had succeeded or that it had failed, it was clear in any case that the purpose of the Canadian initiative had been to weaken the force and effect of Article 10. Originally this had been sought openly, through advocating the article's deletion. When deletion was seen to be impossible, first amendment and then interpretation were sought, always with emphasis on the right of states to decide individually what, if anything, they would do to oppose aggression. The claim advanced by Canada, and by others, that the meaning of Article 10 was unclear, and that only a needed clarification was being sought, was recognized as disingenuous both in Geneva and in Ottawa. Senator J.P.B. Casgrain (Liberal, Quebec), a caustic critic of the League but scornful of the Canadian government's demand for interpretation, put it this way: 'He [Gouin] proposed an interpretation of Article 10 ... to make the Article say what it did not say; for there would be no use for an interpretation which would make the article say what it actually did say. Whenever lawyers desire to insert an interpretation clause, the purpose is to make the document say something other than what people read in it.'[26]

If Casgrain was wrong as to the validity of the interpretation contained in the final version of the Canadian resolution – for it would appear to be a defensible legal interpretation – he was certainly right as to the intent. For it was undoubtedly Canada's intention in its first important initiative at the League of Nations to undermine as completely as possible what Article 10 clearly did say, that all League members, Canada included, had an unequivocal legal obligation to protect all other League members against aggression. To whatever extent the Canadian initiative had achieved success, that 'success' consisted in weakening the collective security aspects of the League system.

That this was the case was specifically recognized and approved by the Department of External Affairs as late as August 1933. At that time O.D. Skelton, the Undersecretary of State for External Affairs, provided the head of the Canadian delegation to the forthcoming League Assembly with background papers which included the following comment: 'The Canadian policy in respect to sanctions, guarantee pacts, etc., from the Peace Conference at Paris to the present, has been clear, consistent and constructive. That policy has opposed putting a club behind the League of Nations or rigid, advance guarantees to come to the assistance of any state, if that state is attacked.'[27]

To other Canadians in the 1930s, the policies which Canada had followed seemed clear and consistent, but by no means constructive. Thus Senator W.A. Griesbach (Conservative, Alberta), after citing the long history of Canada's opposition to Article 10, concluded that 'of all the members of the League Canada was the first to take the move which now appears to have torpedoed the organization, or, to use another metaphor, to have robbed it of any teeth that it had.'[28]

The Department of External Affairs background papers referred to above, using still another metaphor, had reached a virtually identical conclusion: 'Our primary concern was with Article 10, "the heart of the Covenant," as President Wilson called it, but a heart which from the beginning we would have been glad to see stop beating.'[29]

7

The appeal of the 'Six Nations'

Some months before the League of Nations Assembly finally voted on the Canadian proposals regarding Article 10, Canada was embroiled in another controversy involving the League. This was a bizarre affair resulting from complaints against Canada by the Six Nations tribes of Iroquois Indians. Eventually it involved, through the League, a most unlikely collection of states: the Netherlands, Great Britain, Estonia, the Irish Free State, Panama, Persia, and Sweden.

The Six Nations Indians were residents of tribal lands near Brantford, Ontario. So far as the Canadian government was concerned, they were subject exclusively to Canadian law, the same as any other British subjects resident in Canada, and any dispute between them and the Canadian government was a purely internal matter. According to the Six Nations' spokesman, Chief Deskaheh, the legal situation was entirely different. He claimed that the Six Nations were an independent state, bound to Canada only through treaties made between his predecessors and the British government. The fact that the British had indeed made what were officially called 'treaties' with the Six Nations lent some colour of credibility to his claim. The dispute itself had to do with such matters as the ownership of land, hunting and fishing rights, and tribal self-government. Failing to resolve these issues to his satisfaction with the Canadian Department of Indian Affairs, Deskaheh in 1922 decided to attempt to bring the matter before the League of Nations.

As the Six Nations were not a member of the League and, whatever their pretensions, were not recognized as a state by any member of the League, at first glance it might appear merely absurd that they attempt to get the League to take up their grievances. Indeed, Chief Deskaheh's attempts to send petitions directly to the League, or to enter into correspondence regarding the merits of his claims, were regularly rebuffed. The matter was not to be settled that easily, however. Article 11 of the Covenant declared it to be 'the friendly right of each Member of the League to bring to the attention of the Assembly or of the Council any circumstance whatever affecting international relations which threatens to disturb international peace or the good understanding between nations upon which peace depends.' What Deskaheh needed, then, in order to bring his dispute with the Canadian government before the League, was to find at least one member state willing to view the dispute as international in character and to sponsor its discussion at Geneva. Even though there might be little likelihood of many members so viewing it when it came up for discussion, the resulting publicity might well bring some effective pressure to bear on Canada to give more serious consideration to the Six Nations' claims. Such presumably was Deskaheh's strategy, and finding a League member ready to take up the Indians' cause proved not too difficult.

On 15 December 1922, the British ambassador in Washington wired the Canadian government that he had been visited that morning by the Dutch chargé d'affaires, who had been called on the day before by 'a Red Indian who described himself as 'Chief of the Six Nations.' This Chief was accompanied by a white American Attorney and a Red Indian Secretary.' The attorney had discussed the Six Nations' complaints against the Canadian government, had contended that the Six Nations were an 'independent people, allies of the British Crown,' and had alleged that an invasion of their lands by Canadian armed forces was imminent. In conclusion, the attorney announced that the Indians 'had decided to appeal for justice to the Queen of the Netherlands, in view of the fact that they had had pleasant relations with the Dutch settlers in the Hudson Valley in the seventeenth century and asked that their petition should be transmitted to the League of Nations.' The Dutch chargé d'affaires had accepted the petition and agreed to forward it to The Hague. When, the next day, he visited the British ambassador, he appealed to him 'to take steps to avoid the possibility of bloodshed and violence.' If the Dutch chargé was prepared to accept the Indians' account of the situation at face value and to act accordingly, the British ambassador was not. He told the chargé that he was surprised by such action on the part of a representative of a friendly government, and that he had nothing more to say on the matter.[1]

The following April the Canadian government learned that the Netherlands' involvement in the affair had by no means ended at that point. The Dutch minister in London had called at the Foreign Office to discuss the matter. He said that the Dutch Minister for Foreign Affairs (H.A. van Karnebeek, who in 1921 had been President of the League Assembly) 'had been impressed by the confidence shown by this Indian tribe' and wondered whether, without referring the matter formally to the League, he might not send the Six Nations' petition to the Council for advice as to the League's competence to intervene. The British Foreign Office had emphasized to the minister the undesirability of encouraging 'any discontented community to think they could find a remedy against the government of their own country by appealing to the League,' and had suggested that such a practice might lead to the Dutch finding themselves 'arraigned before the Council by some of their East Indian subjects.' The minister was impressed, and said he would try to discourage the foreign minister from taking any further action.[2]

Van Karnebeek was not dissuaded, however, and on 26 April 1923, the Dutch Minister in Bern formally transmitted the Six Nations' petition to the Secretary-General of the League of Nations, with the request that it be communicated to the Council. The petition claimed that there was a threat to the peace resulting from measures taken by Canada in violation of the Six Nations' right to independence. It said Canada had applied its laws to their lands, treated their people as British subjects, opened war on them, invaded their country, imprisoned some of their people, and was planning the extinction of the Six Nations as a separate people. Van Karnebeek, while agreeing to transmit the petition, disclaimed any opinion as to the justice of the complaints or the accuracy of the assertions.[3] The Secretary-General promptly sent a copy of the Dutch letter and the enclosed petition to Ottawa, inviting the Canadian government's comments, but pointing out that it would, in any case, be his duty to circulate the documents to the members of the Council, as requested.[4]

The Canadian reply, sent by Sir Joseph Pope after obtaining Prime Minister King's approval of the wording, was emphatic in rejecting any right either of the Netherlands or the League to intervene. It said that the Canadian government 'utterly repudiates' the suggestion that 'the circumstances are such as to endanger world peace, and so bring the situation within the purview of the League of Nations,' and insisted that 'the claim that the Six Nations are an organized and self-governing people so as to form a political unit apart from Canada, is to anyone acquainted with the actual conditions, an absurd one.'[5]

The Secretary-General next transmitted the Canadian comments to The Hague, before doing anything further to comply with the Dutch request. At this point Van Karnebeek backed off to some extent from his original position. He insisted that his government had no intention whatever to intervene in 'the dispute between Canada and the Six Nations.' His government 'had no other intention but to forward on to its address a document which had been sent to them,' and 'the procedure to follow in the matter is for the League of Nations to decide.'[6]

This reply was, to say the least, equivocal. The question clearly was not merely one of sending a document to its right address. The same and similar documents had already been sent to their 'right address,' i.e., the League Secretariat, with no result because the Six Nations had no right to bring anything officially before the League. But the Netherlands did have such a right and, even though it now disclaimed any responsibility for the procedure to be followed, had not specifically withdrawn its request that its letter and the Indians' petition be sent to the members of the Council.

With Canada adamant and the Netherlands wavering, Joseph Avenol, acting Secretary-General of the League in the temporary absence of Sir Eric Drummond, agreed that 'what must be done is to "enterrer" [bury] the matter. The question is how to do it.' A letter from an official of the Political Section to Dr Joost van Hamel, a Dutch jurist who headed the League's Legal Section and was then in the Netherlands, asked that he find out informally if the Dutch government might be willing to withdraw its request. If not, the documents would be distributed to the Council members for information. In that event, it was 'most unlikely that any Member of the Council would ask that the matter be put on the agenda. The question would be completely buried and never likely to be resuscitated.'[7] Van Hamel wired in reply: 'second alternative preferable avoid every additional publicity.'[8]

With the Dutch no longer seeking any publicity beyond that which was inevitable unless they formally withdrew their request, their letter of 26 April, the enclosed petition from the Six Nations, and the Canadian reply were formally communicated to the ten states then members of the League Council on 7 August 1923, for their information. In a 'personal' letter to Mackenzie King, Sir Herbert Ames, the League's financial director and its ranking Canadian official, explained again that the Secretary-General had no option but to make this distribution, but that the matter would not be placed on the Council's agenda for discussion unless one of the members so requested.[9] The British Foreign Office, after obtaining Canada's concurrence, formally protested the Netherlands' role in the affair, which it considered 'an uncalled for interference in internal affairs of Canada.'[10]

No Council member chose to pursue the matter, and the Netherlands was not heard from again on the subject. However, it was far from buried, and the Six Nations' campaign to bring their grievances before the League had only begun.

The focus of attention for the next phase of the campaign was the Fourth Assembly, which met in Geneva beginning 4 September 1923. Chief Deskaheh wrote the Secretary-General and the President of the Assembly, attempting again to petition the League directly, and again being told that he could not do so.[11] What was needed was still one or more member states willing to bring up the question officially.

While searching for states willing to act on their behalf, Deskaheh and his aides conducted an active publicity campaign in Geneva. Emery Kelen, a political cartoonist in Geneva at the time has given a vivid description of some of the Chief's activities. At their first meeting, Kelen 'was desolate to find him wearing a neat brown business suit and at his side no moccasined brave but a ... vulturous paleface lawyer.' Deskaheh could provide exoticism when necessary, however. He tried to 'register with the League several strips of wampum representing treaties his ancestors had concluded with the paleface; these documents he carried in a buffalo-skin pouch.' He arranged to appear at a local theatre to present his appeal to the people of Geneva. There he appeared in full regalia, feathers and all. He pulled a wooden pipe out of the buffalo-skin pouch and held it high. 'Here is the pipe of peace which my ancestors smoked with the Canadians,' he said. 'And here are the agreements ... The black beads represent my ancestors, the white beads stand for the paleface. With your own eyes you can see that at the end hangs a black and white fringe. This means that the agreement was concluded in accordance with the law.'[12]

Whether because of his publicity efforts or his legal arguments, or for other reasons altogether, Deskaheh was, for the second time, successful in finding the necessary champions for his cause. This time the First Delegates of four states, Ireland, Panama, Persia, and Estonia, wrote jointly to the President of the Assembly on 27 September 1923, requesting that a newly-prepared appeal from the Six Nations be communicated to the Assembly, and suggesting that the League Council request an advisory opinion from the Permanent Court of International Justice as to whether the petition was receivable under Article 17 of the Covenant, which dealt with disputes between 'a Member of the League and a State which is not a member of the League.' The request of the four states was based in part, their letter said, on 'l'intérêt universel qui s'attache à la conservation de l'antique race des Indiens Peaux-Rouges.'* It is worth noting that three of the four signers (the delegates of Panama, Persia, and Estonia) had, only two days earlier, addressed the Assembly in opposition to Canada's efforts to obtain Assembly approval of its Article 10 interpretative resolution (see pp. 87-8).

To this letter the Assembly President replied on 28 September that he could make a request of the Council only on the basis of an Assembly resolution.[13] As the sessions of the Fourth Assembly ended on the following day, there was no opportunity for any further action to be taken.

Even though the attempt to bring the Six Nations' appeal before the Assembly had proved abortive, the Canadian government was disturbed by the developments at Geneva. On his return to Ottawa, George P. Graham, one of the two

---

* 'the universal interest attached to the preservation of the ancient race of Red-Skin Indians'

cabinet ministers who had represented Canada at the Assembly, wrote the Minister of Indian Affairs that 'we had some little trouble with the Six Nation Indians question in Geneva, and at one time it looked as though it would really be brought up before the Assembly ... Chief Deskakeh [sic] was not only there with his Yankee Solicitor, but they issued a Bill to every Member of the League making somewhat serious allegations concerning their treatment by the Canadian Government ...' Graham suggested that a complete reply be prepared which could be forwarded to the League Secretariat,[14] and the Department of Indian Affairs subsequently set to work preparing such a reply.

Before the Canadian reply had been completed, however, the Six Nations appeal had once again become an active matter at Geneva. One of the signers of the 27 September letter to the President of the Assembly had been Prince Arfa-ad-Dovleh, the Persian First Delegate. Just two days earlier, Prince Arfa had cast the one negative vote against the interpretation of Article 10 which Canada was insistently advocating. He was not now to let the Indians' grievance against Canada be dismissed so readily. On 13 December 1923, he wired the President of the League Council, from his villa in Monaco, asking that the 27 September suggestion regarding a PCIJ advisory opinion be transmitted to the Council. In reply, Prince Arfa was requested to indicate specifically if Persia wished to place the matter on the agenda of the next Council meeting, to be held in March 1924, and, if so, to submit his government's observations on the matter. The two letters were circulated to the Council members for information.[15]

With the Six Nations affair now likely to go on the Council's agenda, Sir Herbert Ames again wrote Prime Minister King a letter of explanation, emphasizing that if Persia insisted the Secretary-General was obliged to comply with its request. Ames recounted the activities of Deskaheh and his aides during the Assembly, and said that he understood 'they have been following up this initiative by visiting several European countries.' He thought it necessary that Canada give attention to the matter, urged a serious presentation of the Canadian reply, and offered to serve as 'a channel of unofficial communication.' The writing of this 'personal' letter from Ames to King had been suggested to Ames in a memorandum from F.P. Walters, an assistant to the Secretary-General, and Drummond had himself reviewed and slightly revised the letter before it was sent.[16]

Prince Arfa on 8 January 1924, confirmed the request made in his telegram, but declined to submit any observations on the Six Nations question, beyond what had been already said in the four Assembly delegations' letter, saying that the sole purpose of his request was 'to give a small nation a chance of at least being heard.'[17]

At this point the Secretary-General decided on the highly unusual procedure of challenging whether Prince Arfa was speaking for his government in officially raising the Six Nations question. As the Prince's letters had been addressed to the Council President, Hjalmar Branting of Sweden, Branting's co-operation was essential if such a challenge was to be made. On 18 January Drummond wrote Branting, enclosing a draft letter for his signature asking Prince Arfa to advise him 'whether this question should be entered on the agenda "at the request of the Persian Government." '[18]

Meanwhile, Deskaheh had also written Branting, urging the merits of his case. A Swedish foreign ministry official sent a copy of Deskaheh's letter to F.P. Walters, and said that Branting (who had not yet received Drummond's letter of 18 January) 'thinks it rather hard if the poor Indian cannot be even heard.'

With Branting's decision on the proposed challenge to Prince Arfa's authority hanging in the balance, Walters wrote back defending the Secretariat's position, while indicating a sympathy with the Six Nations' appeal which, to say the least, had not been evident in previous expressions by the Secretariat:

I must say that I rather sympathize with the feeling that it is bad luck on the Indian Chief that he should find such difficulty in getting heard, and if any country were willing to put the matter on the agenda of the Council, my own personal feeling would be one of satisfaction. At the same time I do think it is very important to hold to the principle that in such cases there must be a genuine request from a Member of the League, and not the mere expression of a wish on the part of a delegate who is not clearly and definitely acting for his Government. Do you not agree?[19]

Branting did indeed agree, and before Walters' letter had reached him, had already signed and mailed the letter to Prince Arfa which Drummond had written. Arfa replied that he would, as requested, refer the matter to Teheran. The correspondence between Branting and Arfa was circulated to the members of the League Council for their information, and there the matter rested until such time as the Teheran government should decide its position.[20]

Simultaneously with Drummond and Branting raising the question of whether Prince Arfa had exceeded his authority, the British government brought pressure to bear to assure that the answer would be that he had. On 22 January 1924, while the letter drafted by the League Secretariat was awaiting Branting's signature, the Foreign Office wrote the British minister at Teheran advising him, in case the Persian government should decide to pursue the matter, that its involvement in the affair was regarded as 'impertinent interference.'[21]

With the Persian attitude not yet settled, the question, instead of remaining dormant, promptly reappeared from a new quarter. On 1 March the British minister in Panama wired the Foreign Office that the Panamanian government, whose delegate had signed the letter to the Assembly President in September, wished to obtain a statement of the case from the Canadian standpoint before deciding whether to pursue the matter. The Foreign Office, sounding increasingly vexed, wired back that the 'attempt to reopen the question is resented as impertinent interference in internal affairs of the British Empire. You should make this quite plain.' The British minister then discussed the Six Nations question with the Panamanian foreign minister, carefully refraining, he explained, from using the word 'impertinent.' The foreign minister took it up with the President of Panama, and reported back that 'it was fully realised that the question was purely a domestic one,' and that no further action whatever would be taken.[22]

Evidently fearing that Estonia, also a signatory of the September letter on behalf of the Six Nations, might be considering further action, as had Persia and Panama, Britain sought to forestall any such move. The British consul in Tallinn discussed the matter with the Estonian government, and was told that the Estonian representative at Geneva had acted on his personal initiative and had been instructed to abstain from any further steps.[23]

Meanwhile, the detailed exposition of Canada's views on the merits of the Six Nations' claims, on which the Department of Indian Affairs had started work following the 1923 Assembly, had been completed, and was sent on 23 Feb. 1924, to Sir Herbert Ames.[24] On 18 March it was distributed to all League members, and later was printed in the League's *Official Journal.*[25]

The March 1924 Council meeting had come and gone with still no word from Persia, and with the Six Nations' appeal therefore not on the Council's agenda. Finally, on 10 May the Persian Foreign Ministry gave the British government the answer it had been seeking. It was 'telling its representative in the League that the government does not wish to interfere in the matter and that no further negotiations are to be made on the subject.'[26]

With Persia's abandonment of the case, the attempts to bring the Six Nations' appeal officially before the League of Nations came to an end. Before the year was over, the Canadian government dissolved the hereditary Council of the Chiefs of the Six Nations Indians, thereby depriving Deskaheh of his right to speak for them, and provided for a new elected municipal administration for the Indian reserve.[27]

The Six Nations' campaign had thus ended in failure. While information on the matter had been distributed by the League, and substantial local publicity had been obtained in Geneva, the Indians' appeal had never been placed on the agenda for discussion by either the Council or the Assembly. While several states had made tentative moves to do so, none of them persisted when confronted with strong Canadian and British objections.

This outcome was perhaps to be expected, considering the lack of any serious legal claim for jurisdiction by the League. Nevertheless, it was entirely possible for such a question to be discussed and thereby publicized, even in the absence of any legal basis for action. The successful blocking of any such discussion is revealing, both as to attitudes and as to decision-making processes.

In the first place, one may wonder why such diverse countries as the Netherlands, Persia, Panama, Estonia, and Ireland should show any inclination to champion the Six Nations' cause. To some extent their attitudes may have been a reflection of a sentimental sympathy for the 'noble Red man' allegedly victimized by white greed and duplicity. Such sympathy, however, must have been reinforced by a certain irritation with Canada, and perhaps with Britain as well, for it to have found such positive political expression. So far as Canada was concerned, the frequent assertions by its delegates of a superior moral position must have served as an irritant, and for Canada to be forced on the defensive on the same sort of minorities question as was plaguing so many other League members, must have seemed fair enough. In addition, Canada's insistent attempts through four Assemblies to get major changes in the collective security aspects of the League, through tampering with Article 10 – changes which were clearly not palatable to many League members – must have been a further irritant. Certainly the Persian, Panamanian, and Estonian delegates' disagreement with Canada over Article 10 and their simultaneous interest in the Six Nations' grievances can be assumed to be related.

But if a combination of sympathy with the Indians and irritation with Canada probably produced the initially favourable attitudes on the part of several states to the Six Nations' appeal, in spite of a virtually nonexistent legal basis, those attitudes quickly evaporated when trouble resulted for the states themselves. When adamantly opposed by Canada, and especially by Britain, no state was willing to create difficulties gratuitously for itself when it had no knowledge of nor serious interest in the Indians' situation, and no real quarrel with Canada.

The activities of the League Secretariat in the affair were also revealing. While officially made up of international civil servants rather than national representatives, key officials such as Ames and van Hamel acted as the principal contacts for the Secretariat with their home governments, even when the question dealt with was unrelated to their formal responsibilities in Geneva. While officially neutral in a dispute brewing between League members, top officials of the Secretariat, including Drummond, Avenol, and Walters, clearly exerted strong efforts to keep the matter off the agenda. To what extent Drummond or Walters may have been acting as former (and perhaps future) British officials, and not exclusively as League officials, can only be a subject for speculation.

The British role was, of course, a crucial one, as Britain was far more capable of exerting effective influence, whether at Geneva or directly with individual states, than was Canada. The total absence of any Canadian overseas offices in 1923-4, except in London and Paris, meant that Canada could present its point of view in foreign capitals only through British spokesmen and, indeed, the point of view expressed was likely to be considerably more British than Canadian, as when reference was made in the British protests to interference in 'internal affairs of the British Empire,' rather than to internal affairs of Canada.

In any case, the Six Nations' appeal was unique in that it involved a controversy at the League of Nations in which Canada and its policies were under criticism and attack. It showed at least that this was one of the hazards of the full participation in international organizational affairs which Canada had successfully sought, even for a country whose external policies normally gave no offence.

8
The protection of minorities

In 1929 Canada presented to the League Council a proposal for major changes in the existing system for protection of minority rights. This was only the second important Canadian initiative at the League; the first had been Canada's attempt, in 1920-23, to delete or modify Article 10. The initiative taken in 1929 was very different in that it was aimed at making an important aspect of League activity stronger and more effective. It also reflected a new willingness on the part of Canada to involve itself actively and directly, through its role in the League, in a primarily European question which was the subject of heated political controversy.

While the Canadian government of Mackenzie King was willing to make this substantial change in its approach toward the League and toward involvement in European political controversies, the initiative taken was in fact the result of the efforts of one man, Raoul Dandurand. Dandurand was by 1929 a veteran figure both at Ottawa and at Geneva. A French-Canadian lawyer and corporation director from Montreal, he had been appointed to the Canadian Senate in 1898. Since 1921 he had been Liberal party leader in the Senate and Minister without Portfolio in the King governments. He had been a member of the Canadian delegations to Geneva annually since 1924, President of the League Assembly in 1925, and Canada's regular representative on the League Council since it had become a member of that body in 1927. His proposal to reform the League's procedures for dealing with minority complaints was thus based on full familiarity with the policies of both the League and the Canadian government, and a position of influence in both.

The minorities question itself had been a continuing centre of attention and dispute since the League had come into existence. Normally, under international law, questions regarding the rights of members of minority groups within a nation's own population were the exclusive concern of that nation. However, beginning in 1919, various eastern European states were obliged by the major powers to become parties to treaties bringing their treatment of their minorities under a degree of international supervision. By 1924 minorities treaties or agreements were in effect with regard to thirteen states (Albania, Austria, Bulgaria, Czechoslovakia, Estonia, Greece, Hungary, Latvia, Lithuania, Poland, Romania, Turkey and Yugoslavia), and parts of the territory of two others (Finland and Germany). The treaties had, in effect, been imposed on these states following defeat in the world war, or as a condition of receiving additions to territory or recognition of independence. In general, the treaties required the states concerned to give their nationals equal civil and political rights, without distinction as to race, language, or religion. The minorities were assured the right to use their own language, to maintain their own religious, social, and educational institutions, and to receive an equitable share of state funds provided for the support of such activities.

To assure that these obligations were carried out, they were placed by the minorities treaties under the guarantee of the League of Nations. Article 12 of the Polish treaty of 28 June 1919, provided the procedure by which this guarantee should be implemented: 'Poland agrees that any Member of the Council of the League of Nations shall have the right to bring to the attention of the Council any infraction, or any danger of infraction, of any of those obligations, and that the Council thereupon may take such action and give such direction as it may deem proper and effective in the circumstances.'[1]

The same language was used in the other treaties, and a uniform procedure for handling minorities questions was adopted by the Council (except for complaints from either the German or the Polish portions of Upper Silesia, which were governed by special legal provisions and procedures).

As petitions claiming non-compliance with the treaties obviously required review, they were dealt with initially by the Minorities Section of the League Secretariat. Receipt of the petition was acknowledged, but from that point forward all review by the League was in secret, unless a Council member eventually brought the matter officially before the full Council. The Minorities Section determined whether the petition was receivable, that is, essentially, whether it made allegations which, if true, would constitute a treaty violation. If so, the petition and the Secretariat's analysis were reviewed by a 'Committee of Three,' consisting of the president of the Council (a position rotated quarterly among the Council members) and two other members. The Committee of Three, together with the Secretariat, attempted to work out with the government concerned a solution to any apparent problem of non-compliance with the treaties. If this proved impossible, any member of the Committee of Three might then, if he chose to do so, bring the alleged violation formally and publicly before the Council for action.

From its origins, this procedure had been the subject of constant and vigorous complaint from both the minorities and their governments. The governments routinely denied the validity of the complaints against them, and considered the discussion of such complaints an unwarranted intrusion into their domestic affairs, based on treaties unfairly imposed on a selected few states. The minorities and those governments, such as Germany and Hungary, which championed them, contended on the other hand that the procedures followed gave the petitioners much less than a fair hearing. In most cases, the petitioners received no notification of any kind from the League, except the initial acknowledgement of receipt of their petitions. They were never told officially whether the petitions had been ruled receivable, or what had been the result of a review by a Committee of Three. (Some information might, of course, be obtainable informally from the Minorities Section of the Secretariat or from a member of a Committee of Three.) Similarly, while the Committee of Three might, during its review, obtain comments and additional information from the governments complained against, it did not enter into contact with the petitioners, or give them information about or any opportunity to refute the government's statements.

To complicate matters further, there was substantial reason to doubt the sincerity of most of the governments directly involved in disputes over the minorities treaties. On the one hand, states such as Poland and Romania were most reluctant to carry out the treaties' provisions in good faith. On the other hand, states such as Germany and Hungary were obviously less interested in protecting the rights of individuals than in maintaining cohesive and dissatisfied German and Hungarian minorities in neighbouring states, as a base for eventually regaining control of lost territories.

To Dandurand, himself a member of the French-Canadian minority in his own country, more equitable treatment of the eastern European minorities seemed both desirable and possible. As a lawyer, he was dissatisfied with the procedures followed both by the Secretariat and the Council of the League, procedures which seemed to him weighted in favour of the governments and against the minorities. Obtaining changes would at least, however, be a difficult task. In the first place, such Council members as Poland and Romania, with the important backing of France, with whom they were closely aligned politically, could be expected to oppose any substantial change favourable to the minorities. Secondly, no procedural changes could be made by the Council unless consistent with the minorities treaties, as there was no possibility of obtaining consent to any strengthening of the treaties themselves.

Dandurand's direct personal involvement in minorities questions had begun when he took his place as Canada's representative on the League Council in September 1927. He had already made clear, at the League Assembly, his generally sympathetic attitude toward the minorities and, in the opinion of O.D. Skelton, this had won for Canada the votes of three or four states in the 1927 election of Council members (a contest which Canada had won by only three votes). Skelton, always uneasy about Canadian involvement in the quarrels of others, wrote to Prime Minister King at the time that 'I have told him [Dandurand] it may mean that the Ukrainians and Hungarians and Jews and Chaldeo-Assyrians will hereafter look to Canada to champion them in the Council.'[2]

In December 1927 Dandurand was appointed to his first Committee of Three, along with the Council representatives of France and Chile, to consider a petition from members of the German minority in Poland claiming discriminatory treatment by Poland in carrying out agrarian reform. In the committee Dandurand inquired whether the petitioners did not receive a copy of the government's comments, and was informed that they did not. He then advocated obtaining fuller information from both the Polish government and the petitioners, to resolve the contradictions in their assertions, while Joseph Paul-Boncour of France defended the actions of Poland as correct. Agreement was reached on having the Minorities Section obtain supplementary information from the government only, in keeping with the established practice.[3]

At the next Council session, in March 1928, Pablo de Azcárate of the Minorities Section reported that analysis of the information obtained regarding the Polish agrarian reform did not show a disproportionate taking of land from German landowners in the districts complained about. Dandurand questioned the procedure whereby only the members of the Committee of Three, and not all Council members, were permitted access to the file on a minorities complaint. (Thus, for example, the German government would not have access to the file on this complaint from the German minority in Poland.) Sir Eric Drummond, Azcárate, and René Massigli of France explained and defended the existing procedure; the Committee decided to take no further action on the complaint, and to unofficially so inform the Polish government.[4]

After having challenged several basic aspects of the minorities procedure in his first Committee of Three, Dandurand was not again named to a Committee of Three dealing with German-Polish minority questions, but to committees dealing with problems of the less politically important minorities in Greece and Turkey. In December 1928, as a member of Committees of Three reviewing complaints about compensation for expropriated Bulgarian and Russian religious properties in Greece, Dandurand expressed his dissatisfaction with being unable to inform the petitioners of actions taken as a result of their petitions, and indicated his intention of presenting to the full Council the problems resulting from lack of any contact with petitioners. Drummond said the existing rules did not permit any different action, but added that the Secretariat was studying possible procedural changes. Massigli emphasized the difficulties which would be created for governments if petitioners were informed of actions taken.[5]

Two days later, on 15 December 1928, Dandurand gave formal notice to the full Council that at its next session, in March 1929, he would raise the question of the procedures followed in regard to minorities petitions. He was promptly joined in this statement by Gustav Stresemann, the German foreign minister, who had just been engaged in heated dispute over minorities problems with the Polish representative, and who said that he too would ask that the whole procedural question be reviewed.[6]

During the next three months Dandurand prepared the details of his proposal, and the League Secretariat worked out the specific changes which it would like to see made. The two were quite different. The procedural study to which Drummond had referred, prepared by Azcárate, had recommended changes aimed at achieving greater continuity and a higher degree of expertise in the review of petitions by Committees of Three, a report by the Committee of Three to the full Council when review of a petition was completed, and greater publicity as to the results of reviews. Azcárate's recommendations had been circulated for comment within the Secretariat, but had received mostly negative comments. Sir Eric Drummond, after reviewing the proposals and comments, added the following conclusion on 19 December 1928:

The only point, therefore, that remains is that of publicity, but here I think that we shall have to find some method of remedying to some extent the present situation, perhaps simply by publication of a six-monthly or annual list, setting out the petitions received, and stating very summarily the action taken, i.e., 'examined by a Committee of three, consisting of the representatives of ..., ..., and ...; decision to ask Government for certain further information'; or alternatively, 'decided not to proceed further with matter.'
I think that this is the very utmost that the Minorities Powers will accept ...[7]

The position thus reached by Drummond was firmly adhered to during the subsequent discussions. Some publicity as to the results of completed reviews of minorities' complaints was strongly favoured, as it would help to counteract the impression given by total silence that the League and its Secretariat were doing nothing. Procedural changes aimed at strengthening the minorities' position, however, were not favoured; they would interfere with quiet and informal negotiation by the Minorities Section with the governments concerned, which the Secretariat considered the strongest feature of the then existing system.

His own position having been determined, Drummond next attempted to get it accepted by Canada and presented as the Canadian proposal at the next Council meeting. Writing to the Canadian Advisory Office in Geneva, he explained that he thought it would be unacceptable to the countries with minorities treaties to send information directly to petitioners. However, information could be provided to them in a more roundabout way by publishing annually a list of petitions and a brief indication of action taken. This would also 'help to dissipate the impression that petitions from Minorities were as a rule shelved.' No other amendments to the existing procedure appeared feasible or advantageous. 'If this somewhat limited suggestion commends itself to Senator Dandurand, we should, of course, be at his disposal to prepare a memorandum in the sense which I have indicated ...'[8]

The acting Canadian Advisory Officer, Georges P. Vanier, reported to Ottawa about the same time that Germany was 'playing a waiting game' on the minorities question, hoping that Canada would submit a proposal sufficiently wide in scope to make unnecessary any separate German proposal. Vanier thought it important to find a solution readily acceptable to the Council, thus avoiding 'a controversy in the wake of which the German claims might rise.'[9]

Meanwhile, in Montreal, Dandurand was drafting his own proposal to submit to the March 1929 Council session, without asking assistance from the Department of External Affairs, and ignoring Drummond's offer of assistance, as well as his views as to content. On 21 January Dandurand mailed to O.D. Skelton a completed draft of his proposal, asking an immediate review of it by the Department, and a meeting with him in Ottawa to discuss it. He made it clear that any proposals for extensive changes would not be welcome: 'This narration or argument may perhaps need to be condensed without being weakened.'[10]

The proposal which Dandurand had prepared was even more far-reaching in its changes than might have been anticipated from his comments in the Committees of Three. It provided essentially that minorities' complaints would go first to their own government, and then, if not satisfactorily resolved, to the League Council. Questions of receivability would be determined, not by the Secretariat, but by a committee of three members of the Council. The full Council would then review, and act on, each receivable petition. The proposed procedure would provide publicity in all cases, as the published records of the Council's meetings would indicate the action taken on the complaint. The Council could provide for continuity and expertise by setting up a permanent minorities staff under its direction, if it wished, as had been suggested by the Dutch foreign minister at the 1928 Assembly (a suggestion similar to that proposed by Azcárate of the

Secretariat's Minorities Section, but not accepted by Drummond). The proposed procedure would avoid creating disputes between states, as minorities would not be forced to find some government to take up their case in order for it to be presented to the full Council.[11]

During the next few days Dandurand discussed the text of his proposal with Prime Minister King, Skelton, and Riddell, in person and by phone. Lester B. Pearson, then a junior member of the External Affairs staff, prepared a detailed analysis, which was sent to Dandurand by Skelton.[12] One serious objection to Dandurand's text was found during these reviews. The minorities treaties provided for consideration by the League Council of an alleged violation only after a Council member had brought the matter to the Council's attention. Automatic referral of all receivable complaints to the Council, as provided in Dandurand's draft proposal, would, therefore, go beyond the requirements of the treaties, and would undoubtedly not be agreed to by the states concerned. However, these states had already accepted a prior review by a Council committee (the Committee of Three). Therefore, Dandurand accepted a modification in his text whereby all receivable petitions would be referred, not to the full Council as such, but to a Council 'committee' on which all Council members would be represented. A criticism by Skelton that the full Council, which then had fourteen members, was too large a group for the review of petitions, was met by Dandurand's suggestion that the Council might, if it wished, name a smaller committee of its members for a preliminary study of some cases.

With these changes included, Dandurand's text of a proposed Council resolution, an explanatory memorandum, and an accompanying letter to Drummond, were sent by him on 30 January 1929, to Skelton for a final review. Dandurand pointed out to Skelton, 'Vous constatez que je ne demande pas à Sir Eric son opinion. Je vole avec mes propres ailes tout simplement.'*[13]

Dandurand's proposals were forwarded to Drummond without further revisions. They were distributed by the Secretariat to all Council members on 19 February and, after clearance with the Canadian Advisory Office, given to the press.[14] Meanwhile, the Department of External Affairs had already informed the British, French, and German representatives in Canada, and the German government had indicated a generally favourable reaction.[15]

As might be expected, the substance of Dandurand's proposals was far from pleasing to Drummond. On 4 February, not knowing that the proposed changes had been drafted in final form and were on their way to him, he again wrote the Canadian Advisory Office. His suggestions were even more cautious than before;

* 'You will note that I do not ask Sir Eric for his opinion. I fly with my own wings, quite simply.'

he favoured publicity, for information only, of the results of reviews of minorities petitions, provided it could be done in such a way as not to invite discussion of the petitions by the Assembly.[16] Lester Pearson, forwarding a summary of Drummond's views to Dandurand, commented: 'I presume Sir Eric will cease to worry us about his problem of circulation of information regarding minorities petitions when he receives your resolution on the question. He will have other things to worry about then.'[17]

Indeed he did. Drummond, after receiving the text of the Canadian proposal, referred it to the Minorities Section for analysis, with the comment that he found Dandurand's summary of existing procedures 'incomplete and misleading.'[18] At about the same time the New York Times carried a report from Geneva that Dandurand's proposals 'meet with little favor in the secretariat,' and that 'secretariat circles doubt whether the Council will approve.' When the Canadian Advisory Office inquired, it was assured by the Secretariat that no such disapproval or doubt had been expressed.[19]

Another counter-move was made at this time by Poland, which, the British government advised the Canadian Department of External Affairs, planned to propose a general Minorities Convention applicable to all members of the League. It was hardly likely that Poland expected such a general minorities treaty to be accepted. The real purpose of the proposal was presumably to make it clear that states supporting stronger protection of minority rights meant such protection to be applicable only to Poland and other eastern European states, and not to themselves. If so, it promptly produced the expected reaction in London and in Ottawa. Sir Austen Chamberlain, the British Foreign Secretary, had informed the Polish chargé d'affaires that Britain 'could give no support to such a proposal.' To Canada, the explanation was given that a general minorities treaty was not needed, and 'appeared to threaten interference by the League in the domestic affairs of certain parts of the Empire.' The Canadian reply was 'to the effect that our attitudes were the same on the Polish proposal.' At the same time Canada was told that Chamberlain 'readily acquiesced' in Dandurand's proposed Council resolution, except for the part recommending a committee of the whole Council.[20]

Meanwhile, on 25 February Azcárate completed a detailed analysis of the text submitted by Dandurand. In the first place, he was surprised to find that there was no provision for publicity of the results of review of minorities petitions. (This omission was undoubtedly unintentional. Dandurand's original draft had provided for automatic publicity, as all petitions would be acted on by the Council. When, during the hurried review in Ottawa, the draft was revised to provide instead for action by a Council committee, it was apparently overlooked that the provision for automatic publicity thereby disappeared, as the proceedings of Council committees were not ordinarily published.)

Azcárate's other most serious objection was to the provision for formal, public, adversary-type proceedings between the minority and its government, in place of informal private attempts at mediation by the Minorities Section and the Committees of Three. He thought such a change would be disastrous to the interests of the minorities themselves, and would make most unlikely the obtaining of concessions from their governments. He thought the best course of action would be to follow, instead, Drummond's earlier suggestion for some publicity of the results obtained.[21]

Drummond thought Azcárate's analysis 'excellent' and had it circulated to his key subordinates. He also referred to the Secretariat's Legal Section the question, raised by Azcárate, as to whether reference of all petitions to a 'committee' composed of the full Council was consistent with the minorities treaties. The Legal Section replied that it was not.[22]

After review of the text of Dandurand's proposal, then, the Secretariat's position remained unchanged. It favoured a certain publicity for actions taken, but no other alterations in the minorities procedure. Dandurand's specific proposals it considered either unwise, or contrary to the treaties, or both.

On 4 March 1929, undoubtedly after consultation between Dandurand, who had meanwhile arrived in Geneva, and the Secretariat, a slightly revised, and final, version of the Canadian proposal was circulated to Council members. (The full text is given in Appendix A.) The principal change was to correct the inadvertent omission of provision for publicity, by directly authorizing the 'committee' of the full Council to publicize its actions.

On 6 March the Council took up the Canadian and German requests for a general review of minorities procedures. No specific German proposal had been submitted. Dandurand explained the basis for the Canadian recommendations, emphasizing the inadequacies of the existing procedure:

This procedure has not given satisfaction to the minorities, which never cease protesting through all the channels at their disposal. Although the method has yielded good results, it leaves the minority under the impression that its case has not been heard and that it is being victimised by the inaction or indifference of the Council. The minority complains, but is left ignorant what action, if any, has been taken on its representations. Its complaint is generally referred to its Government, but the latter's reply is never communicated to the minority.

Quite possibly in nine cases out of ten the complainant is in error; but, as this is not made clear to him, he preserves his grievance and loudly proclaims his discontent. That is not what the framers of the minorities treaties intended. Their object was to calm the atmosphere and establish harmony in the newly constituted or reconstituted States.[23]

Stresemann agreed generally with Dandurand, but also presented several recommendations of his own, for example, that all minorities committee reports be presented to the Council and published, and that directly interested parties (such as the German government, in the case of a German minority) should be entitled to participate in the reviews. Of other Council members who commented, only the Finnish representative offered general support to Dandurand. Auguste Zaleski (Poland), supported by Nicolas Titulescu (Romania), said the Canadian proposal involved new obligations which would require the consent of the states concerned, thought publicity might be harmful by creating dissension, and said minorities obligations should, in any case, apply equally to all states.

Sir Austen Chamberlain defended generally the existing procedures, but favoured some additional publicity and greater speed of action; the support by Chamberlain for the Canadian proposals which had been indicated the preceding month did not materialize. The position of Aristide Briand, the French foreign minister, was substantially the same. He generally favoured the existing procedures, but would support some publicity and a system for reporting to the Council.[24]

On the following day the Council referred the Canadian proposal to a committee consisting of Japan, Great Britain, and Spain, to report at the June 1929 Council meeting.[25] Based on the Council discussion, prospects for acceptance of the Canadian recommendations hardly seemed bright. In particular, the fact that Britain and France had already arrived at very similar positions on the question, and that they favoured only minor changes in procedure (primarily in the area of publicity, as advocated by the Secretariat), gave a fairly clear indication of the probable outcome of the Council's deliberations.

Meanwhile, in the March meetings of Committees of Three, the procedural controversy continued. A new complaint from a Russian monastery in Greece was claimed by Greece not to be covered by the minorities treaty. Dandurand contended in the Committee of Three (Chile, Canada, and France) that the facts needed to settle the question could probably be obtained quite readily from the petitioner. Instead, the Committee was able only to follow Drummond's suggestion that the question be referred to the Minorities and Legal Sections of the Secretariat for a detailed review of the relevant documents.[26] In another Committee of Three (Finland, Canada, Spain), set up to consider complaints against Turkey by the Armenian Catholic bishop in that country, Dandurand proposed that a question regarding the legality of confiscation of property by Turkey be referred to the Permanent Court of International Justice for advice. The Committee decided, however, to defer any other action until further information had been obtained from the Turkish government.[27]

Between the March and June, 1929, Council sessions, the committee that had been appointed to review the Canadian proposal met in Geneva and in London, with Sir Austen Chamberlain as the British member. Canada had no part in this review, and Dandurand first learned of the committee's recommendations when he arrived in Madrid for the June meeting.[28]

The committee had, in effect, rejected Dandurand's proposals and recommended instead much more limited procedural changes along the lines already indicated as acceptable to Britain, France, and the Secretariat. To meet the need for greater publicity, the petitioner would be informed if his petition was declared not receivable; all Council members would be informed of the result of each examination completed by a Committee of Three; the Committees of Three could, with the consent of the government concerned, have the results of their examinations published; and the Secretary-General would publish annual statistics regarding the number of petitions received and examined. To speed up the review of petitions, Committees of Three were encouraged to hold meetings between Council sessions.[29]

Notably absent from the committee's recommendations were any assurance that a petitioner would be informed of the action on his complaint, or the basis for it; any procedure for obtaining supplementary information from a petitioner; any means whereby a petitioner might know or comment on his government's statements; and any right of access to the file on a minorities petition for Council members other than those on the Committee of Three.

The German representative expressed general dissatisfaction with the report. He proposed amending it to include on the Committees of Three those states directly involved with complaints, but his amendment was rejected by the Council.[30]

Canada was the only other Council member to indicate dissatisfaction. Dandurand first proposed adjournment of the question to the September meeting, but did not persist in this request. He then concentrated his efforts on an insistence that the right of Committees of Three to obtain supplementary information directly from minorities be explicitly recognized. Titulescu objected to any such procedure. At this point Drummond told the Council that there was a misunderstanding, that the Committees of Three were already 'competent to collect information of any kind and from any source without limitation,' and that already 'a case had occurred' in which a Committee of Three had asked petitioners for further information.[31] This was certainly not the procedure which had normally prevailed in the Committees of Three. As Dandurand later described the meeting, '... l'intervention du secrétaire général fournit la grosse surprise de tout le débat. Son attitude démentait toute la tradition qu'avait suivie les comités de trois ...

Elle allait aussi manifestement à l'encontre du rapport ... que nous étions à étudier ... La déclaration de sir Eric Drummond renversait tout cet échafaudage au grand scandale des opposants. Monsieur Titulesco en parut estomaqué.'*[32]

Agreement was then reached by the Council without further difficulty. Briand thought it 'inadmissible that the League of Nations should become a tribunal before which a subject might plead against his Government,' but was nevertheless willing to accept Drummond's interpretation as to the possibility of obtaining supplementary information. Dandurand said he was satisfied, and made no further proposals to alter the committee recommendations.[33] Stresemann supported the committee report, and credited Dandurand personally with having obtained the determination permitting Committees of Three to contact petitioners. On 13 June 1929, the Council unanimously adopted the committee recommendations, putting the new procedural provisions into force at once.[34]

Dandurand contended, before the League Assembly in September as he had before the Council, that his recommendations had been largely accepted.[35] While this greatly overstated the case, there had nevertheless been some substantial procedural changes agreed upon, primarily as a result of Dandurand's personal interest and persistence. The changes constituted at least a modest strengthening of the system for protecting minority rights, by providing more information to petitioners and to Council members than had previously been made available, and by opening up the possibility of direct communication between the Council committees and the petitioners. The changes went beyond the very limited publicity measures which Drummond had favoured, and which had been aimed more at protecting the Secretariat from criticism than at protecting the rights of minorities, but it had eventually been Drummond himself who had played the key role in finding a compromise satisfactory to all parties. The finding of a mutually acceptable compromise was also due, no doubt, in large part to the fact that neither Dandurand personally, nor Canada as a nation, was directly involved in a partisan way in the often bitter disputes over minorities questions. His success in getting some changes agreed upon, in what had at first appeared to be most unpromising circumstances, was a good illustration of the useful role which small states could at times play within the context of the League of Nations.

The initiative which Canada took in this instance was, however, very much an exception to its usual policy with regard to League affairs. While Canadian government spokesmen, both in Geneva and in Ottawa, repeatedly stressed the value

* '... the intervention of the Secretary-General furnished the great surprise of the entire debate. His attitude refuted the entire tradition which the Committees of Three had followed ... It was also clearly in contradiction with the report ... which we were studying ... Sir Eric Drummond's declaration upset all that structure to the great indignation of those opposed. Mr Titulescu seemed astounded by it.'

of the League as an agency for conciliation rather than coercion, they usually showed no interest whatsoever in taking initiatives in Geneva aimed at conciliation of other states' disputes. Dandurand's personal interest in the minorities question, rather than any interest in it on the part of the Canadian government as such, led to the Canadian proposals of 1929 being made. For the moment Canada found itself in the centre of a debate involving Briand, Stresemann, and Chamberlain – the ranking international statesmen of the day – and dealing with one of the most controversial of European political problems. Once this debate had been concluded, however, the more usual Canadian policy of inactivity in matters not immediately affecting it was resumed.

One striking indication that the Canadian proposals of 1929 were not viewed by the government as a significant policy matter, was the fact that no reference was made to them in the House of Commons, which was in session in the spring of 1929. The same was true in the Senate until Sir George Foster, a Conservative Senator who had just retired as President of the League of Nations Society in Canada, raised the question. 'The first I heard of it,' Foster said on 11 April, 'and I think the first that was heard of it by any of us, was when the news was put upon the wires that the honourable gentleman [Dandurand] had filed a motion on this subject.' No information had been given to Parliament, and there had been no consultation with it. The League of Nations Society, which had been holding its annual session at the time that Dandurand's initiative was reported in the press, had also been unaware of it until then.[36] Following this criticism, Dandurand gave in the Senate a full discussion of the minorities procedure question, and had the text of the League Council's discussions included in the printed Senate Debates.[37]

Another question raised by Foster was whether 'the other member of the Empire who is a member of the Council' had been consulted and was in agreement with the Canadian proposals.[38] It was clear, as a matter of fact, that there had been no meaningful consultation between Canada and Britain either before the proposals were submitted or after. As already noted, Britain was advised of the content of Canada's proposals only after the text had been finally agreed on, and Canada learned of the counter-proposals of the Council committee (of which Chamberlain was a member, and which did its main work in London) only after the text was in final form. In other words, Canada's insistence on formulating its own policies independently of Great Britain had effectively precluded any cooperative approach with Britain on the minorities question, even though the British attitude might well be decisive in determining to what extent the Canadian proposals would be accepted.

Canada's involvement with the minorities question did not, of course, end immediately after the League Council's adoption of procedural changes in June

1929. Dandurand continued as a Council member and as a member of various Committees of Three, and continued to take a lively interest in minorities problems. Thus on 13 June, two days after the adoption of the Council resolution on procedures, Dandurand proposed in the Committee of Three consisting of Chile, Canada, and France, and dealing with the complaint of a Russian monastery against Greece, that the matter be referred to the Permanent Court of International Justice for an advisory opinion, or that a questionnaire be sent to the petitioners to obtain more complete information. Instead, the Committee, on Drummond's recommendation, decided first to allow more time for completion of a study of the situation by the Secretariat, and to authorize the Minorities Section to seek further information from the Greek government.[39] Finally, in May 1930, this and two other pending complaints against the Greeks were resolved to the Committee's satisfaction on the basis of a friendly settlement with the Greek government. Dandurand proposed that the results of the Committee's work should be publicized, and agreement was readily reached that, with the consent of the Greek government, full publicity would be given.[40] Also during the May 1930 Council session, the one remaining Committee of Three of which Dandurand was a member completed its work. With regard to the petition concerning the Armenian Catholic minority in Turkey, Dandurand considered the Turkish government's reply too general, and suggested obtaining more concrete supplementary information from the petitioners. The other two members of the Committee, from Finland and Spain, and also Drummond and Azcárate, objected that the petition itself had been too general, and that the Committee should not attempt to elicit from the petitioners information which would bolster their case. The Committee then decided to consider the matter closed, and to seek the Turkish government's consent to publicize the action taken and the reasons for it. Dandurand favoured such publicity, especially because it would inform the petitioners as to why the Committee had taken no action.

This Council session was the last one in which Dandurand participated. In the Canadian general election of 28 July 1930, the Liberal government of which he was a member was defeated, and later in the year Canada's three-year term on the Council expired. Direct Canadian involvement in review of minorities petitions came to an end at that time, as did Canadian government interest and initiative in such matters, which Dandurand as an individual had provided.

9
The Manchurian crisis

The first great crisis which shook the League of Nations was the Japanese occupation of Manchuria which began in September 1931, and in it Canada played only a minor role. The crisis and how to solve it were considered first by the League Council, then by a Committee of Nineteen named by the Assembly. Canada was not a member of either of these bodies, so its participation in the League's consideration of the crisis was largely limited to statements in the Special Assembly called to deal with it. One of these statements, however, produced for the Canadian government a good deal of unfavourable publicity, both at home and abroad, and led to some serious attention by the government to Canada's international position.

The views of O.D. Skelton, the Undersecretary of State for External Affairs, were clearly formulated at an early stage. In the first place, he was unequivocal in considering Japan the aggressor. Thus in background material which the Department of External Affairs prepared for the Canadian delegation to the Disarmament Conference at the beginning of 1932, it was stated that in the Manchurian crisis 'the proof of aggression was as clear as may ever be expected.'[1] In replying on 23 January to Herbert M. Marler, the Canadian minister in Tokyo, whose reports had fully endorsed the Japanese actions, Skelton used more cautious phraseology, but reached essentially the same conclusion:

I am inclined to think, on a hasty glance, that you have given Japan rather too clean a bill of health. Granted that she had real grievances and vital interests in Manchuria, the question remains whether she did not violate her treaty engagements in the steps taken to assert her rights. I am inclined to think that she has, and the fact that other Imperialist powers have taken similar action in the past does not justify a breach of the higher code of international conduct which the world has been endeavouring to build up since the Great War.[2]

Skelton's views remained the same as the crisis continued. On 29 November 1932, shortly before the Special Assembly was to reconvene to consider the Lytton report, he wrote, 'To the plain man there appears no doubt that Japan has made war on China in Manchuria, and that it is as definitely the aggressor as any country can well be.'[3]

Skelton was equally emphatic, however, in his view that no sanctions, either economic or military, should be applied. This reflected the views regarding sanctions which he had long held, and which he continued to hold when confronted with what he himself considered a clear-cut case of aggression. These views were well summarized in the Disarmament Conference background materials:

It [a policy of security via sanctions] does not appear *desirable*, in so far as it would put the emphasis of League action on force as against conciliation, on punishment as against prevention, and interfere with the slow but steady building up of the method of world publicity, of the formation of the habit of discussion and co-operation.

It may well be argued that the most effective sanction that can be applied, under present conditions, is 'moral force,' the sudden focussing of world opinion on a meeting of the Council of the League, especially convoked to deal with a disturber of the peace.[4]

A variety of additional arguments were advanced in the same document. The automatic application of sanctions to an aggressor might mean going to war against a state whose demands were justified, but not obtainable by peaceful means. The United States was unalterably opposed to a sanctions policy, and Canada, if it followed such a policy, might well become involved in wrangling with the United States over neutral rights. The European states were interested in security only for themselves, not in guaranteeing it for other continents. 'The Manchurian crisis proves this to the hilt; ... what great Power was willing to apply even economic sanctions against Japan? Were we ourselves anxious to stop all exports to Japan and close down the CPR [Canadian Pacific Railway] Pacific service?'[5]

If Skelton's views were clear and consistent, they were, nevertheless, entirely inconsistent with Canada's legal obligations. He considered Japan an aggressor, but thought that nothing should be done about the aggression beyond the application of moral pressure. Canada, however, like all other members of the League of Nations, was legally bound to preserve the territorial integrity of each League member, to treat an attack against any other member as an attack on itself, and to apply full economic sanctions automatically to an aggressor.

As it was impossible to reconcile the views he held and the policies he advocated with Canada's legal obligations, Skelton favoured, in effect, a policy of inactivity and silence, except for a general support of such moral pressure on Japan as might be initiated by others. This approach was in keeping with his general approach toward Canadian involvement in international controversies. 'The Dominion may, with propriety, keep in the background in Conference discussions on most subjects,' the Canadian delegates to the Disarmament Conference were advised as the Conference assembled in February 1932, in the midst of the Manchurian crisis.[6]

Skelton's views were exceptionally influential in determining Canadian policy at this time. The prime minister, R.B. Bennett, showed little interest in foreign affairs, except for questions of trade and tariffs. No other member of the Conservative cabinet had developed any continuing interest or expertise in foreign policy or League questions, as had Lapointe and Dandurand in the preceding Liberal cabinet. Skelton was, in effect, free to continue to enunciate and apply the policies which he and Mackenzie King had developed in the 1920s.

King, now the Leader of the Opposition, gave indirect endorsement to the government's approach in the House of Commons in February 1932, declining to comment on the merits of the Sino-Japanese dispute except to criticize the resort to force, and emphasizing the importance of 'international public opinion' as a means of resolving the crisis.[7] At the same time former Prime Minister Arthur Meighen, now the government leader in the Senate, was stressing that economic sanctions could not be expected to work in the Far East in any case, because of non-participation by Russia and the United States.[8]

Bennett himself studiously avoided any statements of policy on the matter. In April, responding to criticism in the House of Commons by J.S. Woodsworth, he claimed to have insufficient knowledge 'either to blame or praise this country or the other.'[9] In May, again under attack by Woodsworth, he specifically stated his opposition to any use of economic sanctions 'against either China or Japan.'[10] In November, he once more refused to discuss the merits of the situation, contending that any comment would tend improperly to prejudge a matter receiving 'quasi-judicial' consideration by the League Assembly.[11]

Opposition to these policies was limited. Marler, the Canadian minister to Japan, showed a strongly pro-Japanese bias in private, in his despatches and correspondence;[12] J.W. Dafoe in the *Winnipeg Free Press*,[13] and J.S. Woodsworth in the House of Commons, publicly favoured firm action in opposition to Japan. Woodsworth, leader of the new Cooperative Commonwealth Federation (CCF) party, was alone in parliament in advocating the application of economic sanctions. 'I think we might very well have joined with other nations in taking such sanction,' he said, 'and in that case I do not think a general war would have been precipitated. But I would point out that through our inactivity we are laying the foundation for a war in the future.'[14] In general, however, pressure on the government was minimal at home, and Canada was strictly on the sidelines at Geneva.

Sir George Perley, who headed the Canadian delegation to both the Disarmament Conference and the Special Assembly, made clear his government's position on sanctions in February 1932, in the midst of the Manchurian crisis. Canada thought peace could best be achieved '... by emphasizing the prevention of conflict, rather than the punishment of aggression; by building up machinery for conciliation, rather than providing for sanctions; by using the League of Nations as a channel through which international public opinion can express itself, rather than by developing it into a super-State.'[15] Perley's only direct statement at Geneva on the Manchurian crisis, in March, urged a real and effective armistice, and advocated non-recognition of territorial changes brought about in violation of Article 10 of the Covenant,[16] a policy already endorsed by the United States and by the League Council.

Though both Britain and Canada were Pacific powers, as well as members of the British Commonwealth and of the League of Nations, and Britain's role was a key one in whatever action might be taken regarding Manchuria, Canada adhered to its now well-established policy of not attempting to influence British action. As Skelton informed Perley in February 1932, 'while informed by the British Government on each occasion of the action it has taken, there has been no prior consultation at any stage during the recent dispute.'[17]

The major powers and the League decided, of course, to make no attempt to prevent the Japanese seizure of Manchuria, a decision which was entirely acceptable to the Canadian government. The League did, however, send an investigating commission headed by Lord Lytton to report on the affair and recommend action. The report of the Lytton Commission, which in effect confirmed what everyone knew, that Japan was the aggressor, and which called for a negotiated Japanese withdrawal, was presented to the Special Assembly in December 1932, long after the detachment of Manchuria from China had been successfully completed. As no negotiated withdrawal by Japan was in prospect, the question before the League was not really what would be done about the aggression, but only what attitude would the League take toward it.

The Canadian First Delegate at the December Special Assembly, as well as at the preceding regular Assembly in September and October, was C.H. Cahan, Secretary of State in the Bennett cabinet. Cahan's cabinet responsibilities did not involve foreign affairs, and he had not previously represented Canada at Geneva. He was a Conservative member of parliament from Montreal, where he was a lawyer for large corporate interests. He was a figure of some importance in the government party, identified with its most conservative elements. Cahan had, in the past, represented Canadian financial interests engaged in hydroelectric development in Mexico. According to Walter Riddell, the Canadian Advisory Officer at Geneva, he 'had very decided views regarding countries with weak or unstable Governments. He considered that China was one of these countries and therefore he had a great deal of personal sympathy with Japan.'[18]

Cahan's personal bias in the matter was soon evident. In October, he reportedly told a high League official that 'everyone in Canada thinks that China is a chaotic mess and that the only hope lies in backing the Japanese enterprise to the limit.'[19] Discussions with Yosuke Matsuoka, the head of the Japanese delegation to the Special Assembly, served to strengthen Cahan's sympathies with Japan.[20]

The instructions sent by Prime Minister Bennett to Cahan were, however, in keeping with Canada's previous policies, critical of Japan but opposed to action. 'Any discussion of sanctions or action against a party unwilling to accept settlement would be out of place at this stage.' The principles contained in the Lytton Commission report 'appear to constitute the framework of a permanent settlement. Their detailed application would depend on the development of the situation, but, on the whole, the recommendations appear useful and reasonable.' It would be advisable to defer any statement in the Assembly for the time being.[21]

Cahan was unwilling, however, to remain silent. On 7 December he wired that Sir John Simon, the British Foreign Secretary, had urged him to make a short address, and that he proposed to go over a draft with Simon that evening, and to make an address the following day on the lines of Bennett's instructions, unless told not to. He also indicated his 'personal opinion ... that China and Japan are both culpable and that if Assembly acts it should find accordingly.'[22] The same day Skelton and Sir George Perley (acting prime minister during Bennett's absence on a trip to England) wired back that they saw no objection to Cahan's making an address on the lines indicated.[23]

Meanwhile Cahan had prepared the text of his speech, which he declined to show to Walter Riddell, but took with him to show Simon, with whom he was dining. Riddell first saw the text of the speech the next morning, 8 December, shortly before Cahan left for the Assembly to deliver it. He must have read it with some consternation, as its pro-Japanese bias was all too evident, and it clearly was not consistent with Cahan's instructions from Ottawa. As Riddell reported afterwards to Skelton, his hurried reading of the text convinced him 'that there were a number of things that might better not be said. Mr Cahan, however, was not prepared to make any changes. He was very nice about it, but said that he was quite prepared to take all the consequences of his statements ...'[24] At the Assembly, just before delivering the speech, Cahan told another Canadian official, 'There's not a Government here that's prepared to give a man or a gun or a ship' in the service of the League in the Far East; therefore prudence was the better part of valour.[25]

The speech itself went further than that of any other delegate, including Simon, in upholding the Japanese position. Cahan recounted at length the provocations to which Japan had been subject. He found Japan's response similar to that of Britain in 1927 when it was involved in a trade dispute with China (even though Britain had seized no Chinese territory). He questioned whether China even met the requirements for League membership, because of the lack of effective control by a strong central government, an argument which had been strongly advanced by the Japanese. In any case, Article 10 of the Covenant bound League members to oppose only 'external aggression,' and the Assembly should not wholly disregard Matsuoka's statements that Japan had had no connection with the 'independence movement' in Manchuria, which had led to the separation of the province from China and the establishment of the state of Manchukuo. Any discussion of sanctions or other action against Japan would be out of place.[26]

Cahan prefaced these views, which departed so completely from his instructions, with the statement that 'the opinions I am about to express are more or less personal; but nevertheless, I think they are opinions in which my Government will concur.'[27]

The immediate effect of his speech was to remove Canada from the comfortable obscurity which it had sought, and to make it the target of much unfavourable publicity as the defender of Japanese aggression. His remarks were criticized by the Chinese spokesman in the Assembly later the same day,[28] and on the following day, 9 December, the Chinese consul general in Ottawa called on Skelton to lodge a formal protest, unless the Canadian government was prepared to repudiate Cahan's statements.[29] Riddell wrote Skelton that the speech was considered highly pro-Japanese, and that both the Chinese and the United States representatives in Geneva had been upset by it.[30]

Canada was in a particularly embarrassing position with regard to the United States. W.D. Herridge, the Canadian minister in Washington and Prime Minister Bennett's brother-in-law, had discussed the Canadian attitude fully with Secretary of State Stimson prior to the meeting of the Special Assembly, and Stimson had 'expressed much pleasure at noting the position which the Canadian Government was taking.' When news of Cahan's speech reached Washington, 'there was great astonishment in the State Department.'[31] In Geneva, Hugh Wilson, the

American minister to Switzerland, told Riddell that 'he considered it a straight double-cross.'[32]

Cahan meanwhile had sent the text of his speech to Prime Minister Bennett in London. He added that he had been urgently advised by Sir John Simon to speak, and that Simon 'read over my draft address, made several suggestions, and warmly approved of the address as delivered.'[33] The Japanese, of course, also approved. On 12 December Skelton wrote Herridge: 'I met the Japanese Minister yesterday, and was warmly thanked for the attitude the Canadian Government had taken at Geneva. I did not refuse to accept his thanks, thinking we had better keep at least one friend for the time being ...'[34]

Approval was also forthcoming from Marler, the Canadian minister in Tokyo, who wrote the Department of External Affairs indicating his 'very deep satisfaction' with Cahan's speech, which he said expressed his own personal views, and had been 'most favourably commented on in Japan.'[35] This unqualified approval, which was based on summaries of the speech, Marler subsequently modified after receiving the full text, which he thought contained some statements that would have been better omitted.[36]

Prime Minister Bennett was in London at the time Cahan's speech was made, and was joined there shortly afterwards by Cahan. From London he wired instructions to Riddell approving the proposals of the Assembly's Committee of Nineteen, which endorsed the Lytton Commission's findings and proposed further efforts at conciliation. He still wished, however, to avoid any overt criticism of Japan. 'It would seem to me regrettable,' he said, 'if terms of resolution of Assembly could be construed as prejudging or condemning past policy of Japan before every effort has been made to effect conciliation of parties to controversy.'[37]

Cahan apparently experienced no immediate difficulty with the prime minister over the content of his speech. After they had conferred in London, Bennett sailed for Canada and Cahan went to Paris, where he was negotiating a trade treaty. From Paris he wrote Riddell: 'Mr Bennett was quite pleased with my address to the Assembly on Sino-Japanese relations, and he wishes me to keep closely in touch with developments. I shall likely return to Geneva when the Assembly re-convenes in January.'[38]

As a matter of fact, however, Cahan was not to represent Canada again at Geneva, either in January or later. If Bennett had not initially been disturbed by Cahan's actions, Skelton decidedly had been. On 24 December he sent Riddell a detailed analysis of the ways in which he considered that Cahan had departed from his instructions. He also criticized Cahan's having submitted his speech 'on approval' to Simon, and emphasized that Canadian delegates in Geneva could properly present only their government's views, and not personal views.[39]

Upon Bennett's return to Ottawa, Skelton promptly pressed his views on the prime minister. 'The Department had taken the matter much more seriously than Mr Bennett,' Riddell noted after talking with Lester B. Pearson. 'This seemed to be the case until Mr Bennett arrived in Ottawa, when Mr Pearson said that Dr Skelton had had the most serious discussion he had ever had with the Prime Minister, and had convinced him of the seriousness of the situation.'[40]

By 7 January 1933, Skelton had apparently made his point successfully, as he wrote Riddell that Bennett was 'much disturbed by Mr Cahan's action.' It would, however, not be possible for the government to repudiate a cabinet member, and if the matter came up in the forthcoming session of parliament, 'an effort will doubtless be made to smooth it over.'[41]

Even though Cahan was not publicly repudiated, information was soon 'leaked' that his views were not those of the Canadian government. Riddell, for example, confirmed this to Mary Craig McGeachy, a Canadian member of the League's Information Section, on 30 January, 'after two months of looking blank' whenever questioned about it, and Miss McGeachy promptly passed the information along to J.W. Dafoe,[42] whose *Winnipeg Free Press* had vigorously criticized both Cahan and Simon.[43] Herridge apparently explained what had happened to United States officials. According to Skelton, 'it was only the good relations which exist between the Canadian Legation and the State Department which prevented considerable irritation developing' over the incident.[44]

Also on 30 January, the expected embarrassing question was put to Bennett in the House of Commons, when Ernest Lapointe asked whether Cahan 'represented the view of the government of Canada when he spoke at Geneva about the Manchurian question?'[45] Bennett's reply was evasive. He thought that Cahan's speech had been misinterpreted and unfairly criticized. He did not feel that the statement as a whole departed from the government's instructions, though isolated sections of it might give a contrary impression.[46] In effect, Bennett refused either to repudiate Cahan or to defend the specific views Cahan had presented.

Meanwhile, retaliation from China had failed to materialize. In December Skelton had considered an anti-Canadian boycott by China a possibility.[47] Sir Eric Drummond, the Secretary-General of the League, had also been concerned about a Chinese boycott, as noted by Riddell in his diary:

Last night at a dinner given by Sir Eric Drummond he told me that for a few days Mr Cahan's speech in the Assembly had given him a great deal of trouble, but that he was glad to say he thought it was now coming out all right. He said that we had very narrowly averted a British Empire boycott [by China] following the speeches of Sir John Simon, Mr Bruce [of Australia] and Mr Cahan. He went on to say that, if Great Britain lost her trade in China, it would be most disastrous as, since the Japanese boycott [by China], British trade had been very profitable.[48]

The time was fast approaching when Canada would again be called on to indicate its position on the Manchurian affair, as the Committee of Nineteen's recommendations to the Assembly, including approval of the Lytton Commission's findings, were coming up for a vote. Moreover, Riddell was approached by Drummond regarding possible Canadian membership on a new committee to be set up to encourage a negotiated settlement of the Sino-Japanese dispute. An acceptance by Canada could, for the first time, involve Canada actively in attempts to resolve the dispute. Riddell requested instructions from Ottawa, and at the same time advised Skelton, who was in London, of the request.

Skelton's reaction was predictable, as this was precisely the kind of role which he consistently wanted Canada to avoid. He cabled Bennett in Ottawa and Riddell in Geneva, saying that both he and G. Howard Ferguson, the Canadian High Commissioner in London, were doubtful whether Canada would wish membership on such a committee.[49]

In Ottawa, after seeing Skelton's telegram, the Acting Undersecretary of State for External Affairs, Norman A. Robertson, gave Bennett the opposite advice. He favoured acceptance of the invitation to serve on the negotiations committee, as 'a refusal to act might be interpreted as an evasion of responsibility.' Robertson had also consulted with the Chief of the General Staff and obtained his concurrence that Canada should accept the invitation, and had drafted a telegram of acceptance.[50]

Confronted with this conflicting advice from Skelton and Robertson, Bennett adopted Robertson's views, and on 18 February 1933, he instructed Riddell that Canada was willing to accept membership on the negotiations committee.[51] Advising Ferguson and Skelton in London of his decision, he used the language of Robertson's memorandum on the subject, explaining that 'refusal to serve on it might be interpreted as evasion of responsibility.'[52]

Thus before the Manchurian affair was over, Bennett had moved from a position of apparent lack of interest, to one of willingness to accept a more active Canadian role than had previously existed in connection with League efforts to settle a major political crisis. Moreover, although it was Skelton's displeasure with Cahan's indiscretion that had brought Bennett actively into the picture, Bennett quickly accepted a less isolationist approach than that of Skelton, and overruled Skelton on a question of some potential importance. Finally, his willingness to overrule Skelton in this instance was known not only in the Department of External Affairs in Ottawa, but also to Ferguson in London and Riddell in Geneva. This sequence of events indicated both a shift in Bennett's views and a weakening of Skelton's dominance over foreign policy decision-making, changes which were to be strikingly confirmed when the next great crisis in League of Nations affairs arrived.

In this instance, however, the prospective new role for Canada proved abortive. The proposed negotiations committee was never established, as Japan was unwilling to accept it. Instead, an Advisory Committee on the Sino-Japanese dispute was named by the Special Assembly on 24 February 1933, with Canada as a member. This committee, however, found nothing of importance to do, as Japan was firmly in possession of Manchuria, had given notice of its withdrawal from the League, and had no interest in discussing the Manchurian question further.

Japan's notice of withdrawal came after the Special Assembly, on 24 February, adopted the report of the Committee of Nineteen, including its acceptance of the findings of the Lytton Commission, with only Japan in opposition. The Canadian government, besides voting for the report, took advantage of the opportunity to have its spokesman, Riddell, make clear Canada's unqualified support of its findings.[53] Riddell reported that afterwards both the United States and the Chinese representatives in Geneva expressed their appreciation to him.[54] The damage to Canada's reputation done by Cahan's December speech had, at least in part, now been undone. On the same day in Ottawa, Bennett read the text of Riddell's statement to the House of Commons, and received immediate statements of approval from the two principal opposition spokesmen, Mackenzie King and J.S. Woodsworth.[55]

On this note of unanimous disapproval of Japan's actions, combined with an unwillingness even to consider doing anything about them, consideration of the Manchurian crisis by the League of Nations ended. In Canada, the political controversy generated by Cahan's speech had largely subsided, though not completely. The League of Nations Society's publication, *Interdependence*, in its March 1933 issue, abandoning its usual non-partisan and informational approach, published a number of criticisms of Cahan, notably by Sir Herbert Ames, the former financial director of the League of Nations, and by Frederic H. Soward of the University of British Columbia's History Department.[56]

In May, Cahan himself for the first time undertook to explain his behaviour to the House of Commons. He insisted that his remarks in Geneva the previous December had been fully justified, and he repeated the same arguments. He referred to China as '... a politically disorganized Asiatic state, some of whose leaders are evidently actuated by a belief that, under the protection of the international agreements, to which their country is a party, they may persist in hostile and provocative acts against foreigners without fear of retaliation.' He quoted at length the sections of the Lytton report which were critical of China, recounted

the historical record of Canada's opposition to a sanctionist policy, and emphasized that the chief League powers were themselves entirely unwilling to do anything effective in China's behalf.[57]

Other members of the government left Cahan to fend for himself, and took no
part in the debate, except for Sir George Perley, who said only that he thought
discussion of the Far East situation by the House was not desirable.[58] Mackenzie
King, the Leader of the Opposition, had already expressed the same view, and he
declined to comment on the merits of the matter.[59] Only William Irvine (CCF,
Alberta) attacked Cahan's views, contending that the Canadian people had believed it was the League's duty to stop the Japanese invasion of China.[60]

Cahan's self-defence produced a new flurry of press commentaries on his
speech at Geneva. These ranged, according to a survey in *Interdependence*, from
the *Montreal Star*'s conclusion that he had played the statesman's part, to the
Toronto Star's view that his speech 'was a national humiliation. Greater care
should be taken in selecting the men who represent Canada at international
gatherings.'[61]

By the time the Manchurian affair was over, the latter opinion no doubt more
nearly coincided with Prime Minister Bennett's view than the former, even though
he was never willing to say so publicly. Probably the most important result of
the controversy over Cahan's actions was that it brought Bennett into a more
direct involvement in foreign policy questions than had previously been the case,
and in so doing laid the groundwork for some important changes in Canada's
international role.

10

Reappraising Canada's collective security policy

The failure of the powers to observe their commitments under the League Covenant when Japan seized Manchuria in 1931-2 was soon followed by other events indicating a breakdown of the international system constructed in the 1920s and the probability, if this trend continued, of another general war. In January 1933, with the coming to power of Hitler in Germany, the much feared possibility of a stridently nationalist and expansionist German government had become a reality. The attitude of the new government toward the League system was clearly indicated by its withdrawal from both the League of Nations and the Disarmament Conference before the end of the year. The Disarmament Conference itself, after two years of futile discussions, adjourned in 1934 without any agreements having been reached, and the armaments race continued apace.

As the prospect of the general war which it had been established to prevent became greater, the League of Nations was clearly in a weakened position. Of the major powers, only Great Britain, France, and Italy were members, with the United States, the Soviet Union, Germany, and Japan all outside. The first challenge to the collective security system by a major power, Japan, had been an unqualified success, and the credibility of those who insisted that the system might yet work was understandably low. Yet abandonment of the League and of collective security implied an acceptance of the inevitability of a new war which hardly seemed justified by a single major failure.

The years between the occupation of Manchuria and the next crucial challenge to the League, the Italian invasion of Ethiopia in October 1935, were a period, then, of re-examination and reappraisal of the basic idea of collective security and its adequacy as a means of preventing aggression and war. Some were ready to abandon collective security and the League as a proven failure, and seek protection either in isolationism, or in national armaments and alliances. Others saw the only hope in a revitalized and effective League, which would successfully meet future challenges. Governments were thus confronted with conflicting and unreconcilable foreign policy demands, at a time when their main energies and attention were taken up by the worldwide economic depression.

In Canada, the Department of External Affairs remained convinced of the correctness of its opposition to the main features of the League collective security system. A memorandum prepared by Lester B. Pearson and endorsed by O.D. Skelton, the Undersecretary of State for External Affairs, in July 1933, described Canadian policy in these terms:

To us, the chief value of the League of Nations has been the slow but steady building up in Geneva of a medium for world publicity, of the formation of the habit of discussion and co-operation. We think that any attempt to arm the League would interfere with this development ...

Canadian policy has been ... emphatic in its opposition to the development at Geneva of a super-state which would remove from our own Parliament control over questions of peace and war. Such control is the first attribute of national sovereignty, and Canada has never viewed with any favour the transference, at the present time under present conditions, of that control to a League of Nations ...

... We are not willing to give a blank cheque to Geneva or any other international organization by which we might be involved in international commitments ...

It should not be forgotten [that] the doctrine of sanctions has been proved unworkable in the last year ...

We should continue, then, our policy of co-operation through the League, while remaining true to our constructive position, that the League must remain consultative and not executive. The teeth must be kept out of Articles X and XVI and the Geneva Protocol must remain dead; at least until the Anglo-Saxon and Latin groups show a much greater tendency to 'get together' than they do at present.

In short, developments at Geneva in the last six months, far from giving us cause to alter our policy in respect to security and sanctions, warrant us being more firm than ever in pursuing that policy.[1]

The League of Nations Society in Canada, meanwhile, far from considering the League a lost cause, was promoting support for it more actively than ever. In January-April 1934, in the fall of 1934, and again in January-March 1935, series of nationwide radio broadcasts on the League were organized by the Society. Speakers included Sir Robert Borden, Ernest Lapointe, John W. Dafoe, Newton W. Rowell, Robert J. Manion (Minister of Railways and Canals in the Bennett cabinet, and Canadian First Delegate at the 1933 Assembly), as well as a number of other individuals from the universities and public life who were outspoken in support of the League.[2] In general, the Society continued to concentrate its activities on publicizing and building general support for the League as an organization, avoiding controversy over the nature and extent of collective security commitments. The latter question was not always avoided, however. For example, in an address to the Society's annual meeting in September 1933, subsequently published in *Interdependence*, S. Mack Eastman, the ranking Canadian on the staff of the International Labour Organization, criticized Canada's attack on Article 10 of the League Covenant in 1920-23, and concluded: 'The question is whether Canada might not seize some early opportunity to say something for the rehabilitation of Article 10 ... Article 10 should be restored to a place of honour.'[3]

More typical was an address in January 1934 by Ernest Lapointe, the president of the Society, which emphasized public opinion rather than security commitments:

'... public opinion in all countries must insist that governments everywhere keep their plighted word and refrain not only from war but from preparations for war. The League of Nations Society in Canada will devote itself to this work ...

We want to equip our association for intelligent and vigorous participation in the task of creating public opinion in behalf of international co-operation.'[4]

The Society continued to co-operate closely with the League Secretariat, and in the summer of 1935 arranged a study tour to Geneva, which included visits to the new League headquarters buildings and to the ILO, as well as receptions by the Secretariat and by Walter A. Riddell, the Canadian Advisory Officer.[5]

In the House of Commons, J.S. Woodsworth, the Cooperative Commonwealth Federation leader, was more than usually active in trying to generate discussion of League and foreign policy questions, though after the Manchurian affair he was increasingly pessimistic about the League. In March 1934 he summed up his views as follows:

Well, the league has done some good pieces of work, but the league has shown itself very weak indeed because the member nations would not give the league support, and to-day the League of Nations is very much discredited. But having said all that I come back to this point: what, then, is the alternative? ... if we are to go back to the bad old way of fighting it out as individual nations, where will the world be within a very short time? If that takes place, war, and a much more serious war than the last, is inevitable, and that in the not distant future. It seems to me that if we were serious about the League of Nations we would spend a great deal more of our energies in trying to work out, through the league, some of these world policies which might bring us peace.[6]

Again in April 1935 Woodsworth reviewed the international situation, saying that, in his judgment, war would not end, 'until we destroy capitalism, with its social injustice, and imperialism,' and insisting that 'we have to see to it that Canadian boys are not sacrificed on the battlefields of Europe or, I may add, of Asia.' Nevertheless he rejected a policy of attempted isolation, which he did not think would keep Canada out of war, as well as 'the discredited policy of military alliances,' and concluded:

I come then to the third alternative, and I can see no other – that of collective security. It would seem to be the world's only hope. Canada ... is already a member of the league even though we have not taken our obligations very seriously; but if we are to have peace we must be prepared to pay the price and that may be a great deal higher than some of us have yet imagined. It may involve economic sanctions that will mean a very decided sacrifice to us in Canada, but when we consider the sacrifices involved in war, we ought not to hesitate to make great sacrifices in attempting to secure peace.[7]

Woodsworth was not content, however, to give a general theoretical support to collective measures to prevent war, but sought also to find specific things that Canada might do here and now in the cause of peace. In keeping with this interest, he moved in the House of Commons on 21 March 1934, that 'the Dominion government be requested to forbid the export of nickel to be used for war purposes,' and that the League Council be requested to set up the necessary procedures for controlling the private manufacture of armaments and the trade in raw materials used in armaments manufacture. Woodsworth considered nickel an appropriate subject for Canadian action, he explained, because Canada furnished ninety per cent of the world's supply, and because nickel was an important material in armaments manufacture, used in making armour plate to increase the strength and impact resistance of steel. The League of Nations had already set up co-operative international machinery for controlling the production and distribution of narcotics, and similar techniques could be used to control the trade in nickel and other raw materials important in the armaments business.

'It may be said,' Woodsworth told the House of Commons,

that as Canada is such a small nation numerically, she by herself can do very little in world affairs, but the possession of nickel gives us a strategic importance.
Through her virtual monopoly of nickel Canada may speak with a voice that may
be heard around the world. Canada might make a gesture offering to cooperate
with the league in the control of nickel, which might at this critical juncture produce the most far-reaching effects.[8]

Woodsworth was followed by a succession of speakers who opposed his resolution, contending that most nickel was used for peaceful purposes, that its use
in warfare was becoming obsolete, and that his proposal did not in any case deal
with the causes of war. Ernest Lapointe, then one of the principal parliamentary
spokesmen for the Liberal opposition, and also President of the League of Nations Society, said he agreed both with Woodsworth's purposes and with the objections of his critics; the question was, in any case, already under study by
Canada and by the League, as part of a general consideration of international
control of the arms trade. Lapointe's ambiguous position paralleled that of the
League of Nations Society itself, which had discussed the export of nickel at its
annual meeting the preceding year. Following differences of opinion, the national
executive of the Society had adopted a resolution asking the government to investigate the matter.[9] The position of the government was stated by the Minister
of Mines, who opposed any export ban, and thought it would not be of significance in preventing war.[10] Woodsworth then withdrew his motion, no other
member, from his own party or any other, having spoken in support of it.

What Woodsworth had proposed, which involved a voluntary cutting back of
exports and of the related employment, was, of course, more than ordinarily difficult to win support for in a time of severe economic depression. The reception
his proposal received in the House of Commons illustrated clearly, in any case,
how much easier it was to obtain generalized endorsement for peace and disarmament than it was to obtain backing for specific measures requiring some sacrifice.

In the Senate at the same session of parliament a review of Canadian policy
toward the League of Nations was precipitated by a motion by A.D. McRae
(Conservative, British Columbia), 'That this House is of the opinion that Canada
should withdraw from membership in the League of Nations and that no further
money should be voted to the League.'[11] McRae had advocated withdrawal from
the League in a Senate speech in February, because of 'the certainty of war
before us,' and because he could not 'conceive of any developments which would
justify this country in sacrificing the blood of one single Canadian on the future
battle-fields of Europe.'[12] On 21 March 1934, he gave notice of his formal

motion for withdrawal. McRae's sponsorship of the motion was of some importance. He had been a Brigadier General in the Canadian army during the world war, and had been the chief organizer of, and a leading financial contributor to, the Conservative party's successful election campaign in 1930. He had been rewarded by an appointment to the Senate by Prime Minister Bennett in 1931. A few days after McRae presented his motion for withdrawal from the League, Ernest Lapointe raised the question in the House of Commons, suggesting that, in view of 'the publicity that has been given this notice, not only here but also in Europe,' Bennett should disavow it. Bennett promptly did so in unequivocal terms.[13]

McRae's motion was nevertheless scheduled for debate. The ensuing discussion, which began on 17 April 1934, and continued until 31 May, constituted by far the most thorough parliamentary consideration of Canadian policy toward the League of Nations and collective security of the entire period of the League's existence. Eighteen Senators, ten Conservatives and eight Liberals, took part, and the full range of major policy alternatives were forcefully presented.

McRae first reiterated his essentially isolationist position. In addition to withdrawal from the League, he favoured a national referendum prior to entry into any war, except for home defence. 'It is bad enough to send our boys to kill in defence of their country. It is unthinkable that Canadian sons should be sent to Europe to war with ... [the] sons of a decaying civilization.'[14]

Raoul Dandurand, the Liberal party leader in the Senate, immediately replied with an eloquent defence of the League:

'But,' says the skeptic, 'the ideal is unattainable. The proof lies in the failure to maintain peace in Asia and to bring about a reduction of armaments.' It is indeed surprising to see the rapid discouragement of people when confronted with so formidable a problem. It is not to be expected that the habits of the world can be changed in a day. I absolutely refuse to write the word 'failure' because of difficulties and reverses encountered ...

Humanity progresses slowly, imperceptibly, from generation to generation. The League of Nations is still in the experimental and formative stage, and my experience leads me to say that it is full of promise ... The process may be slow indeed, but the world is growing smaller, and more and more it will hear and heed the voice of Geneva ...

The economic sanctions would, I am quite sure, be the sole contribution that Canada would be called upon to make in the case of European war. Our country, to my mind, would not hesitate to sever all trade and financial relations with an aggressor if it were requested so to do by the Council of the League. We surely could not do less in duty to ourselves and to humanity ...

The world is so much in need of peace that pessimism offends its natural aspirations. The League of Nations exists. All our best efforts must be to guard it and to strengthen it. To abolish it would be to abandon humanity to fatalism and despair.[15]

Senator Edward Michener (Conservative, Alberta), president of the Calgary branch of the League of Nations Society, went even further, advocating that military power be given to the League, and that national sovereignty be surrendered to that extent. 'I have not the slightest doubt,' he said, 'that we must be willing to be governed by the majority opinion of the nations as expressed through the League.'[16] In contrast with Michener's internationalist views, Senator W.A. Griesbach (Conservative, Alberta), like McRae a Brigadier General during the world war, favoured reliance on armaments and the British Empire, and considered membership in the League of no importance one way or the other, with regard to war and peace.[17]

For the government, former Prime Minister Arthur Meighen, Minister without Portfolio in the Bennett cabinet and government leader in the Senate, without minimizing the League's failures, made a strong statement in support of the League and of collective security:

I do not quite like the spirit which seems to me too prevalent in our own country, and which I may describe in this way: We are glad to be members of the League, because under article 10 as re-interpreted, with the dissidence of Persia, we do not at any time actually need to fight. We are happy to be within the pale of the Covenant, because all we can be asked to do is to refuse to trade; and we hold up both hands for the League of Nations because of this re-interpretation which will always keep Canada out of war, no matter what to others may result ... Until this country is ready to take the whole consequence of membership in the League, and take its whole part in the enforcement of its covenants, we have no right to rejoice in membership at all ... We say it is no part of our duty to enforce peace; that the worst we could be called upon to do would be to refuse to trade with recalcitrant nations.

In the degree in which that attitude of mind prevails among its members the League will fail to achieve its purpose. Only in the definite knowledge that every country is ready to live up to its whole responsibility for the enforcement of compliance with covenants can the League ever attain its end. I agree entirely ... that when we sought to reduce, abbreviate and attenuate the meaning and force of the covenants we applied the poison from which the League is suffering at this time ...

Let us by our example illustrate what the League can become, not only by contributing to its upkeep, but also, if it becomes necessary to do so in order that the collective will of all the nations within its fold may prevail, by standing ready even to draw the sword on behalf of the collective will.[18]

This strong endorsement of the League system by Meighen was all the more remarkable in that the government which he headed in 1920-21 had conducted the campaign against Article 10 which he now denounced.

At the conclusion of the Senate debate, two Conservative Senators attempted to substitute for McRae's motion a positive expression of support for the League.[19] Their amendment was ruled out of order,[20] and McRae's original motion was then defeated by the Senate, without a recorded vote.[21]

Of the eighteen Senators who took part in the debate, twelve (six Conservatives and six Liberals), including both party leaders in the Senate, had made strongly pro-League statements. Five Senators (three Conservatives and two Liberals) had been primarily critical of the League, but had not specifically supported withdrawal. Only Senator McRae himself had spoken in support of his withdrawal motion. Even though a wide range of views had been presented, the predominant tone of the debate had been one of support for the League, rather than rejection of it, by Senators from both parties.

Later in 1934 a Canadian initiative in applying economic sanctions received an endorsement from a particularly unexpected source, the leader of the Liberal party, former Prime Minister W.L. Mackenzie King. In a speech to the National Liberal Federation on 12 December, King asserted:

... it is not sufficient that we, as Liberals, should express by words and resolutions our support of the League of Nations. We must become militant in our advocacy of those policies which may serve to strengthen the League in its work. I believe that this objective should increasingly become the key-note of all our policies ...

Were a collective and solemn undertaking entered into by the members of the British Commonwealth of Nations, the United States, France, Italy, and Japan, to the effect that they would provide neither arms, nor foodstuffs, nor credits to any nation guilty of disturbing the peace, on actual facts to be determined, we should soon witness the end of war propaganda, and the certain dawn of world peace ...

A policy of the kind, to be wholly effective would require united action. Is there any reason, however, why the nations which believe in the necessity and efficacy of such a step should not begin by adopting it as a part of their own national policy? In this, as in all else, it is necessary that some country should take a lead.

May I ask my fellow Liberals if there is any reason why, in a matter of so great importance to the world, Canada should wait for any other nation to take the lead? This country should definitely declare not only that it will give no succor to any nation which wantonly disturbs the world's peace, but that it will provide neither arms nor foodstuffs nor credits to such a nation.[22]

King's speech was well publicized in the press, the *Toronto Star* featuring it under the headline, 'Boycott Aggressors in All Future Wars, Liberal Chief Urges.'[23] The full text was included in the next issue of *Interdependence*, the League of Nations Society publication. At the next session of parliament, on 1 April 1935, King repeated the same proposals in the House of Commons, urging again that Canada take the lead by announcing a policy of denying munitions, food, and credit to 'any nation which could be shown to have threatened the peace of the world by violating a pact of collective security.'[24] There was no response from any spokesman for the government.

Throughout this period of review and reconsideration of Canadian policy toward the League, the Prime Minister, R.B. Bennett, continued to refrain from any over-all presentation of his government's views to either parliament or the public. However, beginning in 1933, he was himself increasingly involved in League activities. Prior to that time, he had been actively concerned with Canadian and British Empire tariff policy, but had left other aspects of foreign policy largely to O.D. Skelton, the Undersecretary of State for External Affairs. As already discussed, in February 1933, overruling Skelton's recommendation, Bennett had approved Canadian membership on a League advisory committee on the Sino-Japanese dispute, but the committee was inactive because of Japan's unwillingness to co-operate with it. In June-July 1933, Bennett attended the League-sponsored World Economic Conference in London, and in August he presided at an international conference there of wheat exporting and importing countries, also held under the auspices of the League. At these meetings he became acquainted with Joseph Avenol, the new Secretary-General of the League of Nations, and other officials of the Secretariat, and was reported to have been favourably impressed with them and with the League's economic and financial work.[25] Avenol told Walter Riddell, the Canadian Advisory Officer in Geneva, that he had found Bennett 'a man of courage and force, although not very favourable to the League.'[26]

In May 1934 Bennett made a short address at the annual meeting of the League of Nations Society in Canada,[27] and in September of that year he headed the Canadian delegation to the League Assembly in Geneva. He was chairman of one of the Assembly committees, but was ill with influenza much of the time,[28] and took no significant part in the discussions. In January 1935, his government's statement to the opening session of parliament credited a 'renewed determination to make use of the agencies of conciliation and co-operation provided by the League of Nations' with having brought about a lessening of political tension and unrest in Europe, and pledged support to this trend.[29] When Bennett, at the beginning of 1935, launched a major program of domestic and social reform, the so-called 'Bennett New Deal,' the basis for asserting federal government jurisdiction over such matters as minimum wages and unemployment insurance was found through ratifying a number of treaties drawn up in the International Labour Organization, a League of Nations affiliate, and enacting domestic legislation to implement the treaties.

Although it became increasingly involved with the League in positive ways, the Bennett government did not undertake any significant initiatives at Geneva. The prime emphasis in Canadian statements there was placed on support for disarmament, and Bennett in February 1934, in reply to criticism from J.S. Woodsworth of lack of foreign policy discussion in the House of Commons, summarized Canada's policy as favouring the peaceful settlement of disputes, and especially disarmament.[30] Even on that subject, the Canadian government remained wary of appearing simply to be following the British lead. When, shortly before Bennett's statement emphasizing disarmament, the British government had sought Canadian public support of its most recent disarmament proposals, the Department of External Affairs had advised the Canadian High Commissioner in London that it was unwilling to comply:

It must be recalled that the Government of the United Kingdom reached decision on its present policy and communicated it to foreign powers without any prior consultation whatever with our Government, though we have been fully and courteously informed of decisions taken and notes despatched. We do not take objection to this course ... But in light of this fact we do not think it fitting role for Canada to be brought on Westminster stage after main performance ended to act as part of chorus chanting testimonials and unquestioning agreement.[31]

In other circumstances, the Canadian government was prepared to give full support to the initiatives taken by others. Thus while Bennett was in Geneva for the 1934 Assembly, he took part in a major development in League affairs by signing, along with the representatives of twenty-nine other League members, an invitation to the Soviet Union to join the League.[32] Canada subsequently voted in support of admitting the Soviet Union, both in committee and in the full Assembly, though O.D. Skelton made it clear in committee that this was done with some reluctance: 'Canada is one of those countries which find substantial difficulties in the entrance of Soviet Russia into the League, but believe that, under the present world circumstances, its entrance is desirable.'[33]

In March 1935, a new international crisis arrived with the announcement by Germany of the re-establishment of military conscription and of rearmament far in excess of the limitations imposed by the Versailles Treaty. The British, French, and Italian prime ministers met at Stresa and decided, in effect, to do nothing about it except protest. In the League Council they sponsored a resolution which the Council adopted on 17 April 1935, denouncing Germany's action and establishing a committee 'to propose ... measures to render the Covenant more effective in the organization of collective security and to define in particular the economic and financial measures which might be applied, should in the future a State, whether a Member of the League of Nations or not, endanger peace by the unilateral repudiation of its international obligations.'[34] The committee, in other words, was to make specific proposals regarding economic sanctions for future repudiations of treaty obligations, not including the German action just taken, but applicable to future actions of that sort. A Committee of Thirteen was named by the Council the same day, and one of the members named was Canada.*[35]

Walter Riddell, the Canadian Advisory Officer, had been approached by the League Secretariat regarding Canada's being a member, and had requested instructions from Ottawa. Before he had received a reply, however, the committee was officially appointed by the Council, and the list of members made public. Riddell never found out specifically who had suggested Canada as a member.[36] A list of proposed committee members had been prepared by the Secretariat in consultation with Britain, France, and Italy. One official of the Secretariat told Riddell that he thought Canada had been named because of its record of opposition to Articles 10 and 16 of the Covenant, 'and that it was considered better to have Canada's point of view taken into consideration in findings of Committee than to run the risk of our opposition later.'[37]

In any case, it was at first uncertain whether Canada would in fact agree to be on the committee. A memorandum prepared in the Department of External Affairs on 18 April, after receiving Riddell's original request for instructions, concluded: 'The Resolution, in short, is a clumsy and panicky attempt to invoke the authority and resources of the League in solving difficulties of a few of its members. For these various reasons acceptance of the invitation would appear unwise.'[38]

---

*   The members of the Committee of Thirteen were Portugal (Chairman), the United Kingdom, Canada, Chile, Spain, France, Hungary, Italy, the Netherlands, Poland, Turkey, the Soviet Union, and Yugoslavia

The announcement by the League of Canada's membership on the committee, before it had been either accepted or rejected by Canada, was a source of considerable embarrassment in Ottawa, and consideration of the matter apparently produced another conflict in views between O.D. Skelton and Prime Minister Bennett. Riddell recorded being told by Lester Pearson that 'the Department had been very much alarmed and, I later gathered, annoyed that sufficient time had not been given for them to look into the question thoroughly. I gathered that they thought something had been put over on the Department ... He said Dr Skelton felt very strongly against sanctions ...'[39] Bennett told Riddell, whom he saw in London early in May, that Riddell's telegram 'had been brought down to him when he was ill and he had stated at once that it was impossible for us to refuse the invitation.'[40] The decision was made by Bennett just before sailing for England to attend the King's Silver Jubilee celebrations, and it was to accept membership on the Committee of Thirteen.[41] Riddell thought that if it had not been for Bennett's intervention, membership would probably have been refused.[42]

As a member of the Committee of Thirteen, Canada was faced with some difficult policy questions. There was, of course, a long history of Canadian opposition to the economic sanctions provisions of the League Covenant, though it was by no means clear how firmly the Bennett government still adhered to that policy, if at all. However, the subject for the Committee of Thirteen's consideration was not the existing economic sanctions provisions, contained in Article 16, which applied only to cases of resort to war in violation of the Covenant, but the proposed extension of such sanctions to cover treaty repudiation in general, whether or not involving resort to war. (German rearmament, for example, violated the Versailles Treaty, but did not violate the League Covenant, and did not involve resort to war.)

Riddell reported to Ottawa the views of the League Secretariat on this question:

Some of the high officials of the Secretariat are greatly concerned about the outcome of work of Committee of Thirteen. These officials do not consider that French objective to make sanctions applicable in cases of unilateral treaty repudiation can be achieved under the Covenant and are strongly opposed to having it amended for this purpose. They hope that Canada will not agree to any such amendment.[43]

The Canadian government, among others, fully shared these reservations, and its acceptance of membership on the Committee of Thirteen had specified that it did not necessarily accept any such extension of the applicability of economic sanctions, but thought the committee should consider specific proposals for such extension on their merits.[44]

A second major difficulty was that the Council resolution establishing the committee had limited its considerations to the repudiation of treaties related to 'the security of peoples and the maintenance of peace in Europe.'[45] There was no apparent logical reason why different principles and penalties should apply to treaty repudiation in Europe and treaty repudiation elsewhere. It was widely suspected that this limitation had been inserted to prevent discussion by the committee of Italy's dispute with Ethiopia, which had been in progress since a border incident in December 1934, and which already seemed likely to result in an Italian invasion. An official of the Political Section of the League Secretariat confirmed to Riddell that the limitation to Europe had not been in the original draft of the Council resolution as prepared by France, 'but had been put in at Stresa at the request of Italy in order to give the Italians a free hand in Ethiopia.'[46] Riddell discussed his dissatisfaction with the European restriction with Anthony Eden, who 'thought it was an excellent point and said he hoped I would tell some of my Italian friends about it. He said: "They may listen to you; they have ceased to listen to me." '[47]

Detailed instructions from the Department of External Affairs regarding these various questions were wired to Riddell, Canada's representative on the Committee of Thirteen, on 26 May 1935. The Canadian government was opposed to any extension of the applicability of economic sanctions to situations not involving resort to war. It favoured emphasis instead on conciliation and discussion. Objection was also made to any new arrangements applicable to Europe only.[48]

The Committee of Thirteen meanwhile had convened for its first meeting on 24 May 1935. Its activity continued until late July, but it never produced any recommendations on the question referred to it. Besides being faced with basic disagreement among its members over any attempted extension of the applicability of economic sanctions, the Committee was working at a time of steadily increasing probability of an Italian invasion of Ethiopia, with Italy as one of the committee members. The application of economic sanctions to Italy under Article 16 of the Covenant was likely to be a very real and crucial question in the near future, and this possibility more and more dominated the thinking of the committee as it dealt with specific aspects of the organization of sanctions.

Riddell's initial statement to the committee presented the position contained in his instructions.[49] After the opening discussions, the committee decided, on the proposal of the British representative, to set up a legal subcommittee and an economic and financial subcommittee. Riddell proposed that the legal subcommittee be asked to report on 'whether, within the framework of the Covenant, it was legally possible to adopt economic and financial measures in the circumstances contemplated,' that is, in the absence of a resort to war, rather than reporting only on questions of 'machinery, method and procedure.' He was supported in this proposal by the Polish representative, but opposed by the spokesmen for France, the Soviet Union, and the Netherlands, who said that, in any case, if the legal experts concluded that there was no means of implementing the proposed extension of sanctions, they would say so. Riddell did not press the point, on the understanding that that possibility remained open.[50] After this exchange, the membership of the two subcommittees was determined. Riddell wrote O.D. Skelton in Ottawa that:

... in view of the interest the Government had taken in the constitutional questions involved, I felt that they would desire to be represented on the jurists Sub-Committee and might find it possible to send a legal expert from Canada to argue our case. I therefore suggested to the Chairman that we be given representation on the Jurists Sub-Committee. That this was not done was due, I think, to the opposition of these three Great Powers, who probably were a little afraid that our presence might make it difficult to obtain a unanimous report. They may also have considered that our point of view would be represented by Poland.[51]

Canada therefore found itself a member of the economic and financial subcommittee, the task of which was to report on specific limited economic measures which might be effective in inducing a state which was violating its treaty obligations to change its course of action.[52] The subcommittee, established on 29 May, did not meet till 1 July, allowing member states time to study the matter. In Canada, a thorough technical review of the question was undertaken by the Department of External Affairs, including the preparation, with the assistance of the National Research Council, of an annotated listing of key products. This work was not completed in time to be used by Riddell or the subcommittee, but it was available to Skelton when instructions were next sent to Riddell.[53]

Riddell wrote later that by the second week in July a marked change had taken place in the Canadian government's attitude toward the committee's work, because of the deteriorating Italo-Ethiopian situation: 'It will be seen therefore that in the beginning the interventions of the Canadian representative in the work of the Committee, while not altogether obstructive, were highly critical. From this time on my participation in the work of the Committee became much more constructive.'[54]

This change in approach was strikingly reflected in instructions to Riddell approved by Skelton and sent on 8 July 1935:

In sub-committee you should state, therefore, that in any contingency where it is agreed that economic sanctions should be applied withholding key products and raw materials is one important method of applying them. List of such key products and raw materials to be effective should be comprehensive ... [It] would be desirable that any recommendation for withholding key products and raw materials be balanced by equally strong recommendations respecting embargoes on exports from and credit facilities to repudiating country ... The application of such recommendation should also take into account acceptance by all countries from which substantial quantities of key products and raw materials could be obtained. In this way the sanction would be made most effective and the burden of control would be spread as widely as possible over participating countries ...

The question of whether or not sanctions are properly applicable under the Covenant in case of repudiation of international obligations is a separate question which you should not discuss in sub-committee.[55]

The following day Riddell stated this position in the economic and financial subcommittee.[56] He reported to Skelton the subcommittee's reactions, as follows: 'Our emphasis that lists of key products and raw materials to be effective should be comprehensive at first met with some objection, but finally gained support from all except the Italian and United Kingdom representatives. Mr Hawtrey, the United Kingdom representative, favored a very limited list and, while in the end he did not maintain his objections, I gathered he accepted our proposals with some reluctance.'[57]

The subcommittee's report on 13 July to the full Committee of Thirteen discussed in some detail the types of partial economic and financial measures which might be the most effective in deterring 'a country which is assumed to have repudiated its obligations with a view to breaking the peace at an early date, and has engaged in intensive warlike preparations,' an accurate description of Italy's posture at that moment. The question of how comprehensive the withholding of key products should be was avoided, by recommending that lists of specific products be prepared for the committee by technical experts. Canada's other main proposal, that the initial sanctions should include a ban on exports, was dealt with by summarizing the advantages and disadvantages, and leaving the policy question to the full committee.[58]

The Committee of Thirteen met again beginning 24 July 1935 to consider the two subcommittees' reports. (The legal subcommittee had reported its conclusion that the League Council could recommend economic and financial sanctions in situations not involving a resort to war, but had reached no agreement as to whether, under the unanimity rule, the vote of the offending state must be counted in the vote on such recommendations.[59]) On 23 July, further instructions had been wired to Riddell from the Department of External Affairs. On the legal questions, Canada's objections to any extension of the applicability of economic sanctions, as well as to any new type of sanctions applicable to Europe only, were reiterated. However, with the Italo-Ethiopian dispute clearly in mind, the Department instructed Riddell:

In view of gravity of general situation now confronting the League, we do not desire you to emphasize question of whether economic and financial sanctions should be applied in cases of treaty repudiation endangering peace. We fear that such a stand at present might be seized upon by certain members of Committee and made pretext for abandoning discussions which they now find inconvenient and wish to stop on other grounds ...

In the discussion you might emphasize that careful study which has been made by the Sub-Committee into question of applying economic and financial sanctions will constitute a useful contribution to discussion of sanctions to be applied under Article 16 if the occasion arises.[60]

Riddell presented Canada's views, in accordance with these instructions, at the opening committee session.[61] The Italian representative promptly objected to any consideration of sanctions which would be applicable outside of Europe.[62] The following day Riddell presented to the Committee of Thirteen the Canadian arguments for a comprehensive ban both on key products and on exports, which he had previously proposed in the economic and financial subcommittee.[63] Again, the Italian representative objected, especially to the idea of a ban on exports.[64]

At this point the work of the Committee of Thirteen effectively came to an end, a complete impasse having been reached, and no report having been made to the Council. Officially, the Committee decided only to adjourn while technical experts prepared a list of key products, but the technical experts had not yet been named when the Italian invasion of Ethiopia began in October, and the project was never resumed.[65] Riddell reported to Skelton on the final sessions of the committee: 'You will see, therefore, that the work of the Committee has been more or less shelved for a considerable time. My opinion is that both the French and United Kingdom representatives were very glad of a pretext for abandoning a discussion which they found inconvenient and wished to stop on other grounds, as you anticipated might happen ...'[66]

The termination of the Committee of Thirteen's work without a report by no means meant, however, that nothing useful had been done. As the prospective Italian attack on Ethiopia became more and more imminent, the real work of the committee centred increasingly on the advance planning of sanctions which might well be applied to Italy in the near future, as Ottawa's instructions to Riddell on 23 July had recognized. When the attack came, the speed with which the League initially acted had been made possible in part by the Committee's work.

Most remarkable of all, from the Canadian standpoint, was the role of Canada in the July 1935 meetings as an outspoken advocate of comprehensive and effective economic sanctions, in contrast with a hostile Italy and a reluctant Britain and France. The position taken was quite contrary to that with which Canada had for years been identified and which, ironically, had probably led to Canada's selection as a member of the Committee. While Walter Riddell was the Canadian spokesman in presenting these new views, his statements were based on explicit instructions from the Department of External Affairs. Examined more closely, the extent to which Canada was really departing from its long-standing anti-sanctionist position was not entirely clear. Any expansion of the situations in which sanctions would be applicable had been firmly opposed by Canada. What had been clearly advocated, however, was that, if economic sanctions were as a matter of fact imposed, they should be rigorous and effective. And that in itself constituted a striking change of emphasis in Canadian official attitudes toward collective security.

Throughout the period between the Manchurian crisis and the Italo-Ethiopian War both the public and governmental attitudes regarding the League of Nations and collective security had been undergoing a significant reappraisal, in Canada as elsewhere. The prestige of the League and the credibility of collective security had been severely damaged by the failure to act against Japan in the Manchurian affair. By the summer of 1935, however, the prevailing result in Canadian governmental circles of two years of reconsideration of Canada's role and policy was clearly a strengthening of support for the League and for the collective system. This was apparent in the Senate debates on withdrawal from the League, in the development of Prime Minister Bennett's activities and views on League matters, and in the explicit backing of economic sanctions by the leaders of both opposition parties, J.S. Woodsworth and W.L. Mackenzie King, as well as in the policies advocated by Canada in the Committee of Thirteen. At the same time, views favouring isolationism, or reliance on arms and the British Empire, were still strongly held and forcefully advocated. Particularly uncertain was the extent to which theoretical views in support of the League and collective security would be maintained as real support in a real crisis. The complete lack of backing accorded Woodsworth when he urged that something real be done in support of disarmament, through a ban on nickel exports for purposes of arms manufacture, was not an encouraging indication. In any case, the real crisis and test arrived in October 1935, with the launching of Italy's long-expected Ethiopian invasion.

11
The Italo-Ethiopian war

When the Sixteenth Assembly of the League of Nations convened in Geneva on 9 September 1935, the Italian attack on Ethiopia had not yet begun, but it was clearly impending. Relations between the two states had been in a state of crisis since a border incident in December 1934, and Italy had massed troops in its two colonies adjoining Ethiopia, in obvious preparation for an invasion. The matter had been discussed by the League Council intermittently since January 1935, and Britain and France, both within and outside of the Council, had attempted unsuccessfully to find some means of deflecting the Italian dictator, Benito Mussolini, from his apparent purpose.

As the invasion had not yet begun, however, there was still the possibility of preventing it. The meeting of the League Assembly became the occasion for a final determined effort in that direction. Sir Samuel Hoare, the British foreign secretary, opened the general debate on 11 September with a firm statement of support for the League and for collective resistance to acts of aggression. Pierre Laval, the French premier and foreign minister, followed on 13 September with a pledge that, if no peaceful solution could be found, France would fulfill the obligations of the League Covenant.

These statements in effect threatened Italy with the application of economic and, if necessary, military sanctions, in accordance with the legal obligations which all League members had undertaken, if it persisted in its plans to invade Ethiopia. They were no doubt intended primarily to dissuade Mussolini, if at all possible, from going ahead with the invasion, but they also pledged the two most important League powers to apply the collective security provisions of the Covenant if he could not be so dissuaded.

As Canada was not then a member of the League Council, it was not involved in any direct discussions of the Ethiopian crisis at the League until the Assembly met in September 1935. The crisis came to a head at an awkward time, so far as Canada was concerned. The government had dissolved parliament on 15 August, and had called a general election for 14 October. It was generally expected that the Conservative government of R.B. Bennett would be defeated by the Liberals, led by former Prime Minister W.L. Mackenzie King. Bennett had defeated King in the 1930 election, in the first year of the great depression, promising effective governmental action to remedy the economic situation. Now, five years later, the depression still continued and was again the main election issue. Although a Liberal victory was expected, Bennett was conducting a vigorous campaign, and had charted a new course for the Conservative party by enacting into legislation early in 1935 a program of social and economic reforms based on the Roosevelt 'New Deal' in the United States. To further add to the uncertainty, three new parties, each offering a reformist program, were competing in the election with the Conservatives and the Liberals. When the League Assembly met, however, Bennett was still in office, and would be at least until 14 October.

As already noted, Bennett's government had, earlier in 1935, moved strongly in the direction of support of the League system, by accepting membership on the Committee of Thirteen set up to work out specific plans for economic sanctions, and by advocating in that committee that, if sanctions were imposed, they should be comprehensive and effective. On 23 August, O.D. Skelton, the Undersecretary of State for External Affairs, wrote W.D. Herridge, the Canadian minister in Washington that 'The Prime Minister is definitely opposed to undertaking military sanctions, but leans to the imposition of economic sanctions under Article 16 of the Covenant if definite aggressive action is taken by Italy. My personal prejudices are against taking any action, but I am not wholly satisfied that we can avoid the clear implications of our League undertakings. I enclose a copy of a short memo I am going to show the Prime Minister on Monday.'[1]

Skelton's message, besides making clear his continuing disagreement with Bennett over sanctions policy, may also have been intended to generate some pressure on Bennett to modify his views. Herridge was also the prime minister's brother-in-law and his most influential political adviser, and he felt that any suggestion of Canadian involvement in the Italo-Ethiopian dispute would be anything but helpful in Bennett's re-election campaign.[2]

Although the Canadian general election coincided with the crisis over Ethiopia, both the government and the opposition carefully avoided in the election campaign any commitments regarding Canadian policy toward economic sanctions, and in general avoided making policy toward the crisis a campaign issue. King, in his opening campaign statement, denied that Bennett had the right to commit Canada to any policy, and repeated his familiar 'Parliament will decide' formula:

So far as the Ethiopian situation is concerned, and so far as Canada is concerned with it, no government has any right to say what this country will do with respect to war arising out of that situation until there is a new parliament and a new government in office.

So far as the Liberal party is concerned, I say now that if the grave responsibility ever fell on the head of a Liberal government of deciding on war in Europe no decision would be made until parliament was assembled, and the will of parliament would decide.[3]

In campaign speeches on 9 September, King indicated opposition to 'war connected with economic interests in the Near East,' and Ernest Lapointe asserted that 'no interest in Ethiopia, of any nature whatever, is worth the life of a single Canadian citizen. No consideration could justify Canada's participation in such a war, and I am unalterably opposed to it.'[4] In fact, of course, Canadian participation in a war over Ethiopia was the remotest of possibilities. On the immediate question of economic sanctions against Italy, King and Lapointe were silent.

So also was Prime Minister Bennett, so far as his election campaign was concerned. He too put the emphasis on assurances that involvement in a foreign war need not be feared. In his opening campaign speech on 6 September, he promised that Canadians would not be '... embroiled in any foreign quarrel where the rights of Canadian are not involved.

'And I conceive it to be the solemn duty of government, by all just and honorable means, to see that Canada is kept out of trouble. We have bought and paid for security and for peace, and we mean to have them.'[5]

Meanwhile, Bennett's government was faced with the necessity of determining the policy it would follow at the League Assembly. A summary of Canada's views provided to the British government a few days before the Assembly met reflected Skelton's long-held doubts about sanctions:

Public opinion in Canada recognizes the importance of preserving the League from the loss of authority consequent on failure to carry out the undertakings of the Covenant, whether wisely made or not, and the undoubtedly aggressive character of declared Italian policy. From the beginning of the League the prevalent Canadian opinion as regards sanctions has been one of doubt as to the feasibility of their application in the absence of important States from the universal membership contemplated when the Covenant was drafted, and of doubt also as to whether in practice European States which have most strongly urged the automatic application and the extension of sanctions would apply them in any case where their own immediate interests were not in jeopardy.

The Canadian statement went on to encourage Britain in its intention not to go further than France was willing to go in committing itself to sanctions, and noted that Canada was under somewhat similar restraints in its need to consider United States policy.[6]

At the Assembly session which opened on 9 September, the Canadian delegation was headed by G. Howard Ferguson, the High Commissioner in London. Ferguson was a Conservative party politician and a former premier of Ontario, who had been appointed to the London post by Bennett in 1930. He had never before represented Canada at a League Assembly, though he had attended Disarmament Conference meetings briefly in 1933. He had as his principal advisers at the Assembly Walter Riddell, the permanent Canadian Advisory Officer in Geneva, and Lester Pearson, who had recently been reassigned from the Department of External Affairs in Ottawa to the High Commissioner's Office in London.

The first important question confronting the delegation was what statement, if any, Canada should make following the strong stand on behalf of the League Covenant and collective security taken by Hoare and Laval. On 13 September, the day of Laval's speech, Riddell wired for instructions:

Laval's statement satisfactory to British and well received by Assembly. Hoare says 'Laval said 75% what I hoped for.' Laval's last sentence 'Our obligations are written in the Covenant and we will not dishonour them' made distinct impression. Feeling is definitely consolidating in favour of British position. South Africa, in impressive statement, supported British view ... Do you think that in view of above we should make statement reaffirming our adherence to the principles of the Covenant and collective system? We believe that if statement is made anything less than this would be misunderstood and inappropriate in view of developments here. If you desire statement made, please telegraph text today. Debate closes tomorrow, Saturday.[7]

Skelton, predictably, thought nothing should be said. Bennett's concurrence was obtained, and a telegram was sent to Riddell saying that Bennett did 'not consider Canadian statement desirable at this juncture.'[8] But, in fact, the matter was not yet settled. In the evening Bennett, after reading Hoare's speech again and then Laval's speech, changed his mind, and personally drafted new instructions to the Geneva delegation. These instructions not only provided that a statement should be made, but specified one which concluded with the pledge that

'Canada is prepared to join the other members of the League in considering how the provisions of the Covenant may be collectively and effectively carried out.' Acrimonious discussions followed among Bennett, Skelton, and Loring C. Christie, Counsellor in the External Affairs Department. Bennett called Skelton and Christie 'welshers,' because of their unwillingness to carry out the commitments which Canada had undertaken in the League Covenant. Nevertheless, before he left Ottawa late in the evening to begin a campaign trip, he had accepted a redrafting of the statement to be made in Geneva, still positive in tone but less far-reaching: 'Canada is prepared to join the other members of the League in considering how by unanimous action peace can be maintained.'[9]* The new instructions, reversing those sent earlier the same day, were wired to Riddell,[10] and on 14 September the statement of Canada's position was made to the Assembly by Ferguson.[11]

The Geneva delegation had obtained the instructions it obviously wanted, and made clear privately as well as publicly its support for the stand Britain had taken. This in turn strengthened the hand of the more strongly pro-League elements in the British government. Thus Anthony Eden, the minister responsible for League of Nations affairs in the British cabinet, wrote Sir Samuel Hoare later in September, at a time when he saw indications that Hoare might be backing off from a hard-line policy: 'The situation here is difficult, but no more so than usual, and there are even compensating elements. First the Dominions, who, as you will remember, were some of them at least distinctly doubtful in their attitude, are all cordially at one with us. If anything they want the League to be more vigorous than it is. They insist that the pressure must be kept up on Mussolini, and if possible increased.'[12]

In spite of all pressure to the contrary, Mussolini began his invasion of Ethiopia on 4 October 1935, and the long-expected crisis for the League and the collective security system began. It was well understood by all concerned that this was, indeed, a crucial test for the League system; another failure, like that over Manchuria in 1931-2, would undoubtedly mean that the League could hardly be taken seriously any longer as a collective security organization. Chances of success against Italy in 1935 seemed quite good, however. Whereas the Japanese seizure of Manchuria had begun suddenly and without advance warning, Italy's intention to attack Ethiopia had become increasingly apparent over a ten-month period of dispute and preparation for war, and the other powers had had substantial time to decide on their response. Whereas China had been unable to offer any substantial military resistance to Japan, Ethiopia appeared able and willing

---

* The full text of notes by Christie on the discussions of 13 Sept. in the Department of External Affairs and with Prime Minister Bennett is contained in Appendix B

to offer effective resistance for some months at least, allowing time for the other powers to act before being faced with a *fait accompli*. Whereas two important Far Eastern powers, the Soviet Union and the United States, were non-members of the League in 1931 and had not undertaken any commitments to action against Japanese aggression, Britain and France, the only important Mediterranean powers other than Italy itself, were firmly committed both legally, as League members, and by their most recent policy statements, to action against Italian aggression. Moreover, Italy in 1935 appeared particularly vulnerable to League action. Key materials needed to maintain the Italian war effort in Africa could be obtained only through imports. Communications with Africa could be maintained only by sea, and the British and French navies were clearly stronger than the Italian. Italian access to Ethiopia depended on use of the Suez Canal, which was under British control. Surely the power lay within British and French hands to apply the sanctions provisions of the League Covenant and force a halt to the Italian invasion, perhaps even by economic measures alone. And if the practicability of the League system could be demonstrated by its successful application against a major power, the whole threatening trend of treaty repudiation, aggression, and impending general war might well be reversed.

Such were the gains that seemed realistically possible to the League's supporters, if only Britain and France adhered in practice to the firm stand against Italian aggression which they had pledged in advance. Effective power to act against Italy lay essentially with Britain and France, not with the League. But the League provided the mechanism for organizing action, and for mobilizing demands for and support for action, and it was in such activity that the smaller powers, including Canada, had the opportunity to make their influence felt.

When news that war had begun reached Geneva, the initial response was rapid. On 7 October, three days after the invasion began, the League Council, unanimous except for Italy, formally found that Italy had resorted to war in violation of the Covenant. The question of economic sanctions was then considered by the Assembly, which had before it a proposal that a Co-ordination Committee be established to recommend specific sanctions to be applied. The proposed procedure was not that provided in Article 16, whereby all League members were immediately to sever all economic and financial relations with the aggressor state, but rather a procedure patterned, in general, after recommendations adopted by the 1921 Assembly, whereby the application of sanctions would be phased and gradual, permitting steadily increasing international pressure to be put on the aggressor to abandon the aggression.

Once again, but in an even more significant way than in the preceding month, Canada was faced with the necessity of taking a public stand, with a general election and possible change in government less than a week away. To Walter Riddell's cabled request for instructions, O.D. Skelton replied on 8 October that he would be discussing the whole question with Prime Minister Bennett that night at Cornwall, Ontario, where Bennett was campaigning. At their meeting, Skelton apparently urged successfully on Bennett the view that it would be improper to make any firm commitment to applying sanctions until after the election.[13] The next day, 9 October, instructions were sent from Bennett that Howard Ferguson should make the following statement:

The Canadian delegation is instructed to refrain from voting at the present juncture. The Canadian Government consider the decision to be taken is one of the greatest moment for the future relations of Canada to the League. In view of fact that the Canadian Parliament has been dissolved and that a new Parliament is to be elected next Monday, it is not considered advisable to anticipate in any way the action of that new Parliament.[14]

These instructions were received with dismay by the Geneva delegation. There was no question but that Italy was guilty of aggression; near unanimity was being reached at Geneva on formal recognition of that fact, and on the application of economic sanctions. Only a few client states of Italy's were expected to abstain in the voting on the Assembly resolution. Ferguson wired back immediately to the Department of External Affairs the strongest objections to the instructions to abstain, concluding: 'Our acceptance today fact of Italian aggression would, of course, be without prejudice to our attitude towards any scheme of sanctions which might be later produced. Hope you realize Canada's abstention under these conditions will without question be misinterpreted here and its importance magnified. Have discussed the matter fully with our Canadian delegation and all agree with above views.'[15]

Ferguson's telegram was phoned to Bennett's private secretary, who was with Bennett campaigning in Ontario, and Skelton later in the day sent a memorandum upholding his position. He insisted again that Canada should not, prior to the election, make any commitment to apply economic sanctions.[16]

Meanwhile, Ferguson had decided not to wait for a reply to his telegram, but to telephone Bennett from Geneva in an attempt to get the instructions reversed. Bennett was reached in Lindsay, Ontario, and the situation was explained to him by Ferguson, with Walter Riddell and Lester Pearson present. Bennett promptly agreed to let Ferguson use his own judgment on the matter, and said to ignore the earlier instructions.[17]

The next day, 10 October, in a heated telephone conversation with the prime minister, O.D. Skelton again sought at least a statement by Canada denying any commitment to apply sanctions. Bennett refused. Skelton implied that Bennett was merely following British policy, and Bennett implied that Skelton was following Mackenzie King's old policies. The conversation closed with an emphatic refusal by Bennett to consider any further change: 'No one in Canada is going to deny Italy guilty or object to our saying so. If they did, not going to wriggle out if it meant I didn't get one vote.'[18]

Once again, through Bennett's support, the Canadian delegation in Geneva had obtained the instructions it wanted. On 10 October, when the vote was taken in the Assembly on the resolution recognizing the fact of Italy's aggression and setting up the Co-ordination Committee to recommend economic sanctions to be applied, only Italy voted in opposition, and only Austria and Hungary abstained.[19]

Having obtained the most direct evidence that Skelton's views lacked the support of the prime minister, Ferguson ceased to be restrained by the instructions Skelton had sent, and for the moment Skelton lost any effective control over the expression of Canadian policy at Geneva. This undermining of his authority was, of course, something which Skelton had brought on himself. He had been well aware for some time that the policy toward the League and collective security which he and King had developed in the 1920s was no longer fully supported by Bennett. However, in the Italo-Ethiopian crisis, Skelton repeatedly tried to insist on his own views, unmodified by those of the prime minister or of dissidents within the Department of External Affairs. The result, as might have been expected, was the overruling or ignoring of his instructions. No doubt, of course, Skelton was encouraged in his reluctance to defer to the prime minister's views by the approaching general election, and the strong possibility that Bennett would soon be removed from the scene.

On 10 October, the day the Assembly voted to set up the Co-ordination Committee on sanctions, instructions were sent to Ferguson regarding Canadian membership on it, which reflected all of Skelton's usual reserve toward League activity: 'As Committee is to consist of all members of Assembly, no objection to accepting membership with arrangements you suggest ... As practically all Ministers are out of town it will, however, be impossible to send instructions until beginning of week, and no definite attitude should be taken until further communication is sent.'[20]

Ferguson promptly accepted membership not only on the Co-ordination Committee, as authorized, but also on the smaller and more important Committee of Eighteen, which was to do the real work of preparing specific sanctions proposals.* Skelton's instructions were not asked regarding membership on the Com-

---

* The members of the Committee of Eighteen were: Portugal (Chairman), South Africa, Argentina, Belgium, the United Kingdom, Canada, France, Greece, Mexico, the Netherlands, Poland, Romania, Spain, Sweden, Switzerland, Turkey, the Soviet Union, Yugoslavia

mittee of Eighteen,[21] and his instructions to take 'no definite attitude' were ignored. At the first meeting of the Committee of Eighteen on 11 October, Ferguson urged immediate action:

The delegations had already stated their position with great unanimity and emphasis in the Assembly. They had declared who was the aggressor, and the proceedings that must be taken followed as a matter of course.

The sole problem before the Committee was to decide what sanctions the delegations could all agree upon that afternoon and put into application immediately. Let them show the world that the League was no longer to be scoffed or laughed at, but that it meant business, and that when a breach of its Covenant took place it proposed to deal with the aggressor in the proper way.[22]

As a first step, he suggested announcement that same day of a complete embargo on arms shipments to Italy. Anthony Eden, the British representative on the committee, said he 'would emphatically endorse what the Canadian delegate had said.' He then offered a formal proposal for an arms embargo, 'on the basis of the remarks of the Canadian delegate,'[23] and before the end of the day the proposal had received the approval of both the Committee of Eighteen and the full Co-ordination Committee, and had been formally recommended to all League members. Canada was thus in the forefront of states demanding prompt and effective sanctions against Italy, as it had been in July in the Committee of Thirteen, when considering the application of sanctions in a more theoretical way.

On 14 October the Committee of Eighteen considered a proposal to prohibit all financial transactions with Italy, which was backed strongly by Eden. Giuseppe Motta of Switzerland objected to any prohibition on transfers of funds or credits to the Italian branches of foreign-owned firms, and Enrique Ruiz-Guiñazú of Argentina expressed doubt as to how promptly his country would be willing to apply sanctions. Ferguson gave full backing to Eden, criticizing the Swiss and Argentine statements as 'tantamount to a refusal to co-operate' as soon as some sacrifice was involved. Not too accurately in historical terms, he gave an emphatic statement of Canadian support for sanctions:

Canada had joined the League, as he assumed all other Members had, with a full knowledge of her undertakings, and fully appreciating the obligations imposed upon her and the risks she was running ...

When they signed the Covenant, the Canadian people had realised that, if ever they were asked to implement it, they would be substantial sufferers ... If she had to restrict the market of her mineral industry, the second most important industry in Canada, and to drive thousands of men out of employment, in order that she might fulfil her obligation, she was ready to do so, because she was prepared to carry out her promise ...[24]

Once again, action was prompt. Eden's proposal for a complete prohibition of financial transactions with Italy, to be completely in operation by 31 October, was approved by both the Committee of Eighteen and the Co-ordination Committee before the day was over.

On that same day, 14 October 1935, the Canadian electorate chose a new parliament. The result was a crushing defeat for Bennett and the Conservatives, who won only forty seats out of a total of 245. The victory for Mackenzie King and the Liberal party was equally decisive, the party winning 173 seats. None of the three new parties made an impressive showing, J.S. Woodsworth's Cooperative Commonwealth Federation winning only seven seats in its first electoral test.[25]

News of the election results reached Geneva on 15 October, and was of more interest than usual because of the active role Canada had been taking. Mary Craig McGeachy of the Information Section of the Secretariat wrote J.W. Dafoe of the *Winnipeg Free Press*:

I have sent up a note to the S.G. [Secretary-General] on the provisional figures and (in the midst of a meeting of the Committee of Coordination on Economic Sanctions!) have a note back asking for final results as soon as possible and a 'note on the probable attitude of the new administration toward problems of foreign policy'! ...

Ferguson has been very useful in the Coordination Committee. He has twice cut across rambling apologies and withdrawings and has made it clear to everyone that the Canadians are determined to see the collective system put in motion in this case. It has been a great comfort to the UK and to the other Dominions ...

It will be most useful if this firm attitude can be maintained.

Given Ferguson's attitude in the Committee it would be very deplorable if the new Government should appear to relax from this firmness. But I am sure there is no fear of that.[26]

The most immediate result of the election, so far as Canadian foreign policy decision-making was concerned, was to leave a vacuum, for the moment, at the political level. Bennett continued in office on a caretaker basis, but took no policy initiatives, until King had formed his cabinet and was ready to assume office, which did not take place till 23 October. Howard Ferguson left Geneva for London to wind up his affairs as High Commissioner, assuming, quite correctly, that he would not be retained in that post by King. Lester Pearson also returned to the London office.

Thus, by default, Walter Riddell was suddenly left as the ranking Canadian representative in the development of economic sanctions policy in Geneva, assisted only by the regular staff of his own office. And if policy formation had temporarily come to a halt in Ottawa, such was not the case in Geneva. On 14 October Riddell had reported to the Department of External Affairs that Canada had been named to a Sub-Committee on Economic Measures, and concluded: 'Would appreciate full instructions on economic sanctions.'[27] Skelton was now freed from any concern about Bennett's views, and the instructions sent on 15 October sounded a familiar refrain: 'In view of results of general election of yesterday and of fact that new Government cannot take over for some days, it will not be possible for you to take position on any further proposals in the meantime.'[28]

Abandonment of the highly active role which Canada had been playing, in favour of taking no position, was not a palatable change to Riddell. He wired back on 15 October: 'Unless advised to the contrary, I shall continue to express in Co-ordinating Committee and Sub-Committees Canadian policy regarding sanctions as defined in your communication concerning Committee of Thirteen.'[29] Skelton's reply, quite remarkably, pleaded ignorance of what Riddell was talking about: 'I do not understand your reference to our policy regarding sanctions defined in our communication concerning Committee of Thirteen. Only instructions regarding sanctions were those contained in our telegram of 10th October stating that no definite attitude should be taken until further communication was sent.'[30] Riddell, still unwilling to accept instructions to say nothing, replied: 'My reference was to Sanctions Committee of Thirteen set up April 17th in particular to your telegrams ... July 8th and July 23rd.'[31]

There was no further response from Skelton. The instructions of 8 and 23 July 1935, which Riddell obviously wished to follow now, had, in a striking departure from previous Canadian policy, expressed the view that economic sanctions, if their application should be decided on, should be as comprehensive and effective as possible. When reminded of the instructions by Riddell, Skelton did not specifically repudiate them, but told Riddell in unambiguous terms to take no position on any further proposals. Whatever the origin of the 8 and 23 July instructions may have been, they clearly did not represent Skelton's views now, and of course the incoming government of Mackenzie King had had no responsibility for them.

The newly-acquired habit of ignoring Skelton's instructions was apparently a difficult one to break, however, and Riddell did not return to a policy of silence and negativism. On 15 October, and again on 17 October, in the Sub-Committee on Economic Measures, he advocated including processed materials as well as raw materials in any embargo recommendations adopted.[32] The same question arose in the Committee of Eighteen on 19 October, with regard to whether iron and steel finished products, as well as iron ore and scrap iron, should be embargoed.

Riddell favoured including them all: 'The Canadian delegation had always held the view, which he had expressed in the Committee of Thirteen, that any scheme of economic sanctions should be comprehensive.'[33]

Riddell was, in other words, continuing to base his actions on the instructions received in July, rather than those received in the last few days. In this instance, Riddell's view was opposed by Britain and France, among others, and iron and steel products were omitted from the recommended embargo list for the time being.

During these same days Riddell was also reportedly active regarding the question of nickel, the one key raw material that was primarily under Canadian control. Miss McGeachy wrote J.W. Dafoe on 18 October: 'This might be a useful thing to know: that the Canadians themselves have taken the initiative in getting nickel placed on the list of raw materials to be withheld from Italy under economic sanctions ... The Canadians yesterday got nickel moved from List II to List I [for immediate embargo].[34]

The Co-ordination Committee then, on 19 October, adjourned until the end of the month, having recommended a ban on arms shipments to Italy, and on all financial transactions with and all imports from Italy. It had also recommended a ban on export to Italy of a selected, but not comprehensive, list of raw materials.

On 23 October, shortly after the Co-ordination Committee completed the first phase of its work, the new Canadian government took office in Ottawa. So far as foreign policy questions were concerned, the key personnel were exactly the same as in the Liberal governments of the 1920s. W.L. Mackenzie King was again prime minister and Secretary of State for External Affairs. Ernest Lapointe was again Minister of Justice and King's unofficial deputy. Raoul Dandurand was again Minister without Portfolio, and the only cabinet member besides King and Lapointe with a strong interest in foreign policy. In the Department of External Affairs, O.D. Skelton continued as Undersecretary and promptly resumed his old role as an exceptionally influential adviser to the prime minister.

It remained to be seen, of course, whether the policies as well as the personnel would also be the same as in the 1920s. King, in policy statements in December 1934 and April 1935 on Canada's role in the League of Nations, had advocated Canadian initiative in applying comprehensive economic sanctions against an aggressor. His policies while in office in 1921-30 had been distrustful both of economic sanctions and of Canadian initiatives. Returning to office in the midst of the League's first attempt at applying sanctions, he was faced with the necessity of making important policy decisions almost immediately.

The first decision to be made was whether to accept and put into effect the first group of sanctions against Italy recommended by the League. In a statement given to the press on 29 October, King announced that Canada would adopt the recommended measures, but he also reviewed the history of Canadian opposition to a sanctionist policy, and said that 'the Government's course in approving economic sanctions in this instance is not to be regarded as necessarily establishing a precedent for future action.'[35]

In Geneva, Riddell found the government's acceptance of the sanctions proposals 'without any reservations whatsoever ... a heartening surprise,'[36] and continued his active participation in the preparation of further proposals. On 1 November, in the Sub-Committee on Economic Measures, he was outspoken in disagreement with Walter Stucki of Switzerland, who had proposed that exceptions be made to the embargo on all imports of Italian goods:

The issue at stake was tremendously serious ... They were called upon to make Article 16 effective through economic sanctions and without resort to war. That was the biggest experiment ever yet tried among the nations. He had the impression that some nations wished to play their part at little or no cost to themselves; but, as the Canadian representative at a previous meeting had said, the thing could not be done without cost ...

Believing that his Government felt as he did on this matter, he would consider he was betraying them if he weakened on these proposals, and must frankly say he could not associate himself with any attempt to undermine what, not only now, but in the future, would be found to be the most effective sanction of all ...

... he therefore felt the Committee should not approve of any exceptions. If a State so desired, let it act as it wished on its own responsibility, without expecting to receive approval of its actions from others.

Stucki then withdrew his proposal, in view, he said, of the Canadian representative's reaction to it.[37] At a meeting of British Commonwealth representatives later that day, Sir Samuel Hoare opened the discussion by complimenting Riddell on his speech, and Anthony Eden and the South African representative also commented favourably on it.[38]

Meanwhile, although the King government had assumed office on 23 October, Riddell had received no instructions since that date regarding what position to take in the session of the Committee of Eighteen which had just resumed, although he had sent repeated requests emphasizing the urgent need for instructions. Finally on 2 November, after approval by Prime Minister King,[39] instructions were sent. Regarding 'inclusion of finished products as well as raw materials' in the ban on exports to Italy, which Riddell had already advocated, '... you should not raise question further. As to inclusion petroleum and copper not desirable to make statement but you may support majority view.'

'Regarding press despatches reporting your taking prominent part in committee discussions yesterday, no position should be taken on any question of importance in committee without definite instructions.'[40]

The new government had determined its policy, and it was the same policy of avoidance of any initiatives and of any encouragement of effective sanctions which had characterized King's previous governments, with no reflection of his contrary statements of more recent years. Indeed, the instructions constituted not so much a statement of policy as an abandonment of any policy: say nothing, and vote with the majority.

The 2 November instructions, however, arrived too late. Riddell, like many others, had become convinced that the successful use of sanctions against Italy was essential to the continued existence of the League system and to the prevention of general war, and that the key to success was the extension of the ban on exports to Italy to include the principal raw materials omitted from the first list: oil, coal, iron, and steel. 'By this time,' he later wrote, 'I had become thoroughly convinced that this was the last and best chance that the Member States would have of preventing a European collapse and another world war; that it was therefore imperative that the Member States should accept their obligations not only willingly but generously, as any losses they might suffer would be a mere bagatelle in comparison with the losses in the event of a break-up of the Collective System.'[41]

On 2 November, at a meeting of the Committee of Eighteen, Riddell concluded that the time was ripe for acceptance of sanctions on oil and the other key products, and that if someone did not act promptly the opportunity would be lost. No one else appeared ready to take the initiative. He wired Ottawa again, asking for specific instructions regarding the proposal he had in mind. He then drafted the proposal, and showed it to Robert Coulondre and Anthony Eden, the French and British representatives on the committee. Both were prepared to support it. Riddell asked Eden 'if he saw any objection to my making this proposal and he said "No" and then, after a moment, "I wish you would." '[42] With time running out, and no instructions yet from Ottawa, he discussed with his two assistants at the Canadian Advisory Office whether he was justified in going ahead and making the proposal; their advice cancelled out.[43] He decided to proceed, and introduced his proposal, as follows:

In execution of the mission entrusted to it under the last paragraph of Proposal IV, the Committee of Eighteen submits to Governments the following proposal:

It is expedient to adopt the principle of the extension of the measures of embargo provided for in the said proposal to the following products:

Petroleum and derivatives;

Coal;

Iron, cast iron and steel.

As soon as it appears that the acceptance of this principle is sufficiently general to ensure the efficacy of the measures thus contemplated, the Committee of Eighteen will propose to Governments a date for bringing them into operation.[44]

Later the same day Riddell received the instructions from King and Skelton telling him to make no statement regarding a further extension of sanctions, and criticizing the much less important initiatives which he had previously taken.

Action on 'the Canadian proposal' in the Committee of Eighteen was prompt. With a minimum of debate, after a rewording which did not alter its substance, the proposal was adopted by the Sub-Committee on Economic Measures and, on 6 November, by the Committee of Eighteen, with no expressed opposition to it, and was recommended to states for adoption.[45]

The significance of the 'oil sanction' proposal was recognized by all. If put into effect, it would close the large gaps in the economic sanctions already adopted and put maximum collective economic pressure on a vulnerable Italy. It would mean applying the League collective security system in earnest, forcing Italy to halt its aggression in Ethiopia, if that could be done, and there was excellent reason to think it could. Yet nothing would happen unless someone first took the initiative. As Sir Samuel Hoare later wrote, 'Behind ... the apparent unanimity of the League States, there persisted many doubts and hesitations that came to a head when the Canadian representative proposed to extend the comparatively mild embargoes to include oil ... [The] proposal, once made, forced the issue into the forefront of the League discussions.'[46]

Riddell explained his objective later the same month, in a letter to Newton W. Rowell, who had written, 'I hope the good work at Geneva will be continued, and that the League will work out such a system of sanctions as will compel Mussolini to desist.'[47] Riddell replied: 'As far as one can learn, petroleum is the key product most essential for Italy to carry on the war, and, if an effective embargo can be put on this substance, the hope expressed in your letter may be realised.'[48]

The reason Riddell's proposal had not specified an effective date for the new sanctions was that the co-operation of non-League powers, especially the United States, would be needed for the embargo on oil, in particular, to be effective. The United States government had already publicly indicated its willingness to apply pressure on its private firms in behalf of an oil embargo, and Riddell had found the American representative in Geneva, Prentiss Gilbert, 'convinced that his Government would not allow the export of their products to nullify any sanctions undertaken by the League.' The German government's representative in Geneva had told him that Germany had decided not to take any part either for or against sanctions, and would not be likely, at least for the time being, to increase its exports to Italy.[49]

It is ironic that when Canada did take this major initiative at the League of Nations, at a moment when other states hesitated to act, it was taken contrary to the instructions of the Canadian government. Riddell insisted, both at the time and afterwards, that he had adequate grounds for considering his proposal consistent with his government's policy, and that he had been, in any case, speaking only as an individual, but his arguments are not convincing. He cited his instructions as Canadian representative on the Committee of Thirteen in July 1935, which advocated comprehensive and effective economic sanctions, and the fact that the only specific information he had been sent as to the King government's attitude was the press release in which the government agreed to all the sanctions which had at that time been recommended by the League. This was true as far as it went, but in addition Riddell had received the most specific instructions from Skelton not to take any position until directly authorized to do so. His mention of the Committee of Thirteen instructions to Skelton had produced a response which made it clear that those instructions no longer represented Skelton's views on sanctions, and the terms of King's acceptance of the sanctions already recommended by the League in no way implied that further measures were advocated.

In the case of other Canadian representatives at Geneva, such as Cahan in 1932, failure to follow instructions could perhaps be explained by lack of experience. Such was certainly not the case with Riddell. He had been continuously involved in League affairs since 1920, first as an official of the International Labour Organization, and since 1925 as the permanent Canadian representative to the League and the ILO. He had served as dean of the diplomatic corps of permanent representatives to the League since it had first organized as a corps in 1932, even though he was not its senior member, and he had been its regular spokesman in dealing with the Secretariat.[50] In October 1935 he had begun a one-year term as Chairman of the Governing Body of the ILO. He was thoroughly familiar with the views and attitudes of Mackenzie King, under whose direction he had worked for five years, and of O.D. Skelton, who had been his immediate superior for ten years. He had been present at Geneva throughout the Cahan episode, and was undoubtedly well aware that any formal proposal he made could only be made as the representative of Canada, and not simply as an individual. He was, in short, thoroughly experienced in League affairs and as a Canadian government representative, and it must be assumed that in making his oil sanction proposal, he knew very well he was acting in a way not authorized by his government.

Why, then, did he do it? The only realistic answer would seem to be that he thought, with much justification, that the issue was of vital importance and that the right timing was essential, and that he therefore decided to follow his own views, even without the authorization of his government, a certain protection being provided by the confusion and contradiction in the instructions which he had been sent.

Riddell's unauthorized proposal of oil sanctions was not, of course, a single, isolated incident, but rather the culmination of a process that had been going on throughout the Italo-Ethiopian crisis. Initially, while Bennett was in office, it had been Skelton, not Riddell, whose views were in conflict with those of the prime minister. Because the Geneva delegation was headed by a political appointee, Howard Ferguson, who could by-pass Skelton and deal with Bennett directly, this was brought into the open and Skelton's authority was temporarily undermined. The Geneva delegation then had the heady experience of being able to ignore unwelcome instructions, and respond as it wished to that 'spirit of Geneva' which was operating with full force in an hour of crisis for the League. This situation was changed completely with Bennett's defeat at the polls, but Riddell either did not realize this, or perhaps thought that what could be accomplished for the League and collective security was worth the risks involved.

Prime Minister King first learned of 'the Canadian proposal' for oil sanctions when he read about it in the newspapers.[51] A brief statement of the action taken was received from Riddell.[52] King's response was prompt, but private. Nothing was said in public. Riddell was told on 4 November, by telegram, that King had 'noted with much surprise' that 'without authorization you took the initiative in moving certain additional articles' be added to the sanctions list. Riddell was reminded that he could act only as the representative of the government of Canada, and that he 'should not take action on any question of importance such as those recently considered without definite and positive instructions.'[53] When Riddell made an attempt to justify his action, the reply was emphatic: 'I have noted your explanation but must insist that position which you took was not in my judgment in conformity with important factors in Canadian situation and not within the scope of your authority.'[54]

At this point active Canadian participation in the League's consideration of sanctions and the Italo-Ethiopian crisis came to an abrupt halt. Riddell continued to represent Canada in the committee meetings, but said nothing. On 8 November he wrote the Secretary of the Co-ordination Committee, requesting that the word 'Canadian' be deleted from references to 'the Canadian proposal' for additional sanctions in the draft minutes of the various committee meetings, and this was done.[55] It must have been apparent at Geneva that something was amiss, even though the Canadian government had said nothing publicly to indicate that Riddell had not been speaking for it.

Mackenzie King evidently hoped, quite characteristically, that if he kept quiet about Riddell's proposal, Canada's and the world's attention would quickly turn to something else, and the whole matter would soon be forgotten. Such was not to be the case, however. The crucial importance of cutting off Italy's supply of oil, if the League's sanctions were to be a success and the Ethiopian invasion halted, was increasingly recognized. The oil sanction had been recommended to states by the Committee of Eighteen on 6 November 1935; the committee was to meet again on 12 December to consider states' replies, and was expected then to set a date for bringing the sanction into force.

The press, both in Canada and elsewhere, repeatedly credited Canada and the King government with authorship of the proposal and with being in the forefront in support of sanctions, much to King's annoyance. A listing of 'press references to oil embargo as a Canadian proposal' prepared for the prime minister cited a long list of Canadian, American, and British sources. The *Montreal Gazette*, for example, had used as headlines, 'Canada Urges Wider Embargo,' and 'League Adopts Canadian Plan.' The London (England) *News Chronicle* had referred to the 'ban on these exports, proposed by the new Liberal Government of Canada.'[56] Vincent Massey, the new Canadian High Commissioner in London, wrote King on 29 November, almost four weeks after Riddell's proposal was made:

... they are so commonly referred to in the press as the 'Canadian proposals' that this designation is on the way to being, if it has not already actually been, accepted as their appropriate description ...

... whatever may be the exact nature and status of the action taken at Geneva in this matter, the parentage of that action is, in this country, ascribed to Canada.[57]

Before Massey's letter was received, King had acted to correct that impression. He and Skelton, after getting the new administration under way, had visited Washington, DC, and then gone on to Sea Island, Georgia, for several weeks' vacation, leaving Ernest Lapointe as Acting Secretary of State for External Affairs, and Laurent Beaudry, a career official, as Acting Undersecretary.

With the next session of the Committee of Eighteen in view, Skelton wrote Beaudry on 26 November that it would be well to 'make it clear to Riddell that he is not to vote or take any position on the question before reporting precisely what the proposal is and receiving definite instructions thereon. It is evident the question is going to be full of dynamite, and in view of Riddell's previous unfortunate actions, he must not be allowed to act at his own discretion or pull any more of Mr Anthony Eden's chestnuts out of the fire.'[58]

Lapointe, however, thought something more was needed, and on 28 November Beaudry wired to Skelton: 'Mr Lapointe is disturbed by headlines in Press emphasizing initiative taken by Canada and is wondering whether some course of action could be adopted to counteract this effect.'[59]

Skelton discussed Lapointe's request with King, and King decided that Riddell's initiative should be publicly repudiated. He thought that Lapointe should arrange to be interviewed by the press, and should state that the Canadian government 'has taken no initiative in subject and that opinion expressed by Canadian member of Committee of Eighteen represented only his opinion as member of Committee.' Also, Massey should be informed that Riddell had acted without authorization, and should so inform the British government 'in view of misleading references and emphasis in press upon Canadian initiative.'[60]

Lapointe and Beaudry promptly agreed, and made a further suggestion: 'Massey is being instructed accordingly. Interview by the press will also be arranged. Would Prime Minister consider sending Dandurand to next meeting of League Committee with special instructions to survey situation and prevent further commitment. He is in Paris.'[61] King's reaction to being represented by a cabinet minister notably sympathetic to the League was blunt: 'Prime Minister thinks would be most unwise to send person named.'[62]

Lapointe's press statement, published on 2 December 1935, disclaimed all responsibility for the oil sanction proposal:

The suggestion which has appeared in the press from time to time, that the Canadian Government has taken the initiative in the extension of the embargo upon exportation of key commodities to Italy, and particularly in the placing of a ban upon shipments of coal, oil, iron and steel, is due to a misunderstanding. The Canadian Government has not and does not propose to take the initiative in any such action; and the opinion which was expressed by the Canadian member of the Committee – and which has led to the reference to the proposal as a Canadian proposal – represented only his personal opinion, and his views as a member of the Committee, and not the views of the Canadian Government.[63]

Riddell thought that Lapointe and Beaudry bore the main responsibility for repudiating his action,[64] but this is clearly not correct. While they raised the question with King, the decision to publicly repudiate Riddell, the way in which it should be done, and the essential content of the statement were all determined by King and Skelton. There was also widespread speculation that Italian pressure had had much to do with the repudiation. Riddell thought this was probably the case,[65] and Joseph Avenol, the Secretary-General of the League, suggested to him that 'it was probably done through pressure from the Papal See through the

Church in Quebec.'[66] The files of the Department of External Affairs do not reveal any evidence of Italian pressure having been brought to bear. The Italian government had protested against any application of sanctions to Italy, but seems not to have raised the question of Canada's initiation of the oil sanction proposal. The decision to publicly repudiate the proposal would appear to have been based almost entirely on irritation and annoyance at the continuing press references to the 'Canadian proposal,' when in fact it had not been initiated by the Canadian government and did not reflect its views.

The repudiation announcement was the occasion for another round of press comment, both in Canada and abroad, on Canadian policy. Summaries prepared by the League of Nations Society[67] and by the Department of External Affairs[68] reported favourable comments in most French-Canadian papers, and unfavourable or mixed comments in most English-Canadian papers. British anti-sanctionist newspapers approved, while British pro-sanctionist papers attempted to minimize the importance of the repudiation, or to explain it as a domestic political gesture.

A United Press dispatch from Rome on 2 December quoted foreign office spokesmen there as expressing pleasure at Canada's latest action. Canadian papers critical of King's policy featured the Italian reaction under such headlines as 'Rome Is Jubilant Over Lapointe Declaration,' and 'Mussolini Is Delighted Canada Has Backed Down.'[69] The Canadian legation in Washington reported that one newspaper there had featured Prime Minister King's picture with the caption, 'Afraid to Ban Oil.'[70]

In the *Winnipeg Free Press*, J.W. Dafoe, who had vigourously supported King and the Liberals in the recent election, at first opposed the government's action, then was somewhat less critical, on the grounds that the government had not repudiated sanctions, but only Riddell's unauthorized initiative.[71] Newton W. Rowell, like Dafoe a prominent advocate of sanctions, made a statement to the press on 2 December urging support for the oil sanction, and expressing regret that the Canadian government was not entitled to the credit of having proposed it.[72] At the same time he sent a telegram to Lapointe saying he was surprised and disappointed at his statement: 'To [repudiate Riddell] now in face Mussolini's threat is to encourage the aggressor and weaken the forces working for peace and maintenance of collective system ... Quite frankly I was shocked by the government making such an announcement at this critical time.'[73] Rowell also wrote Riddell expressing sympathy and support.[74]

Raoul Dandurand wrote Lapointe his views, from Paris: 'Votre communiqué a fort réjoui tous les amis de l'Italie en France – ils sont fort nombreux – qui ont vu un désaveu non seulement de l'initiative de Riddell mais de l'action consécutive du Comité.'[75]* He enclosed a newspaper clipping of a press statement he had made, attempting to correct the latter impression.

The League of Nations Society in Canada devoted an entire issue of *Interdependence* to the question of sanctions, but took no stand as an organization for or against the repudiation of Riddell's initiative. Earlier, on 8 November, when the oil sanction proposal was believed to be government policy, the Society's National Council had met and attempted to establish a position. The result was a demonstration of the lack of consensus within the Society on the sanctions issue.

At the meeting Escott Reid, National Secretary of the Canadian Institute for International Affairs, moved a resolution recommending that Canada initiate action through the League to encourage the meeting of Italy's economic needs and, unless such action were taken, should refuse to apply sanctions, and that Canada also give notice of withdrawal from the League unless exempted from Articles 10 and 16 of the Covenant. Tom Moore, president of the Trades and Labour Congress of Canada, and Newton W. Rowell attacked the idea that Italy's invasion of Ethiopia had any economic motivation, citing Italian economic nationalism, diversion of production to armaments, and promotion of an increased birth rate. J.S. Woodsworth, who was now having second thoughts about the economic sanctions system which he had previously advocated, supported Reid. Rowell, seconded by J.W. Dafoe, moved a substitute resolution giving full backing to the government's actions in support of sanctions, and accepted an added provision that action should be taken to make effective the disarmament and treaty revision provisions of the League Covenant.

Woodsworth then moved a further amendment, stating the belief that 'sanctions unaccompanied by a determined effort to discover and remove the causes of the present and coming wars offer by themselves no solution of the problem of organizing peace,' which was adopted by a vote of eleven to ten. Then Rowell's substitute motion, as amended, was defeated, and Reid's original proposal was also defeated. The National Council had reached a complete impasse, none of the views presented obtaining majority support. Rather than accept this outcome, a drafting committee was appointed, and it produced two comparatively innocuous resolutions. One endorsed 'the action of the Canadian government in agreeing to co-operate in the imposition of economic and financial sanctions in order to restore peace in the present crisis.' It was adopted by a vote of fourteen

---

* 'Your statement greatly delighted all the friends of Italy in France – they are very numerous – who saw a repudiation not only of Riddell's initiative but of the subsequent action of the Committee.'

to four, with Woodsworth still in opposition. The second resolution, favouring initiation of proposals to discover and remove the causes of war, was carried unanimously.

At this critical time in the League's history, the League of Nations Society not only failed to apply any pressure on the government in behalf of the collective security system, but only with difficulty found it possible to give a mild endorsement to what the government had already done.[76]

If organized pressure on the government was absent, still the amount of individual and newspaper criticism of the repudiation of Riddell's oil sanction proposal was impressive. King and Lapointe attempted to counter it by emphasizing that they had not repudiated the oil sanction, and had an open mind on the question, but had only repudiated an unauthorized initiative. Lapointe, who only the preceding February had left office as President of the League of Nations Society, attempted to reassure the Society's National Secretary: 'My attitude is far from being one of no cooperation with the other members of the League but I claim that on any question which involves the question of peace and war the Canadian representative at Geneva must first secure the authorization of the Canadian Government before making such a momentous proposal.'[77] To Rowell's criticism he replied that there was no intention 'of conveying the impression that we are not prepared to consider on its merits' the oil sanction proposal.[78] King, in a press conference on 6 December, sounded the same theme: the government's statement had had reference to the origin of the proposal only and not to its merits.[79]

As to what the Canadian government did think of the merits of the oil sanction, the prime minister was resolutely silent. The proposal had been submitted to states for comment, but Canada, together with most other states, sent none, waiting first to see what the major powers would do. The secretary of the League's Co-ordination Committee inquired of Riddell whether, in view of Italian propaganda claiming that the Canadian government's attitude revealed a breach in the united front of the sanctionist states, some statement to the contrary might not be made from Ottawa.[80] Ottawa considered King's 6 December press statement sufficient, and refused to say more.[81]

In Geneva, as the next session of the Committee of Eighteen approached, the atmosphere was still optimistic, and Riddell's part in pressing the key issue was appreciated. F.P. Walters, head of the Secretariat's Political Section, told Riddell that he 'was confident the Canadian Government within two or three weeks would be trying to claim some credit for having proposed the embargo on oil; and that when the history of the whole dispute was being written the most important place would be given to the initiative of the Canadian representative.'[82]

Joseph Avenol said to Riddell that he and the chairman of the Committee of Eighteen 'should be pleased with the attention we were receiving from the Italian

Press.' Avenol was convinced that when the committee met on 12 December a date would be set for bringing the oil sanction into effect, 'and he was confident that Italy was already defeated, and that the League had won a great victory. He said that in his mind once the sanctions had been applied there had never been any doubt as to the successful result.'[83]

It was at this point, before the Committee of Eighteen had met, that the Hoare-Laval proposals to appease Mussolini, through the cession to Italy of large parts of Ethiopian territory, became known. The proposals produced a storm of criticism and were abandoned, without ever having been accepted by Mussolini in any case. Even though Sir Samuel Hoare was replaced as British Foreign Secretary by Anthony Eden, the leading British spokesman for a sanctionist policy, it was impossible any longer to accept at face value the protestations of Britain and France of their determination to prevent the Italian aggression from succeeding. The idea of effective economic sanctions, including the oil sanction, was not abandoned, but was repeatedly postponed. The Committee of Eighteen met in December 1935 and again in March 1936, but no further action was taken. After Hitler's reoccupation of the Rhineland in March, Britain and France lost whatever interest they may still have had in bringing Mussolini to terms, and by May 1936 his conquest of Ethiopia had been successfully completed.

For Canada, the revelation of the Hoare-Laval proposals meant that the focus of world attention had now shifted, and Canadian policy was no longer a subject of major interest. Canada was now able to retire into the comfortable obscurity so much desired by Mackenzie King. At the December 1935 meeting of the Committee of Eighteen, the Canadian representative was Lester Pearson, because Walter Riddell, in his capacity as chairman of the Governing Body of the International Labour Organization, was presiding at a regional ILO meeting in Chile. At the meetings, Pearson wrote Skelton, he 'maintained an impressive silence.' He was, he reported, 'naturally asked by a good many people there to explain Canada's actual policy with respect to collective action against Italy, but was fortunately able to take refuge in the fact that being a new man only recently sent to Geneva I was, naturally, quite ignorant about it all!'[84]

Riddell again represented Canada at the March 1936 meeting, and was equally silent. At both meetings, the Canadian representatives had instructions authorizing them to concur in bringing further sanctions into effect, including the oil sanction, should there be general agreement in the committee on doing so, but telling them to take no initiative in discussion or in suggesting action.[85] The Canadian government had had no advance information about the Hoare-Laval proposals. It authorized Pearson in December to concur if Britain and France wished a postponement of further action on sanctions while the proposals were considered, but told him to express no opinion as to their merits.[86]

In February 1936, the first session of the new Canadian parliament met. There had been no parliamentary session since the previous July, so this was the first opportunity for discussing or questioning the government regarding any aspects of its policy toward the Italo-Ethiopian War. The war itself was still in progress, and at the moment application of the long delayed oil sanction seemed a real possibility.

R.B. Bennett, now Leader of the Opposition, reviewed the 'Riddell incident' and made a vigorous attack on the government's having taken action which, in effect, weakened the sanctionist position: 'I regret more than I can say that the Minister of Justice saw fit to make the observations he did. They were made in a moment of crisis, at a moment of great difficulty, at a moment when we should have stood with every other member of the league. It weakened our position to give succour and support, not physical but moral, to Italy and she was not slow to represent our attitude to all the world.'[87]

Mackenzie King replied with a detailed account of the affair. By now, however, instead of insisting that it was only the unauthorized initiative and not the proposal itself that had been repudiated, King was beginning to take credit for having stopped a dangerous move. He was appalled at the idea that Canada should 'attempt to regulate a European war and to say what other countries are to do with respect to the manner in which a European war is to be carried on.' He thought that 'by pressing the matter of oil sanctions at that stage, a situation might have arisen in Europe the like of which has not been known since the great war,' and concluded: 'I am not at all sure that, when the whole story comes to be told, it may not be discovered that, but for the action of the government of Canada in this particular matter, at that particular time, the whole of Europe might have been aflame to-day. What would then have been said of "Canada's proposal"?'[88]

Bennett, while making clear his general support for the League and for economic sanctions against Italy, did not pursue the matter further. However, T.C. Douglas (CCF-Saskatchewan), a newly elected member, made a forceful presentation of the case for stronger support of a sanctionist policy. In his first speech in the House of Commons, Douglas asserted that Riddell had been right, that effective sanctions were essential, and that the most effective sanction would be on oil.[89] On 2 March 1936, he moved a foreign policy resolution urging, among other things, that Canada initiate 'the prohibition of direct or indirect export to an aggressor nation of all raw materials and manufactured articles necessary for war purposes.'[90]

J.S. Woodsworth, the leader of Douglas' party and formerly the most articulate parliamentary critic of King's foreign policy, commented at length on the motion, but his position remained somewhat ambiguous. He doubted that an isolationist position could be successfully maintained, but thought it might be the best available alternative, if Canada was threatened with being dragged into a war. There was danger of war if sanctions were applied to an aggressor, and also if they were not applied. He condemned Italy's action in Ethiopia, but was conscious that other nations had sinned in much the same way.[91] No member who spoke supported Douglas on the sanctions question, and debate was ended without any statement on the subject by the government.

Walter Riddell, meanwhile, shortly before the parliamentary session had begun, had spent a few days in Ottawa following his ILO meeting in Chile. He was invited to have dinner with King, Skelton, and Lapointe, at King's home, and after dinner they discussed the events of the previous November. King was personally cordial, but was annoyed when Riddell defended his actions. Lapointe seemed less friendly, and had little to say to him.[92]

However annoyed they may have been with Riddell, King and Skelton were not vindictive. Riddell continued in his post as Canadian Advisory Officer in Geneva until late in 1937. At a special Assembly session in June 1936, he was named only an adviser to the delegation, instead of being given his usual rank of delegate or substitute delegate, but at the following Assemblies his previous status was restored. On leaving Geneva, he continued his diplomatic career at the Canadian legation in Washington, and as High Commissioner to New Zealand. Skelton later looked back philosophically on the 'Riddell incident,' and wrote Riddell: 'The proposed oil embargo and the whole subject with which it was connected has now passed into history. Through your part in it, you too, have achieved a niche in the hall of fame.'[93]

The point of view which Riddell's attempted initiative represented was, however, firmly rejected by the King government, even more emphatically in private than in public. The Ottawa correspondent of the *Winnipeg Free Press* sent J.W. Dafoe a revealing account of King's views in mid-December 1935:

Had a few words with Mr King re the Italo-Ethiopian settlement and he spoke with surprising frankness ... King complained angrily about Dr Riddell's gasoline, steel and coal proposal. 'I am certainly going to give him a good spanking,' was the way he put it ... He is very dubious about foreign commitments, and, also, about getting into the League too deeply. He said that the only real difference of opinion he had ever had with Lapointe was with regard to Canada's acceptance of the presidency of the League Assembly.* He had opposed it on the ground

* Reference was undoubtedly intended, not to Canada's acceptance of the presidency of the Assembly, but to its acceptance of membership on the Council, which had been the actual occasion of King's difference of opinion with Lapointe

that it would stimulate League thought in Canada, tend to lead us more deeply into League affairs and, possibly, foreign commitments.[94]

Early in May 1936, with the fall of Addis Ababa to the Italian armies, and the flight of the Ethiopian emperor from the country, the Italo-Ethiopian war came to an end with a complete victory for Italy. Despite the legal commitments in the Covenant, and the threats and promises of the key powers, the League's sanctions system had been only partially and half-heartedly applied, and had neither deterred aggression nor prevented its success.

Canada's part in this crucial test of the League system had been, for Canada, an unusually active one. As a small power, it had no opportunity to play a determining role. However, it did have substantial opportunity to attempt to influence British policy, and to a lesser degree French policy, and Britain and France were in the key decision-making positions.

While R.B. Bennett was prime minster, Canada offered vigorous support in Geneva to the collective security system, taking a leading role in urging the prompt and effective application of sanctions. The initiative did not come primarily from Bennett, but from the Canadian delegation in Geneva. However, when support was needed from Bennett to overcome the opposition of O.D. Skelton, the Undersecretary of State for External Affairs, it was provided. When Mackenzie King succeeded Bennett, this support disappeared. Walter Riddell attempted to continue, and to pursue still further, the sanctionist policy which Canada had been following, but he quickly found that this was unacceptable to the new government. At a time when British policy was wavering between applying full economic sanctions to Mussolini or attempting to appease him, Canadian backing was dramatically and publicly withdrawn from the sanctionist position. Canadian influence, then, was exerted first on one side and then on the other in the controversy over sanctions, finally settling down into a policy of silence, inactivity, and support of whatever consensus others might reach.

The Bennett government was often suspected by its critics of simply following British policy. Certainly most Canadian advocates of acceptance of British leadership in foreign policy were to be found in the Conservative party, and in September-October 1935 official British policy was virtually identical with a pro-League collectivist policy. Bennett's own sympathies with Great Britain were well known; in 1939, after relinquishing the leadership of the Conservative party, he moved to England; he obtained a peerage through the influence of his long-time personal friend, Lord Beaverbrook, and concluded his political career in the House of Lords. Nevertheless, the evidence does not support a conclusion that Bennett's policy was merely one of backing Britain. His government, for example, had urged a policy of comprehensive economic sanctions in the Committee of Thirteen in July 1935, when Britain was unwilling to do so. In 1936 he opposed the removal of sanctions from Italy, when Britain favoured doing so. His private statements in the fall of 1935 indicate a primary concern that Canada should carry out in good faith the collective security obligations it had undertaken, rather than an interest in following British policy in whatever direction it might lead.

The policy reversal which took place after King assumed office has often been attributed to the influence of an alleged French-Canadian isolationism. Again, the evidence is not convincing. The position which King and Lapointe adopted in 1935 was consistent with the policies which they had followed when previously in office. Neither in the 1920s nor in 1935 were these policies apparently based on responsiveness to any peculiarly French-Canadian demands. Indeed, a wide range of foreign policy views had been presented by French-Canadian political spokesmen, as by their English-Canadian counterparts. King had just won an overwhelming victory at the polls, another election was not required for five years, and his political position could hardly have been more secure. When, four years later, he favoured following Britain's lead into war with Germany, he did so without hesitation and without any major political difficulties in French Canada. His public and private statements in 1935 indicate that his principal motivations were distrust of sanctions and of Canadian initiatives in world affairs, plus great irritation at false assumptions being made about his policies because of Riddell's unauthorized initiative.

Perhaps the most striking characteristic of Canadian foreign policy formation at the time of the Italo-Ethiopian war was the extent to which policy, and policy reversals, were determined by the prime minister and the merest handful of advisers, subject to no effective pressures except, of course, the prime minister's evaluation of the eventual political effect, if any, of his decisions. Both Bennett and King kept sanctions policy out of the election campaign. Parliament was not in session when the key decisions were taken. The principal potentially influential outside organization, the League of Nations Society, was immobilized by its own lack of agreement on sanctions. Bennett determined policy, and then reversed his initial determinations, after consultations involving only O.D. Skelton, Howard Ferguson, and their immediate staffs. King decided on a major reversal of policy while away from Canada and in contact only with Skelton and his staff, and with Ernest Lapointe. The fluctuations in Canadian policy at this critical time were great, but reflected essentially the personal views of Prime Ministers Bennett and King and their key advisers, including the strong disagreements among those advisers, and the basic difference in the attitudes of the two prime ministers themselves toward the League of Nations and collective security.

12
The final years of the League

After the failure, in 1936, of the effort to apply effective economic sanctions against Italy, the League of Nations was dead as a collective security organization. The provisions of the Covenant remained unchanged, but the League played no significant part in the remaining crises and aggressions that preceded the outbreak of the second world war. The Council and the Assembly continued to meet, however, until December 1939, and the League's various economic and social functions continued in full operation.

The League, in short, not by design but through the collapse of its efforts in security matters, had become much the kind of organization that Prime Minister Mackenzie King had long advocated: it still offered opportunities for discussion and conciliation in political affairs and its technical operations continued, but it no longer attempted to exercise any coercive functions.

It was in the context of this new situation that King, on 18 June 1936, for the first time in his years as prime minister gave to the House of Commons a detailed statement of Canadian policy toward the League. He began by insisting, in effect, that he had been right all along in opposing a League based on commitments to use economic or military force, and in favouring instead a view which 'laid emphasis upon prevention rather than punishment, urged the peaceful remedy of grievances rather than making war upon a country resorting to war, questioned the readiness of European countries to give as well as to receive aid.' As examples of this policy he cited, among others, the attempt to revise Article 10, the rejection of the Geneva Protocol, acceptance of the compulsory jurisdiction of the Permanent Court of International Justice, and efforts to provide a fair hearing for minorities protected by the peace treaties.[1] For the future, he summarized his views of the League's role as follows:

There is undoubtedly much that is attractive and persuasive in the conception of a world united to prevent by force a breach of the peace by any aggressor. It has been stoutly contended that if all nations would undertake to make war upon an aggressor, and carried out that undertaking, war would never occur. That may well be, but unfortunately it is only a hypothetical argument; it bears no relation to the actualities of to-day. It may be that eventually some such rule of law will be established in the international as has been established in the national field, or at least in those countries where law and the free expression of the people's will still prevail. But clearly that time has not yet come, and to pretend that it has is only to make for disillusionment and misdirected effort ...

Under such conditions it is clearly impossible for a country like Canada to make binding commitments to use economic force or military force ...

But that does not mean that there is not a great part for the league to play. If it cannot become the international war office, neither need it become a mere debating society. It can emphasize the constructive side of its task.[2]

King suggested, as major areas for future constructive activity by the League, the providing of permanent machinery for conference and conciliation, developing 'the habit of working together on small tasks leading to greater,' forcing public defence by governments of their policies, encouraging disarmament or at least the halting of the arms race, providing conciliation and arbitration in specific disputes, and discussing economic grievances.[3]

In September 1936 King headed the Canadian delegation to the League Assembly, and stated the same conclusions in Geneva:

But there is to-day also a widespread conviction, born of experience, that, at this stage in the evolution of the League, emphasis should be placed upon conciliation rather than upon coercion. There is a general unwillingness of peoples to incur obligations which they realise they may not be able in time of crisis to fulfil, obligations to use force and to use it at any place, any time, in circumstances unforeseen, and in disputes over whose origin or whose development they have had little or no control ...

The coercive and punitive provisions of the Covenant have operated in the past as a deterrent to the kind of collaboration which must serve as an intermediate stage to a League of Nations which will be universal. By emphasizing the mediation and conciliation aspects of the Covenant, we can help to transform the collective system from a hope into a reality.[4]

The reaction to King's statements of policy toward the League were, predictably, quite varied. In parliament, R.B. Bennett, leader of the Conservative opposition, made a pro-League statement essentially in harmony with what King had said, finding the League still useful as a place for discussion and negotiation.[5] J.S. Woodsworth, leader of the Cooperative Commonwealth Federation, said he was generally in agreement with King, though his support for a policy of conciliation rather than coercion went much further. 'Personally,' he told the House of Commons, 'I think Canada should declare her firm intention not to participate in any overseas conflict, whatever.'[6]

In contrast, many who had championed the League as a collective security organization were outraged that King, after refusing it support at a crucial time, should now claim that its failure was inevitable, and found his concept of its future role entirely inadequate. T.C. Douglas (CCF, Saskatchewan), in the parliamentary session following King's Geneva speech, was the prime minister's most scathing critic:

A league such as is envisaged and talked about by the Prime Minister would be ... as effective as a ladies' aid meeting. To take the teeth out of the league, to take from the league all capacity to enforce its decisions, is to make the League of Nations null and void ...

To suggest that if we take the teeth out of the League of Nations they may all get together in good fellowship is like suggesting that if we rescinded all the laws in Canada, we and the criminals could fraternize and have no more hard feelings against each other.[7]

Douglas advocated a collective security system 'involving, if necessary, collective economic sanctions' against an aggressor, but leaving 'to those located in affected areas the task of supplying, where necessary, military force.'[8] King's response was scornful. Those who shared Douglas' views, he said, 'would have a league that relies on force, but they are quite eager to see that other nations are the ones to supply the force and that we are to continue to enjoy security and to be kept entirely out of the situation.' Use of economic force, he contended, sooner or later meant use of military force. 'If we are to rely for peace upon force, let us squarely face the situation and realize that we as well as other nations must be prepared to make our contribution in terms of force.'[9] Ernest Lapointe, the Minister of Justice, joined in rejecting any coercive functions for the League: 'I do not think war should be avoided by means of war ... I say I am opposed to force being exercised by the League of Nations, but I believe we should help the victim against the aggressor, economically, diplomatically or otherwise.'[10]

Douglas returned to the attack, opposing the increase in Canadian armaments now recommended by King:

... I feel they are the price the Canadian people are being called upon to pay for the weakness and spinelessness of those who have been responsible for Canada's foreign policy ... As a matter of fact we had imposed other sanctions, and if sanctions lead to war why did we impose the first sanctions? If we were afraid of war why did we impose any sanctions? Why did we impose some and not others? ... And now, when we see the Minister of Justice and the Prime Minister shedding crocodile tears over the demise of the League of Nations, I feel that the situation is ironic indeed ... We have created this situation and now we are proceeding to ask the Canadian people to pay with their money for the folly and the weaknesses of the foreign policy of this government and the British National government.[11]

J.W. Dafoe's editorials in the *Winnipeg Free Press* were no less caustic. He characterized King's Geneva speech as saying

... that by the simple procedure of its members repudiating any obligations under the Covenant which appear onerous to them and by acceptance of the rule that each article in the Covenant means nothing to any nation which desires to ignore it, the League will be transformed into something to which Canada can belong ...
    In the light of Japan's action in 1931 and Italy's within the last twelve months, how can Mr King think that the League can keep the peace by methods of conciliation?[12]

The League of Nations, Dafoe wrote, 'with assurances of the most distinguished consideration, was ushered out into the darkness by Mr Mackenzie King.'[13]
    Whatever the potential usefulness may have been of a League of Nations not claiming coercive powers, the prime minister's critics had substantial grounds for challenging his sincerity in championing such a League. While King, throughout his years as prime minister in the 1920s, had often spoken in support of the League's conciliatory functions, Canada's record was almost totally devoid of any initiatives in the exercise of such functions. It soon became clear that King had no intention of actively seeking to construct a new kind of League of the type he was now advocating.
    In private, King expressed an increasingly greater distaste for the League and all its works. While at the 1936 Assembly session, he recorded in his diary: 'One felt the absurdity of entrusting the affairs of one's country directly or indirectly to an aggregation of the kind which one sees in the Assembly Hall. Countries named by the dozens of which one has seldom or never heard ...'[14] On his return from another trip to Europe in 1937 he wrote: 'I wish the League of Nations could be gotten out of the way altogether. Every feeling I had had about the mis-

chief being wrought through the intrigues of that institution has been intensified by what I have seen and heard while abroad.'[15]

The consequence of this attitude, and of King's long-standing distrust of Canadian initiatives, was to leave Canada's representatives as silent and frustrated spectators at League meetings. Hume Wrong, who succeeded Walter Riddell as Canadian Advisory Officer at Geneva in 1937, recorded in that year 'a plan for the perfect representation of Canada at Conferences': 'Our delegate would have a name, even a photograph; a distinguished record, even an actual secretary – but he would have no corporeal existence and no one would ever notice that he was not there.'[16]

Vincent Massey, King's appointee as Canadian High Commissioner in London, had similar reactions to his membership in the 1937 Assembly delegation. He was a member of the committee dealing with budgetary and administrative matters, but in 'the absence of any instructions from Ottawa ... had no contribution whatever to make.'[17] He wrote in his diary at the time:

I am increasingly conscious of the futility of my existence in Geneva ... In fact I cannot help feeling that I might more appropriately hold a visitor's ticket ... than a delegate's ...

The real difficulty is the state of funk in which the Govt. or rather the PM lives vis à vis international affairs ...

We under the present administration have decided to maintain an absolutely negative attitude in international affairs even when an opportunity offers itself to help in an important piece of international conciliation.[18]

The new situation must have been doubly difficult for Canadian representatives who had been actively involved in League affairs in happier days, such as Raoul Dandurand, who was a member of the Assembly delegation headed by King in 1936, and was once again First Delegate in 1937. Massey recorded in 1937 that 'Dandurand enjoys playing about with European byways but nothing is further from his mind than a serious preoccupation in the work of the League.'[19] The year before, just after Italy had completed its conquest of Ethiopia, Dandurand had written to Walter Riddell: 'They were happy days which we passed together at the League meetings between '24 and '30. It will be something else henceforth! There were ideals to strive for. I would, with a stout heart, return to the task if free to express my own views.'[20]

In these circumstances, it is hardly surprising that Canada's record at the League in its final years was largely a negative one, in spite of Prime Minister King's statements implying a readiness to act constructively, so long as coercion was not involved.

The first problem confronting the League after the conclusion of Italy's conquest of Ethiopia was whether to terminate or to continue the partial economic sanctions then in effect against Italy. To terminate the sanctions would be a humiliating admission of failure, and might be interpreted as a readiness to accept the legitimacy of Italy's actions; to continue the sanctions, however, could hardly be expected to produce any useful results. J.S. Woodsworth, as early as 13 May 1936, a week after the end of the war in Ethiopia, had raised in parliament the question of whether sanctions would be continued by Canada. King refused to discuss the matter, except to deny that there had been any consultations with Britain on the subject.[21] In London, Vincent Massey had been instructed not to take part in any such consultations, and had noted in his diary: 'Ottawa is apparently panic-stricken & seeks to protect itself by an ostrich-like policy of not even wanting to know what is going on.'[22]

On 18 June, after receiving word that Anthony Eden, the British Foreign Secretary, had formally announced that Britain would propose the lifting of sanctions at a forthcoming special Assembly meeting, King told the House of Commons that Canada's policy would be the same, but that the Canadian decision was 'arrived at before we had any information as to what the British action would be.'[23] Only R.B. Bennett objected, saying that if Canada joined in removing sanctions from Italy, 'we undoubtedly have put a direct premium upon the violation of international agreements.' He thought consideration should be given to supporting a continuation of sanctions, as South Africa was advocating, regardless of Britain's attitude.[24] At the Assembly, however, Massey, the Canadian spokesman, endorsed the removal of sanctions since, in his government's view, 'continuance of the ineffective economic pressure would not secure the original objective and would be worse than useless.'[25] Almost all the other members agreed, and the League's sole effort at coercion through application of economic sanctions was brought to an end.

In succeeding Assemblies a principal subject of attention was 'reform' of the League, an attempt to define a new role for the organization, with its emphasis on conciliation rather than coercion. Among the proposals considered were revision of the unanimity requirement under Article 11 of the Covenant, which enabled a party to a dispute to prevent an unwelcome recommendation from being made; strengthening the League's organization for carrying out economic and social functions; and formally deleting provisions for sanctions from the Covenant, or declaring them inoperative. Nothing of consequence was accomplished in the brief time remaining to the League. All members were preoccupied with the approaching general war, some hoped eventually to revive the system of sanctions against aggressors, and there was always opposition to any specific proposal for change.

Canada, represented first by Raoul Dandurand and then by Hume Wrong, was one of twenty-eight members of a Committee to Study the Application of the Principles of the Covenant which met in 1936-8 and sought unsuccessfully to reach agreement on specific reform measures. Prime Minister King at the 1936 Assembly had indicated that he did not think formal amendment of the Covenant was needed, and had supported the view that unanimity could not reasonably be required for the approval of conciliation efforts under Article 11.[26] Canada continued to support these views, but took no active part in developing reform proposals. At the committee's final session in February 1938, Wrong was able to contribute only the suggestion that 'the only possible course is to keep the League operating as effectively as possible within the scope which experience has shown to be practicable,' and to refer again to King's statements at the 1936 Assembly.[27]

With regard to the sanctions provisions of the Covenant, King told the House of Commons in May 1938 that the government had concluded that they 'have ceased to have effect by general practice and consent, and cannot be revived by any state or group of states at will.'[28] When, however, the British government asked the Dominions' opinion on the advisability of an Assembly interpretative resolution declaring the sanctions provisions no longer operative, Canada was opposed. If 'the Assembly were recognized to have any authority to suspend the application of sanctions it would also have authority to re-apply them – a position which the Canadian Government would not desire to see established.' It would be preferable for the Assembly merely to take note of 'the position at which the League has now arrived' through convention and usage. However, 'the Canadian government, it should perhaps be added, do not contemplate initiating any procedure themselves at Geneva.'[29]

While not proposing adoption of any resolution on the subject, Ernest Lapointe, Canada's First Delegate at the 1938 Assembly, did make clear his government's view that, by 'practice and consent, the system of sanctions under the Covenant had ceased to have effect. Sanctions had become non-automatic and non-obligatory.'[30] A majority of League members expressed similar views, but there was sufficient opposition to prevent any attempt being made to obtain formal approval by the Assembly.[31]

Also at the 1938 Assembly, Britain sponsored an Assembly resolution providing that the votes of parties to a dispute should not be counted in determining whether unanimity had been obtained for certain types of conciliation proposals under Article 11 of the Covenant. The Canadian government, which had already advocated this change in principle, was now fearful that it might increase the possibility of coercive action being recommended. It therefore suggested adding to the proposed resolution a further limitation: '... provided, however, that such recommendations shall not involve the application of measures of coercion against a State which has not resorted to war.' When this amendment was not accepted, Canada abstained in the voting on the British proposal, both in committee and in the full Assembly, where the resolution was defeated by negative votes cast by Hungary and Poland.[32]

During these same years, though the League of Nations had no significant part in the succession of major political crises which immediately preceded the second world war, there was occasionally an attempt to find some role for it. Thus in September 1937, after Japan had begun a full-scale invasion of China, a meeting was called of the League's advisory committee on Sino-Japanese relations, which had been set up in 1933 in the aftermath of the Manchurian occupation, but had been largely inactive. Canada was a member of the committee, and was represented on it in 1937 by Dandurand. According to Vincent Massey, before the committee met Dandurand was asked by Anthony Eden, the British Foreign Secretary, if Canada would take the chairmanship. Dandurand cabled Ottawa for instructions. 'The answer was an unequivocal "no." Ottawa also said if our membership could be assigned to Australia or some other state they would have no objection ...'[33] As it turned out, the advisory committee once again found nothing useful to do, because of Japan's refusal to co-operate.

Another political question before the 1937 Assembly was the vote on Spain's re-eligibility for election to the League Council. The Spanish Civil War had begun over a year before; Spain was represented at the League by the Republican government. A two-thirds vote, in a secret ballot, was required to permit a non-permanent member of the Council to seek re-election. Spain had obtained this authorization in 1931 and 1934, and sought it again in 1937. Dandurand, acting on his own authority, cast Canada's vote in favour of Spain's re-eligibility. The necessary two-thirds majority, however, was not obtained. Although the vote was secret, the rumour spread that Canada was one of the states which had voted against the Spanish Republican government. Prime Minister King refuted this in a statement to parliament in 1938, and revealed how Canada had voted, quoting the text of a letter to him from Dandurand.[34]

While King, during these years, explained his foreign policy to the House of Commons more fully than he had previously been willing to do, and answered some specific questions, he was no less reluctant than before to permit any general parliamentary debate of his policies. J.S. Woodsworth, as he had done for over a decade, continued to demand such debate, and in particular discussion of possible Canadian initiatives in world affairs: 'I cannot see why someone else should always lead. The Prime Minister said recently that a very difficult situation confronts European statesmen at the present time. Why cannot we understand that it confronts the world and Canada and not merely European statesmen?'[35]

King firmly rejected the idea that Parliamentary debate was desirable: '... there was the possibility of a debate in this house arousing adverse comment and possibly more in the way of misunderstanding in Europe. That would not have helped the situation there ... I believe this parliament has contributed to the solution of that situation, in so far as there has thus far been a solution, much more effectively by its silence, up to the present – so far as it has been silent – than it would have contributed by any prolonged discussion.'[36] While refusing to engage in debate on foreign policy in parliament, King nevertheless continued to reiterate his 'Parliament will decide' formula, even expounding it in his 1936 speech to the League Assembly.[37] As previously discussed (see Chapter 3), the real meaning of this formula was not to give any effective decision-making role to parliament, but rather to leave the government a completely free hand to determine future policy as it saw fit. The emptiness of the formula was cited by Arthur Meighen, Conservative leader in the Senate, in an attack on King's Geneva speech:

I have read an address delivered at the last meeting of the League of Nations by the Prime Minister of our country. I wish I could compliment him ... on the adequacy of the message which he there expressed. There are few passages in it to which I can attach any meaning at all; if meaning was intended, I do not know what it was ... If the League is only to be told by spokesmen for this Dominion that whatever happens Canada's Parliament will decide what Canada is to do, then I affirm that the League is told exactly and absolutely nothing.[38]

In January 1937, Woodsworth attempted to force a foreign policy debate in the House of Commons by moving that 'under existing international relations, in the event of war, Canada should remain strictly neutral regardless of who the belligerents may be,' that Canadians should not be permitted to make profits out of supplying munitions, and that the Canadian government 'should make every effort to discover and remove the causes of international friction and social injustice.'[39] The government allowed time for debate of Woodsworth's motion, but in the debate made no commitments as to its future policy on the matters covered by it. The motion was then defeated, without a recorded vote.[40]

In fact, King's policies had virtually nothing in common with those favoured by Woodsworth. While repeatedly speaking in favour of conciliation in international affairs, King was not prepared to take any initiatives in that direction. While opposed to the international organization of coercive measures in the League of Nations, he was not necessarily opposed to coercion, or unwilling to take part in it. While unwilling to make any commitments to support British policy, he was not necessarily unwilling to follow the British lead. Thus when

Britain declared war on Germany in September 1939, in a decision which King had not attempted to influence and was not committed to follow, Canada declared war also. In effect, King had simply opted out of any attempt to avert war, or to influence the course of international events. When, however, war 'came,' as if it were some sort of uncontrollable and unpredictable natural disaster, he was fully prepared to take part in it. The decision was not, at that point, a politically controversial one. All parties supported it in parliament, with only Woodsworth recorded in opposition.

There remained one more full-scale League of Nations meeting in Geneva, sessions of the Council and the Assembly called in December 1939 to consider an appeal by Finland following its invasion by the Soviet Union. Canada, whose Assembly delegation was headed by Hume Wrong, was now at war with Germany, and in alliance with Britain and France. The principal measure under consideration was the expulsion of the Soviet Union from its League membership, and Wrong was instructed that if 'the United Kingdom supports the resolution for expulsion you should also support it.'[41] On 14 December a resolution condemning the Soviet aggression and inviting Council action on expulsion was adopted by the Assembly, with Canadian support,[42] and later the same day the Council expelled the Soviet Union from the League.

The Council never met again, and the Assembly met only once more, after the war was over. The Secretariat continued in Geneva on a caretaker basis, with certain of its technical activities transferred to Britain and the United States. Canada provided a wartime home for the International Labour Organization, which temporarily moved its main headquarters from Geneva to Montreal.

In October 1939, Hume Wrong, whose title had been changed in 1938 from Canadian Advisory Officer to Permanent Delegate of Canada to the League of Nations, was transferred to London, and in 1940 the Canadian office in Geneva was permanently closed.

The final Assembly of the League met in Geneva in April 1946, and formally dissolved the organization. Wrong, now a top official of the Department of External Affairs in Ottawa, was again the Canadian First Delegate. His statement at the final Assembly, comparing the new United Nations with the League, provided a cogent summary of the lessons which might, or might not, have been learned:

The United Nations starts with an enormous advantage that the League never had: there is no powerful State left outside ... All the countries possessing substantial power to-day are Members of the United Nations. But the question remains which, with greater justification, haunted the meeting-rooms and corridors of Geneva: Have they the will to use their power to support the principles and procedures of the Charter? ...

The troubles of the world are not, and never have been, at bottom a question of the nature of the existing international machinery, of the processes whereby issues are brought forward for discussion and settlement, of the Covenant or the Charter, of the rule of unanimity or the veto power. What the League of Nations could do, was and is what the States Members agree should be done. The League of itself could accomplish nothing. The United Nations of itself can accomplish nothing. Both are instruments for collective action of their States Members ...

Now, in 1946, we have less confidence that the Charter will succeed than we had in 1919 that the Covenant would succeed. Those who have lived through the terrors and glories of two great wars are bound to be disillusioned. Disillusionment, in its literal sense of the absence of illusions, is a good thing. It should mean that we see more clearly, not that we have lost hope ... We must, nevertheless, keep the hope and faith of the founders of the League of Nations that we can, by concerted effort, banish from the earth the most irrational of human pursuits, the waging of war.[43]

13

Postscript: an evaluation of
Canadian policy

Depending on the criteria applied, evaluation of Canadian policy toward the League of Nations can be a simple or a complicated task. The most important continuing themes in Canadian policy were an interest in promoting a fully independent status for Canada at the international level, a desire to minimize as much as possible Canada's commitments under the collective security system, and an insistence that the League not become involved in questions, such as tariff and immigration policy, which the Canadian government wished to treat as purely domestic matters. In each of these areas, Canada's success in getting what it wanted was quite striking. By 1926 there were no longer any external restraints on Canada's developing and following its own foreign policies, either within the League or outside it. In 1923 Canada had achieved a substantial, if partial, success in its campaign to weaken the binding nature of the commitments under Article 10 of the League Covenant to preserve the territory and independence of all members. During the crises of the 1930s, no unwilling participation in coercive measures had been forced on Canada, and by 1936 the sanctions provisions of the Covenant had become, for the time being at least, inoperative. The only attempt of any consequence to use the League as an instrument for intrusion into Canada's internal affairs, the 'Six Nations' affair of 1923-4, had been successfully resisted by Canada. An entirely free hand had been retained in tariff and immigration matters.

From the above facts, one might be tempted to conclude that Canadian policy toward the League of Nations was an unqualified success, and a prime example of the skillful accomplishment of foreign policy goals. Any such conclusion seems highly unsatisfactory, however. By the late 1930s, though Canada had ceased to be bound by British foreign policy decisions, it was in fact following British policy, without attempting to influence the content of that policy. Though it had been able to avoid international interference with its tariff policy, it was still in the midst of a worldwide economic depression and was still having great difficulty in finding markets for its exports. Most importantly of all, though Canada had successfully evaded binding security commitments which might drag it into war, it had nevertheless become, in September 1939, one of the initial participants in the second world war, less than twenty-one years after the conclusion of the first world war. In short, even if Canada's policy goals had been successfully achieved, the resulting situation was thoroughly unsatisfying. This suggests, of course, that the policy goals were themselves misguided or inadequate, or perhaps that Canada had no capacity to influence the course of world events.

A related problem which is raised by any attempt to evaluate foreign policy solely in terms of its success in achieving specific policy goals is that the goals do not tend to be clearly defined and unchanging. Canadian policy toward the League of Nations, for example, was characterized by repeated endorsements of an important League role in conciliation and mediation of international controversies, but was not characterized in practice by a willingness to take initiatives in developing such a role. Which should be taken as constituting Canada's policy in this area? In 1935, there were important changes in Canadian policy toward collective security. In the final months of the Bennett government, Canada was in the forefront of those League members demanding effective economic sanctions. Shortly afterwards, this position was abandoned. Which represented the 'real' Canadian policy? There are, of course, no answers to such questions. Canadian policy was not entirely clear and consistent, and therefore there is no entirely clear and consistent policy the success of which can be determined.

There remains the further problem of a possible inconsistency in policy goals. The essential purpose of the League of Nations was the prevention of future wars, which was certainly consistent with Canadian policy. On the other hand, more limited and specific Canadian policy objectives may, or may not, have been consistent with that goal. To the extent that they were not, their successful accomplishment may have encouraged international violence, and have been more a defeat than a victory for Canada.

In effect, to produce realistic results a different approach to the evaluation of Canadian policy toward the League of Nations is necessary, one which compares what might have been accomplished with what was in fact accomplished. This in turn involves a consideration of what potential the League of Nations had as an instrument for desirable change in the international system, what opportunities there were for Canadian policy to affect the success and usefulness of the League, and the extent to which these opportunities were realized in practice.

The League of Nations, within twenty years of its creation, had clearly failed as a collective security organization. A new world war had begun, and the League itself was soon to be dissolved. How real had the possibility been of a different outcome? Might the collective security system have been a success? Any realistic answer would seem to require a rejection of the more extreme claims of the League's advocates, who found in the League a panacea for all international conflict, a capability of preventing war or defeating aggression in all circumstances. It would likewise seem to require a rejection of the more extreme claims of the League's critics, who were certain it would be unable to prevent any conflict in any circumstances.

The pertinent question would appear to be, under what circumstances might the collective security system have worked successfully, in preventing or defeating aggression? Here the starting point must be that the League of Nations itself at no time possessed any coercive power, which instead continued to be monopolized by individual states. The League's role was then, necessarily, that of a means whereby persuasion and pressure could be applied to the possessors of power, in an effort to get them to modify their behaviour. There was the possibility, in the long run, of modifying states' behaviour through institutionalized processes of multilateral debate and discussion of questions of common interest; through the establishment of new legal norms demanding the peaceful settlement of disputes; through providing, and encouraging the use of, new agencies of conciliation and judicial settlement. Efforts in all of these areas were made through the League, with varying degrees of support from the various member states. The difficult, but crucial, question remained, however, of what could be done when the system was challenged, techniques of peaceful settlement were rejected, and aggression was threatened or actually begun.

When faced with a specific threat of aggression, the effectiveness of the League system depended primarily, of course, on the response of those states possessing economic or military power which could be quickly and effectively applied to the immediate situation. This meant that the key roles were those of the major powers. For example, in the Sino-Japanese crisis of 1931-2 the only other substantial possessors of power in the Far East were Great Britain, the United States, and the Soviet Union, and their policies were thus all-important in determining whether or not any effective measures would be taken against Japan. In the Italo-Ethiopian crisis of 1935-6, this position was held by Great Britain and France, and to a lesser extent by the United States as a potential supplier of oil to Italy.

Whether the collective security system could work successfully, then, when confronted with specific aggressive actions, depended essentially on the configurations of power relative to the immediate situation, and the policies of those states possessing effective power. In some cases the system might have the potential of working as intended, and in other cases it might not. It is difficult to imagine in the 1920s and 1930s, for instance, the successful application of League sanctions against Great Britain or the United States, had either of those states undertaken a war of aggression. Against other powers, however, the potential for success was very high, and a few successes for the League system against would-be aggressors might well have had a major impact on the international system, serving as a deterrent against further resorts to violence.

The great tragedy of the 1930s was the failure to apply the League system in circumstances in which it could very well have worked successfully. Japan and Italy were, at the time of their aggressions, extremely vulnerable economically, and inferior to the other key powers in the naval strength which was crucial to their military operations. Germany, when Hitler came to power, was still almost completely disarmed, and in no position to threaten anyone until first permitted by the other powers to rearm. While situations can readily be visualized in which the collective security system could not have worked, there would appear to be nothing inevitable about its failures in the 1930s. Those failures can, rather, be attributed to a lack of commitment to the League system, and a failure of nerve in dealing with the aggressors, on the part of the political leaders in Britain, France, the United States, and the Soviet Union.

The role available to smaller powers, including Canada, in the League system was certainly less than that of the major powers, but was by no means without substance. Indeed, one of the important changes in the international system brought about by the founding of the League of Nations was that it gave all member states the opportunity to take part regularly in discussion of the full range of current international problems. Through their own advocacy and example, smaller powers had the opportunity to help build the new international structures for peaceful settlement of disputes, and thus to modify the previously prevailing patterns of international behaviour. In crisis situations, with a few major powers in the key decision-making roles, the smaller powers might be able to bring some effective pressure to bear on those major powers.

The extent to which minor powers could be influential in serious crisis situations was, of course, limited by the specifics of the situation. If the major powers had firmly and unequivocally decided on their own policies, there was little the minor powers could do. If, however, the major powers were undecided or uncommitted, there might well be substantial opportunity for minor power influence to be exerted. In the Manchurian crisis, there would appear to have been little that the smaller powers could have done. However vulnerable Japan may have been, neither Britain, the United States, nor the Soviet Union apparently had any intention of doing anything more than protest the Japanese actions. In the Italo-Ethiopian crisis, however, the situation was quite different. Britain and

France, the major powers with the key roles, were both subject to strong, but conflicting, internal political pressures regarding what action they should take. Both had substantial commitments to the collective security system, and an interest in maintaining it for the usefulness it might have to them in anticipated difficulties with Germany. The uncertainty in British and French policy, in combination with the structures for discussion and recommendation provided by the League, gave a great deal of room for small power influence to be exercised.

Canada's policy toward the League of Nations may be examined, then, in terms of what it, as a small power, might have done, and what it did do, to help bring about the successful functioning of the League in achieving its primary objective of preventing future wars. One type of activity which might have been undertaken was the active development of the League's conciliatory functions. Here the Canadian record was not substantial. Verbal endorsement was given to these functions, but not much else. Some initiative was taken in encouraging acceptance of the compulsory jurisdiction of the Permanent Court of International Justice, though not in actual use of the Court. An initiative of some importance was undertaken in 1929 through an attempt to strengthen the League's protection of minority rights in eastern Europe, but the initiative was really that of Raoul Dandurand, with no more than the acquiescence of the Mackenzie King government. Otherwise, Canadian policy was typically one of refusing to become involved in what were viewed as other people's problems. If Canada did not obstruct or interfere with the operation of the League's conciliatory functions, it also did little to promote or develop them.

Another related means of developing the League system in a positive way would have been to encourage discussion and co-operation through the League on matters of international concern, even though areas of what had traditionally been considered domestic jurisdiction were infringed on. Here Canada's record was almost entirely negative. Its main interest was in preventing League discussion and recommendation on such questions as tariffs, immigration, and minority rights as they related to Canada.

With regard to security questions, a positive contribution could be made by smaller powers through exerting as much influence as they could bring to bear to get the major powers to take seriously the Covenant's strong legal commitments to prevent successful aggression. Here Canada's influence was initially an emphatically negative one. From 1919 to 1923, the Borden, Meighen, and King governments led in an effort to undermine the security guarantees of Article 10, and to encourage League members to feel free to ignore them. In subsequent years, Canadian opposition to the attempts of other states to strengthen the collective security system, through the Treaty of Mutual Guarantee and the Geneva Protocol, represented the same point of view. By the summer of 1935, however, this approach had changed, and in the Committee of Thirteen considering the general question of economic sanctions, Canada was advocating that, if economic sanctions were to be applied, they should be comprehensive and effective.

In the Italo-Ethiopian conflict, the crisis which led finally to the collapse of the League system, the representatives of the Bennett government took a leading part in applying pressure to the British and French governments, through the League, to take the action that the Covenant called for. When King succeeded Bennett, this pressure was no longer exerted, except for the unauthorized actions of Walter Riddell, but was replaced by a policy of inactivity, neither obstructing nor encouraging the attempts of other states to make the collective system work. The repudiation of Riddell's oil sanction proposal, coming as it did when British policy was still wavering, in effect served to publicly withdraw any pressure on Britain to observe its obligations under the League Covenant.

Canadian policy toward the League of Nations was, then, primarily either neutral or harmful in its effects on the League's development and exercise of a capacity to prevent wars. This was not exclusively the case, however, and Canadian policy was not as consistent and undeviating as is sometimes assumed to be the case, as indicated by the Canadian initiative on the eastern European minorities question in 1929, and by the leading role briefly taken in support of economic sanctions in 1935.

The conclusion is nevertheless inescapable, in terms of the above frame of reference, that Canada's role in the League of Nations was indeed predominantly a negative one. The reasons for this have been discussed in the preceding chapters, but, in conclusion, may be summarized as follows:

1 During most of the period of the League's existence, Canada gave no more than a formal acceptance of the basic obligations of members, and often not even that. From the beginning, League membership was viewed primarily as a useful device for establishing Canada's right to a distinct and independent status internationally.

2 This approach to the League was essentially an expression of an isolationist policy, by political leaders who felt that Canada was free from danger, and had no important interests at stake in other parts of the world. Paradoxically, this isolationism was combined with a demand for full participation in the League system, for reasons unconnected with the basic objectives of that system.

3 Other, more constructive, alternatives were available within limits to Canada, as to other smaller powers. In particular, Canada was in a position to exert substantial influence on Britain because of the strong British desire for a common Empire foreign policy. This opportunity was seldom used, and British-Canadian relations were marked instead by trivial disagreements centring on policy details and status considerations.

4 The Canadian political system in effect left major foreign policy decision-making up to the prime minister, his civil service advisers, and those of his cabinet colleagues who were both influential with him and individually interested in foreign policy questions. A prime minister with strong foreign policy views along different lines from those which usually prevailed could probably have substantially reshaped Canadian foreign policy in this period. Important changes had begun to take place in 1935, because of a willingness of Prime Minister R.B. Bennett to support the collective security system, but came to an end when Mackenzie King succeeded Bennett. In general, in the absence of any strong, organized demand for change, there was probably nothing for a prime minister to gain politically and perhaps much to be risked by taking such initiatives.

5 Alternative policies were actively advocated by various individual Canadian political figures throughout the period under consideration, largely, however, on an unorganized and personal basis, and without any significant effect. Perhaps the most that can be said is that the policies that were followed in practice by the Canadian government cannot be attributed to a lack of awareness of alternatives.

6 If Canadian foreign policy in its relationship to the League of Nations can be viewed only as a failure, perhaps the essential reason was the very peripheral role which foreign policy played in Canada's political system. The exclusive or predominant concern of organized political bodies with domestic policy questions left the prime ministers a virtually free hand, and made the avoidance of 'unnecessary' foreign entanglements and controversies appear politically desirable.

In such circumstances, only the truly exceptional political leader could be expected to attempt to force difficult foreign policy decisions to be taken, or even to recognize the need for taking them. The prevailing political leadership in Canada was not that exceptional, any more than it was in most of the other powers, large or small. Such difficult decision-making could have been imposed on the political leaders who did hold office only by effectively organized, foreign policy-centred political action, if at all, but in Canada in the years between the great wars, as in so many other countries, no effective political action of that type existed.

Appendices

A. PROPOSED RESOLUTION OF THE LEAGUE COUNCIL,
REGARDING PROCEDURES FOR THE REVIEW OF
MINORITIES PETITIONS, SUBMITTED BY THE REPRESENTATIVE
OF CANADA (RAOUL DANDURAND), 4 MARCH 1929[1]

Petitions concerning racial, religious or linguistic minorities whether individual or collective, of a country which has signed a Minorities Treaty and originating either in that State or outside it, must be addressed to the Government concerned, with the request that it forward them to the Secretariat of the League of Nations within thirty days of receipt, if the Government does not feel it desirable to reply to the petitioners direct.

If the Government fails to satisfy the complainants, the latter, having received its reply, must give their reasons for maintaining their claims, and may at the same time request the Government concerned to forward all the correspondence which has been exchanged to the Secretariat of the League of Nations within thirty days of receipt of their final reply.

The Government must comply with this request and inform the petitioners that it has done so. It will at the same time communicate to them any additional observations it may think fit to add to the file.

If, within forty days following their request that their complaints and the whole of the file be forwarded to the Secretariat, the petitioners do not receive notice that this has been done, they may themselves forward to the Secretariat of the League duplicates of the documents forming the file, or simply their complaint alone, should they have received no reply from the Government.

In an exceptional case of extreme urgency the petitioners may in addressing their petition to the Government concerned, inform that Government that a copy of the petition has been addressed at the same time to the Secretary-General. The latter may take the steps laid down in the procedure now in force for urgent cases.

In order to be considered by the Council such petitions must conform to the following conditions:

(*a*) They must concern the protection of minorities as provided in the treaties;

(*b*) In particular, they must not be presented in the form of a demand for the rupture of the political ties between the minority in question and the State of which it forms part;

(*c*) They must not come from an anonymous or insufficiently specified source;

(*d*) They must be expressed without violence of language;

(*e*) They must contain information or state facts which have not recently formed the subject of a petition to the Council.

Should the Government concerned contest for any reason the receivability of a petition, the Secretary-General will lay the question of receivability before the Committee of the Council, as constituted below, which may if it thinks fit appoint a Sub-Committee to make a preliminary examination of this question.

To examine these petitions and the documents accompanying them, as described above, the Council decides to form a Committee, composed of all the members of the Council or their substitutes.

Special meetings of this Committee will be held on dates to be fixed by the Committee itself.

In investigating those petitions, the Committee of the Council may, if it thinks fit, refer the question to the Council, which will deal with it in such manner and will give such directions as may seem proper and effectual in the circumstances of the case.

If neither the Committee of the Council, nor any member of the Committee makes a report to the Council, the Committee shall decide in what cases and under what conditions a public communication shall be made.

B. 'NOTES BY L.C.C. [LORING C. CHRISTIE]
ON DISCUSSIONS WITH PRIME MINISTER BENNETT
RE CANADIAN POLICY IN THE ITALO-ABYSSINIAN CRISIS'[1]

Friday 13th September 1935 – 9.30 a.m. Skelton, Macdonald, Robertson* & myself meet at S. office. Hoare's speech at the Assembly Geneva is before us. We conclude Canada should say nothing at this stage of the affair – this being the lesser evil (though M. – a whole hog Leaguer – 'peace is indivisible' – would like us to jump in – and R. suggested R.B.B.† should say what he has to say in his Toronto campaign speech tomorrow night the 14th)

Later in the day the Cabinet meet and decide to say nothing. Canadian delegation are so informed by cable.

10.55 p.m. at Roxborough Apts. I am pulled out of bed and asked to join Skelton at East Block. R.B. has switched. At 9.30 p.m., having sent for Skelton, he says that after reading Hoare's speech again and then Laval's speech (which appeared in this afternoon's papers), he cannot welsh. Laval's last sentences have particularly got under his skin, namely:

He calls S. a 'welsher.' He drafts a cable to the Delegation at Geneva authorizing them, after a brief preamble, to give the following pledge:

'If unfortunately etc Canada is prepared to join the other members of the League in considering how the provisions of the Covenant may be collectively and effectively carried out'

I arrive at 11.10 to find this picture & that R.B. is taking the train at 11.45 to begin his campaign trip & will not be here again until the 25th. I point out that even South Africa has made her pledge conditional on 'unanimous action.' I go to the Rideau Club & get a copy of the afternoon 'Journal' carrying South Africa's pledge as follows:

I return to find S. on the 'phone with R.B. – S. reads to him South Africa's pledge. After some palaver Canada's pledge is redrafted over the phone to read:

'Canada is prepared to join the other members of the League in considering how by unanimous action peace can be maintained.' We then write in 'assured' as an alternative to 'maintained.'

R.B. wants this sent to the train, so he can have a final look at it before it is put on the wire. No messenger available, so S. asks me to take it down. I find Rod Finlayson‡ at the private car on the Toronto train. Rod, who had been wor-

---

* O.D. Skelton, J. Scott Macdonald, and Norman A. Robertson of the Department of External Affairs
† Prime Minister R.B. Bennett
‡ Bennett's private secretary

ried by the other formula, thinks this one all right. R.B. heaves in sight. He shakes hands & greets me as a 'welsher.' We go in the car. I tell him no other messenger was available, so I brought the thing along, but that I never did anything with greater regret or distaste. He prefers 'maintained' to 'assured.' He preaches about 'contracts,' he hurls Beauharnois* at me, taunts me with my insistence on the sanctity of the power contracts – says if he never did anything else in his life he would stand by Laval and Hoare. I tell him he is overriding the whole of previous Canadian interpretation of the Covenant & making a joke of our conceptions of parliamentary control of the issues of peace & war. He repeats 'welsher' – says if we're not ready to live up to our 'contracts' we had better get out etc. A lady arrives to say goodbye. She takes the stage and so I bring the message back to Skelton. It is turned over to the code clerk for dispatching.

S. and I review the day & find it farcical.

R.B. had no opportunity to consult his Cabinet about his change of mind. Rod Finlayson thought somebody else might have got at him but this is uncertain & not very likely in view of his known movements & engagements during the day.

---

* The Beauharnois Power Corporation, by whom Christie had recently been employed as legal adviser

Notes

CHAPTER 1

1 Glazebrook, *A History of Canadian External Relations*, I, 131-7; II, 94
2 *Ibid.*, I, 201-2, 212-3
3 *Ibid.*, II, 12
4 Glazebrook, *Canada at the Paris Peace Conference*, 138
5 Canada, Department of External Affairs, *Documents on Canadian External Relations, Volume 2, The Paris Peace Conference of 1919*, Ottawa 1969, 142. Hereafter cited as Canada, External Affairs, *Documents*, II
6 Borden, ed., *Robert Laird Borden*, II, 952
7 Canada, External Affairs, *Documents*, II, ii
8 Borden, ed., *Robert Laird Borden*, II, 946
9 Canada, External Affairs, *Documents*, II, 135
10 Borden, ed., *Robert Laird Borden*, II, 946
11 Canada, External Affairs, *Documents*, II, 138
12 *Ibid.*, 139
13 *Ibid.*, 136
14 *Ibid.*, 142
15 *Ibid.*, 147
16 Borden, ed., *Robert Laird Borden*, II, 952
17 Canada, External Affairs, *Documents*, II, 152
18 Glazebrook, *Canada at the Paris Peace Conference*, 60-1
19 Donnelly, *Dafoe of the Free Press*, 98
20 Canada, External Affairs, *Documents*, II, 225
21 Borden, ed., *Robert Laird Borden*, 955
22 *Ibid.*, 933
23 Canada, External Affairs, *Documents*, II, 225
24 Borden, ed., *Robert Laird Borden*, II, 959-60
25 Canada, External Affairs, *Documents*, II, 48

26 League of Nations, Document
c.215.M.154.1921, 4, 7-8
27 Canada, External Affairs,
Documents, II, 78-9. Canada,
House of Commons Debates,
2 Sept. 1919, 18
28 Miller, David Hunter, 'The Making
of the League of Nations.' In
Edward M. House and Charles
Seymour, eds., *What Really
Happened at Paris*, New York
1921, 411
29 Canada, External Affairs,
Documents, II, 93
30 *Ibid.*, 122
31 *Ibid.*, 120

CHAPTER 2

1 Canada, Department of External
Affairs, *Documents on Canadian
External Relations, Volume 2,
The Paris Peace Conference of
1919*, Ottawa 1969. Hereafter
cited as Canada, External Affairs,
Documents, II
2 Borden, ed., *Robert Laird Borden*,
II, chaps. 36-8
3 Wallace, *Sir George Foster*, 210
4 Canada, Department of External
Affairs, *Documents on Canadian
External Relations, Volume 3,
1919-1925*, Ottawa 1970, 172.
Hereafter cited as Canada, External
Affairs, *Documents*, III
5 Graham, *Arthur Meighen*, II, 55
6 *Ibid.*, III, 18-25
7 Canada, *House of Commons
Debates*, 19 Feb. 1929, 240-1
8 Dawson, *Mackenzie King:
Biography*, 403

9 *Ibid.*, 402
10 *Ibid.*, 428
11 Neatby, *Mackenzie King: The
Lonely Heights*, 194
12 Pickersgill, *Mackenzie King Record*,
I, 683
13 Canada, External Affairs,
Documents, II, 113
14 Dandurand, *Mémoires*, Québec
1967, 297-8
15 League of Nations Archives, file
27/61907/61907 (memorandum
of Distribution Branch, 27 Sept.
1927)
16 Canada, Department of External
Affairs, *Documents on Canadian
External Relations, Volume 4,
1926-1930*, Ottawa 1971, 623
17 Dandurand, *Mémoires*, 298
18 Neatby, *Mackenzie King: The
Lonely Heights*, 195
19 Canada, *House of Commons
Debates*, 12 April 1928, 1960-1
20 League of Nations, *Records of
the Fifth Assembly, Plenary Meetings, Text of the Debates*, 2 Oct.
1924, 222
21 Eayrs, '"A Low Dishonest Decade,"'
66-7
22 Pickersgill, *Mackenzie King Record*,
6-7
23 Neatby, *Mackenzie King: The
Lonely Heights*, 192
24 Eayrs, *The Art of the Possible*, 47
25 Canada, External Affairs,
Documents, III, 48-9
26 Eastman, *Canada at Geneva*, 4
27 Ollivier, Maurice, ed., *The Colonial
and Imperial Conferences from
1887 to 1937*, 3 vols. Ottawa
1954, III, 146

28 Keenleyside, H.L. 'Canada's Department of External Affairs.' *International Journal*, summer 1946, 204
29 Canada, *Senate Debates*, 3 March 1932, 73
30 Riddell, *World Security by Conference*, 175-6

CHAPTER 3

1 Canada, *House of Commons Debates*, 2 Sept. 1919, 18
2 *Ibid.*, 8 Sept. 1919, 78-9
3 *Ibid.*, 9 Sept. 1919, 140
4 *Ibid.*, 11 Sept. 1919, 230
5 *Ibid.*, 191
6 *Ibid.*, 198
7 *Ibid.*, 9 and 11 Sept. 1919, 130-31, 199-202
8 *Ibid.*, 8 Sept. 1919, 99-100
9 *Ibid.*, 11 Sept. 1919, 239-40
10 Canada, *Senate Debates*, 4 Sept. 1919, 51
11 Canada, *House of Commons Debates*, 1 Feb. 1923, 33
12 *Ibid.*, 21 June 1926, 4762
13 *Ibid.*, 12 April 1928, 1974
14 *Ibid.*, 15 June 1923, 3993
15 *Ibid.*
16 *Ibid.*, 3993-8
17 *Ibid.*, 8 April 1930, 1390-1
18 *Ibid.*, 25 May 1932, 3435
19 Eayrs, *The Art of the Possible*, 118; Canada, *House of Commons Debates*, 11 May 1931, 1466
20 Canada, *Senate Debates*, 15 March 1923, 196
21 *Ibid.*, 12 March 1925, 112-3
22 *Ibid.*, 31 March 1927, 237-9
23 McNaught, *A Prophet in Politics*, 82-5

24 *Ibid.*, 310-2
25 Canada, *House of Commons Debates*, 15 June 1923, 3996
26 *Ibid.*, 26 June 1925, 5047-8
27 *Ibid.*, 8 April 1930, 1393
28 *Ibid.*, 25 May 1932, 3438
29 *Ibid.*, 27 March 1934, 1856-7
30 Neatby, *Mackenzie King: The Lonely Heights*, 327-8
31 *Ibid.*, 387-90
32 Williams, John R. *The Conservative Party of Canada: 1920-1949*, Durham, NC 1956, 111-12
33 *Ibid.*, 123-5
34 Canada, Committee on Election Expenses, *Studies in Canadian Party Finance*, Ottawa 1966, 161-2, 165, 168
35 Canada, Committee on Election Expenses, *Report of the Committee on Election Expenses*, Ottawa 1966, 250-1; Williams, *Conservative Party*, 124-5
36 Cook, ed., *The Dafoe-Sifton Correspondence*, 45. Sifton to Dafoe, 19 Nov. 1920
37 *Ibid.*, 70-71. Dafoe to Sifton, 18 May 1921
38 Donnelly, *Dafoe of the Free Press*, xxiii
39 *Canadian Annual Review*, 1923, 45
40 Canada, *House of Commons Debates*, 29 May 1928, 3515
41 *Canadian Annual Review*, 1923, 44
42 League of Nations Archives, file 22/34072/5635. H.G. Richardson to J.H. Bieler, 17 Jan. 1924
43 *Ibid.*, file 22/34072/5635. H.G. Richardson to Sir Eric Drummond, 1 Nov. 1924

44 *Ibid.*, file 50/14121/14121.
J.H. Bieler to Secretary-General,
23 Aug. 1929
45 *Ibid.*
46 Canada, *House of Commons
Debates*, 22 June 1920, 3961-3,
3975-7
47 League of Nations Archives, file
22/8491/8491. F.P. Walters to
Pierre Comert, 13 Nov. 1920;
Walters to W.A. Riddell, 22 Nov.
1920
48 *Ibid.*, file 40/11288/9990. Sir
Herbert Ames to Sir Eric Drummond, 3 May 1921
49 *Ibid.*, file 22/8491/8491. Ames to
N.W. Rowell, 28 Oct. 1921
50 *Ibid.*, file 40/16842/9990
51 *Ibid.*, file 26/19738/19738. Ames
to W.L.M. King, 9 Feb. 1922
52 *Ibid.*, file 40/16842/9990. Ames
to Sir Robert Borden, 28 Feb.
1922
53 *Ibid.*, file 26/19738/19738. Ames
to Drummond, 13 March 1922
54 *Ibid.*, file 40/16842/9990. Ames
to Raoul Dandurand, 4 June 1925
55 *Ibid.*, file 50/14121/14121.
J.H. Bieler to Secretary-General,
23 Aug. 1929
56 *Interdependence*, March 1933, 3
57 League of Nations Archives, file
50/9965/9965. Report by Miss
McGeachy, undated
58 *Ibid.*, file 50/17785/17785.
C.P. Meredith to H.R. Cummings,
12 March 1930
59 *Ibid.* Meredith to Drummond,
8 May 1930
60 *Ibid.* E.J. Tarr to H.R. Cummings,
3 April 1930

61 University of Manitoba Archives,
Dafoe Papers. Dafoe to J.H. Woods,
24 Aug. 1935
62 *Ibid.* McGeachy to Dafoe, 22 Aug.
and 5 Sept. 1932
63 League of Nations Archives, file
50/9965/9965. Report by Miss
McGeachy, undated

CHAPTER 4

1 League of Nations, *Records of the
First Assembly, Plenary Meetings*,
8 Dec. 1920, 328-9. Hereafter
cited as League of Nations, First
Assembly Debates
2 League of Nations, Fifth Assembly
Debates, 2 Oct. 1924, 221
3 League of Nations, Ninth Assembly
Debates, 7 Sept. 1928, 59-61
4 Canada, Department of External
Affairs, *Documents on Canadian
External Relations, Volume 5,
1931-1935*, Ottawa 1973, 314. R.B.
Bennett to C.H. Cahan, 2 Dec. 1932.
Hereafter cited as Canada, External
Affairs, *Documents*, v
5 League of Nations, *Records of the
Special Session of the Assembly
convened in virtue of Article 15 of
the Covenant at the Request of the
Chinese Government*, vol. III, 59
6 League of Nations, First Assembly
Debates, 10 Nov. 1920, 171
7 League of Nations, *Records of the
First Assembly, Meetings of the
Committees*, II, 191; League of
Nations, First Assembly Debates,
17 Dec. 1920, 646-8
8 Canada, *House of Commons
Debates*, 18 Feb. 1921, 117

9 Canada, Department of External Affairs, *Documents on Canadian External Relations, Volume 3, 1919-1925*, Ottawa 1970, 73-4. Hereafter cited as Canada, External Affairs, *Documents*, III

10 League of Nations, First Assembly Debates, 16 Dec. 1920, 589

11 League of Nations, Second Assembly Debates, 27 Sept. 1921, 458; League of Nations, Third Assembly Debates, 22 Sept. 1922, 204

12 Canada, Department of External Affairs, *Documents on Canadian External Relations, Volume 4, 1926-1930*, Ottawa 1971, 604-7. Hereafter cited as Canada, External Affairs, *Documents*, IV. W.A. Riddell to O.D. Skelton, 22 March 1926, 605-7; Riddell to Skelton, 14 April 1926

13 Wallace, *The Memoirs of the Rt. Hon. Sir George Foster*, 216

14 Canada, *House of Commons Debates*, 22 June 1925, 4628

15 *Ibid.*, 17 Feb. 1927, 385-6

16 *Ibid.*, 14 May 1928, 2965; 16 May 1928, 3064

17 Walters, *A History of the League of Nations*, 148

18 Canada, External Affairs, *Documents*, III, 444

19 *Ibid.*, 450

20 *Ibid.*, 455

21 Canada, External Affairs, *Documents*, IV, 691-2

22 League of Nations, *Records of the Eleventh Ordinary Session of the Assembly, Meetings of the Committees, Minutes of the Third Committee*, 66

23 Walters, *A History of the League of Nations*, 223

24 Canada, External Affairs, *Documents*, III, 533-4. Sir Joseph Pope to Secretary-General, 26 April 1923

25 *Ibid.*, 534. Ernest Lapointe to W.L.M. King, 12 June 1923

26 *Ibid.*, 534-5. Pope to Secretary-General, 19 June 1923

27 League of Nations, *Records of Fifth Assembly, Minutes of Third Committee*, Annex 3, 145-6

28 Walters, *A History of the League of Nations*, 276

29 League of Nations, Fifth Assembly Debates, 2 Oct. 1924, 222

30 Dandurand, *Mémoires*, 273-4

31 Canada, External Affairs, *Documents*, III, 549. Informal Interdepartmental Committee on the Protocol of Geneva to W.L.M. King, 2 March 1925

32 Dandurand, *Mémoires*, 274

33 Canada, External Affairs, *Documents*, III, 552. W.L.M. King to Secretary-General, 9 March 1925

34 Canada, *House of Commons Debates*, 9 Feb. 1925, 12, 24

35 Canada, *Senate Debates*, 12 March 1925, 112-3, 115

36 *Ibid.*, 29 April 1925, 167-9

37 *Ibid.*, 6 May 1931, 188

38 *Ibid.*, 19 May 1921, 509

39 Dandurand, *Mémoires*, 274

40 Ollivier, Maurice, ed., *The Colonial and Imperial Conferences from 1887 to 1937*, vol. III, Ottawa 1954, 157

41 Canada, *Senate Debates*, 31 March 1927, 237-9

42 Canada, *House of Commons Debates*, 28 May 1928, 3459, 3461

43 Canada, *Senate Debates*, 13 April 1927, 400

44 Canada, *House of Commons Debates*, 28 May 1928, 3473-4

45 Canada, *Senate Debates*, 17 April 1934, 249

46 Canada, External Affairs, *Documents*, IV, 639-40. Secretary of State for External Affairs to Dominions Secretary, 23 Jan. 1929

47 Canada, *House of Commons Debates*, 19 Feb. 1929, 248

48 Canada, External Affairs, *Documents*, IV, 640-1. Dominions Secretary to Secretary of State for External Affairs, 9 Feb. 1929

49 *Ibid.*, 644. Secretary of State for External Affairs to Dominions Secretary, 7 March 1929

50 Canada, *House of Commons Debates*, 7 May 1929, 2299

51 Canada, External Affairs, *Documents*, IV, 649-50. Ramsay MacDonald to W.L.M. King, 22 June 1929

52 League of Nations, Eleventh Assembly Debates, 30 Sept. 1930, 163

53 *Ibid.*, 164-5

54 Public Archives of Canada, R.J. Manion Papers, vol. 81

55 Canada, *House of Commons Debates*, 8 Feb. 1932, 59

56 League of Nations, *Records of the Conference for the Reduction and Limitation of Armaments, Series B. Minutes of the General Commission*, I, 134

57 League of Nations, *Records of the Conference for the Reduction and Limitation of Armaments, Series A. Verbatim Records of Plenary Meetings*, I, 102

58 Eastman, *Canada at Geneva*, 6-8

59 League of Nations, First Assembly Debates, 10 Nov. 1920, 170

60 *Ibid.*, 178

61 League of Nations, *Records of the First Assembly, Meetings of the Committees*, I, 132

62 Walters, *A History of the League of Nations*, 233

63 League of Nations, *Records of Eleventh Assembly, Minutes of Second Committee*, 50, 84, 88

64 League of Nations, Eleventh Assembly Debates, 1 Oct. 1930, 184

65 League of Nations, *Records of Twelfth Assembly, Minutes of Second Committee*, 38, 54

66 League of Nations Archives, file 5B/4523/2381. Joseph Avenol to Massimo Pilotti and F.P. Walters, 1 July 1933; Avenol to R.B. Bennett, 22 Aug. 1933

67 Canada, External Affairs, *Documents*, III, 433. O.D. Skelton to W.A. Riddell, 20 April 1925

68 *Ibid.*, 433. Austen Chamberlain to W.L.M. King, 11 June 1925

69 *Ibid.*, 434. W.A. Riddell to O.D. Skelton, 9 Sept. 1925

70 *Ibid.*, 392. Colonial Secretary to Governor General, 22 Jan. 1920

71 *Ibid.*, 408. Administrator to Colonial Secretary, 26 April 1930

72 *Ibid.*, 420. Minute of Meeting of British Empire Delegation, 8 Nov. 1920

73 *Ibid.*, 395. Memorandum by L.C. Christie, 9 Feb. 1920
74 *Ibid.*, 399. Memorandum by C.J. Doherty, 17 Feb. 1920
75 *Ibid.*, 409-10. Administrator to Colonial Secretary, 1 May 1920
76 League of Nations, *Minutes of Council, Thirty-Second Session*, 9 Dec. 1924, 128
77 Canada, External Affairs, *Documents*, III, 551-2. Governor General to Colonial Secretary, 8 March 1925
78 *Ibid.*, IV, 611. Raoul Dandurand to O.D. Skelton, 26 June 1926
79 *Ibid.*, 621-2. Governor General to Dominions Secretary, 18 May 1927; Dominions Secretary to Governor General, 27 May 1927
80 Dandurand, *Mémoires*, 306
81 *Ibid.*, 270
82 *Ibid.*, 272
83 *Ibid.*, 281
84 *Ibid.*, 341
85 *Ibid.*, 333
86 League of Nations, First Assembly Debates, 16 Dec. 1920, 589
87 Dandurand, *Mémoires*, 270; Canada, *Senate Debates*, 29 April 1925, 165
88 Borden, ed., *Robert Laird Borden*, II, 1011-2
89 Canada, External Affairs, *Documents*, IV, 614. W.H. Walker to Sir George Foster, 5 Aug. 1926
90 League of Nations, *Minutes of the Conference of States Signatories of the Protocol of Signature of the Statute of the Permanent Court of International Justice*, 29-32
91 Canada, External Affairs, *Documents*, IV, 700-1. W.L.M. King to United States Minister, 30 May 1928
92 League of Nations, First Assembly Debates, 170; League of Nations, Records of First Assembly, Meetings of the Committees, I, 132
93 Canada, *Senate Debates*, 29 April 1925, 167-9

CHAPTER 5

1 League of Nations, *Records of the First Assembly, Plenary Meetings*, 4 Dec. 1920, 275. Hereafter cited as League of Nations, First Assembly Debates
2 *Ibid.*, 6 Dec. 1920, 279-81
3 League of Nations, Document C.110.M.62.1921.V
4 League of Nations Archives, file 40/11360/4368
5 League of Nations, First Assembly Debates, 17 Dec. 1920, 648
6 League of Nations Archives, file 40/12043/4368
7 League of Nations, Document C.215.M.154.1921
8 Canada, *House of Commons Debates*, 21 Feb. 1921, 158
9 *Ibid.*, 3 March 1921, 521
10 *Ibid.*, 20 April 1921, 2367
11 *Ibid.*, 2368
12 *Ibid.*, 21 April 1921, 2371-2
13 League of Nations, Committee on Amendments to the Covenant, A.C. Procès-Verbaux 9A
14 League of Nations, Document A.24(1).1921.V., 10-14

15 League of Nations, Committee on Amendments to the Covenant, Third Meeting, Minutes of the Third Session

16 League of Nations Archives, file 40/15482/4368

17 League of Nations, Document A.24(1).1921.v., 4

18 *Ibid.*, 3

19 League of Nations, *Records of the Second Assembly, Meetings of the Committees*, I, 191-3

20 *Ibid.*, 109, 113

21 *Ibid.*, 109-13

22 *Ibid.*, 114

23 League of Nations, *Records of the Second Assembly, Plenary Meetings*, 4 Oct. 1921, 834

24 Scarrow, Howard A. *Canada Votes: A Handbook of Federal and Provincial Election Data*, New Orleans 1962, 34-5

CHAPTER 6

1 Canada, *House of Commons Debates*, 19 June 1922, 3170

2 League of Nations, *Records of the Third Assembly, Meetings of the Committees, Minutes of the First Committee*, 24

3 *Ibid.*, 23

4 *Ibid.*, 12

5 *Ibid.*, 24-6

6 *Ibid.*, 32

7 League of Nations, *Records of the Third Assembly, Plenary Meetings, Volume I, Text of the Debates*, 23 Sept. 1922, 212-15

8 *Ibid.*, 216-7

9 *Ibid.*, 217-8

10 Canada, *Report of the Canadian Delegates to the Third Assembly of the League of Nations*, 3-4

11 League of Nations, *Records of the Fourth Assembly, Meetings of the Committees, Minutes of the First Committee*, 44-53

12 *Ibid.*, 11

13 *Ibid.*, 14-18

14 *Ibid.*, 24-8

15 League of Nations, *Records of the Fourth Assembly, Plenary Meetings, Text of the Debates*, 24 Sept. 1923, 75

16 *Ibid.*, 76

17 *Ibid.*, 25 Sept. 1923, 80

18 *Ibid.*, 81-5

19 *Ibid.*, 85-6

20 *Ibid.*, 87

21 League of Nations, *Records of the Seventh Ordinary Session of the Assembly, Meetings of the Committees, Minutes of the First Committee*, 25

22 Ollivier, Maurice, ed., *The Colonial and Imperial Conferences from 1887 to 1937*, vol. III, Ottawa 1954, 35

23 Canada, *Report of the Canadian Delegates to the Fourth Assembly of the League of Nations*, Ottawa 1924

24 Canada, Department of External Affairs, *Documents on Canadian External Relations, Volume 4, 1926-1930*, Ottawa 1971, 701

25 Walters, *A History of the League of Nations*, 259

26 Canada, *Senate Debates*, 12 March 1925, 122

27 PAC, R.J. Manion Papers, vol. 81, file 49
28 Canada, *Senate Debates*, 1 May 1934, 329
29 PAC, R.J. Manion Papers

CHAPTER 7

1 Archives of the Department of External Affairs, file 1362-22. Sir Auckland Geddes to Governor General, 15 Dec. 1922. Hereafter cited as External Affairs Archives
2 *Ibid.* Colonial Secretary to Governor General, 7 April 1923
3 League of Nations, Document C.500.1923.VII
4 External Affairs Archives, file 1362-22. Sir Eric Drummond to Secretary of State for External Affairs, 3 May 1923
5 *Ibid.* Sir Joseph Pope to Secretary-General, 25 May 1923
6 *Ibid.* Van Panhuys to Drummond, 13 July 1923
7 League of Nations Archives, file 11/29540/28075. G.H.F. Abraham to Van Hamel, 31 July 1923
8 *Ibid.*, Van Hamel to Abraham, 3 Aug. 1923
9 External Affairs Archives, file 1362-22. Ames to King, 4 Aug. 1923
10 *Ibid.* Colonial Secretary to Governor General, 30 Aug. 1923; Governor General to Colonial Secretary, 4 Sept. 1923
11 League of Nations Archives, file 11/30035/28075. Deskaheh to Drummond, 6 Aug. 1923; Avenol

to Deskaheh, 14 Aug. 1923; *ibid.*, file 11/30626/28075. Deskaheh to de la Torriente, 4 Sept. 1923; Drummond to Deskaheh, 7 Sept. 1923
12 Kelen, *Peace in Their Time*, 147-9
13 League of Nations Archives, file 11/31340/28075
14 External Affairs Archives, file 1362-22. Duncan C. Scott to Sir Joseph Pope, 19 Oct. 1923
15 League of Nations, Document C.770.1923
16 League of Nations Archives, file 11/32700/28075. Ames to King, 28 Dec. 1923, and attached memoranda
17 League of Nations, Document C.21.1924.VII
18 League of Nations Archives, file 11/32700/28075. Drummond to President of Council, 18 Jan. 1924
19 *Ibid.*, file 11/33556/28075. Deskaheh to Branting, 10 Jan. 1924; Erik Boheman to Walters, 21 Jan. 1924; Walters to Boheman, 24 Jan. 1924
20 *Ibid.*, file 11/32700/28075. Branting to Drummond, 24 Jan. 1924; League of Nations, Documents C.21.1924.VII. and C.70.1924.VII
21 External Affairs Archives, file 1362-22
22 *Ibid.*, Colonial Secretary to Governor General, 12 March 1924, and enclosures
23 *Ibid.* Foreign Secretary to Minister in Esthonia, 7 March 1924; Consul at Reval to Minister at Riga, 7 April 1924

24 League of Nations Archives, file 11/32700/28075. Pope to Ames, 23 Feb. 1924

25 League of Nations, *Official Journal*, June 1924, 829-42

26 External Affairs Archives, file 1362-22. Chargé d'Affaires in Teheran to Foreign Secretary, 10 May 1924

27 *Ibid.* Clipping from Toronto *Globe*, 8 Oct. 1924

CHAPTER 8

1 H.W.V. Temperley, ed., *A History of the Peace Conference of Paris*, vol. 5, London 1924, 442

2 Canada, Department of External Affairs, *Documents on Canadian External Relations, Volume 4, 1926-1930*, Ottawa 1971, 627

3 League of Nations Archives, Section Files, Minorities Section. Hereafter cited as League of Nations Archives, Minorities Section Files

4 *Ibid.*

5 *Ibid.*

6 League of Nations, *Official Journal, Minutes of the Council, Fifty-Third Session*, 68, 70. Hereafter cited as League of Nations, Minutes of Council Session

7 League of Nations Archives, file 4/9900/3418

8 Archives of the Department of External Affairs, file 235-27. Drummond to Georges P. Vanier, 10 Jan. 1929. Hereafter cited as External Affairs Archives

9 *Ibid.* Vanier to O.D. Skelton, 11 Jan. 1929

10 *Ibid.* Dandurand to Skelton, 21 Jan. 1929

11 *Ibid.*

12 *Ibid.* Skelton to Dandurand, 26 and 30 Jan. 1929 PAC, Collection of Papers from the Office of the Under Secretary of State for External Affairs, vol. 103, Skelton to Philippe Roy, 14 Feb. 1929. Hereafter cited as PAC, Skelton Papers

13 External Affairs Archives, file 235-27. Dandurand to Skelton, 30 Jan. 1929

14 League of Nations Archives, file 4/9513/3418; League of Nations, Document C.51.1929.I

15 PAC, Skelton Papers, vol. 103. Skelton to Philippe Roy, 14 Feb. 1929; Skelton to Dandurand, 14 Feb. 1929

16 External Affairs Archives, file 235-27. Drummond to Vanier, 4 Feb. 1929

17 *Ibid.* Pearson to Dandurand, 6 Feb. 1929

18 League of Nations Archives, file 4/10751/3418. F.P. Walters to Minorities Section, 21 Feb. 1929

19 External Affairs Archives, file 235-27. Clipping from *New York Times*, 19 Feb. 1929; Canadian Advisory Officer to Secretary of State for External Affairs, 26 Feb. 1929

20 *Ibid.* Pearson to Skelton, 20 Feb. 1929, reporting conversations with British High Commissioner's Office

21 League of Nations Archives, file
4/9513/3418. Azcárate to Aguirre
de Cárcer, 25 Feb. 1929
22 *Ibid.* Note by Drummond, 26 Feb.
1929. Buero to Drummond,
1 March 1929
23 League of Nations, Minutes of 54th
Council Session, 516
24 *Ibid.*, 522-30
25 *Ibid.*, 541
26 League of Nations Archives,
Minorities Section Files
27 *Ibid.*
28 League of Nations, *Official Journal,
Special Supplement No. 73, Documents Relating to the Protection
of Minorities by the League of
Nations*, Geneva 1929, 6-7. Hereafter cited as League of Nations,
Minorities Documents
29 *Ibid.*, 30-32
30 *Ibid.*, 7-9, 15
31 *Ibid.*, 6-7, 12-13, 15
32 Dandurand, *Mémoires*, 329
33 League of Nations, Minorities
Documents, 15-16, 24
34 League of Nations, Minutes of
55th Council Session, 1006-7
35 League of Nations, *Official Journal,
Records of the Tenth Ordinary
Session of the Assembly, Plenary
Meetings, Text of the Debates*,
4 Sept. 1929, 43-4
36 Canada, *Senate Debates*, 11 April
1929, 94-5
37 *Ibid.*, 98-101, 116-7
38 *Ibid.*, 95
39 League of Nations Archives,
Minorities Section Files
40 *Ibid.*

CHAPTER 9

1 PAC, R.J. Manion Papers, vol. 81,
file 49
2 Archives of the Department of
External Affairs, file 786-31.
Skelton to Marler, 23 Jan. 1932.
Hereafter cited as External Affairs
Archives
3 PAC, Collection of Papers from the
Office of the Under Secretary of
State for External Affairs, vol. 10.
Memorandum by Skelton, 'Manchurian Question,' dated 29 Nov.
1932. Hereafter cited as PAC,
Skelton Papers
4 PAC, Manion Papers, vol. 81, file 49
5 *Ibid.*
6 *Ibid.*
7 Canada, *House of Commons
Debates*, 8 Feb. 1932, 30
8 Canada, *Senate Debates*, 8 Feb.
1932, 11
9 Canada, *House of Commons
Debates*, 7 April 1932, 1826
10 *Ibid.*, 25 May 1932, 3440
11 *Ibid.*, 21 Nov. 1932, 1369-70
12 Eayrs, *The Art of the Possible*, 135
13 Donnelly, *Dafoe of the Free Press*,
146
14 Canada, *House of Commons
Debates*, 25 May 1932, 3437
15 League of Nations, *Records of the
Conference for the Reduction and
Limitation of Armaments, Series A.
Verbatim Records of Plenary
Meetings, Volume I*, 13 Feb. 1932,
102-3
16 League of Nations, *Records of the
Special Session of the Assembly*

convened in virtue of Article 15 of the Covenant at the Request of the Chinese Government, vol. I, 74. Hereafter cited as League of Nations, Special Assembly Records

17 Canada, Department of External Affairs, *Documents on Canadian External Relations, Volume 5, 1931-1935*, Ottawa 1973, 307. Secretary of State for External Affairs to Perley, 27 Feb. 1932. Hereafter cited as Canada, External Affairs, *Documents*, V

18 Riddell, *World Security by Conference*, 73-4

19 University of Manitoba Archives, J.W. Dafoe Papers. Mary Craig McGeachy to Dafoe, 20 Oct. 1932

20 Riddell, *World Security by Conference*, 74

21 Canada, External Affairs, *Documents*, V, 313-14 Bennett to Cahan, 2 Dec. 1932

22 External Affairs Archives, file 786-31. Cahan to Acting Prime Minister, 7 Dec. 1932

23 *Ibid.* Acting Prime Minister to Cahan, 7 Dec. 1932 (initialled by Skelton)

24 Canada, External Affairs, *Documents*, V, 322. Riddell to Skelton, 13 Dec. 1932

25 Eastman, *Canada at Geneva*, 93

26 League of Nations, Special Assembly Records, III, 57-9

27 *Ibid.*, 57

28 League of Nations, Special Assembly Records, III, 65-6

29 External Affairs Archives, file 786-31. Li Tchuin to Skelton, 9 Dec. 1932

30 *Ibid.* Riddell to Skelton, 10 and 13 Dec. 1932

31 Canada, External Affairs, *Documents*, V, 328. Skelton to Riddell, 7 Jan. 1933

32 Riddell, *World Security by Conference*, 77

33 PAC, R.B. Bennett Papers, vol. 429, 272783. Cahan to Bennett, 9 Dec. 1932

34 Canada, External Affairs, *Documents*, V, 321. Skelton to Herridge, 12 Dec. 1932

35 *Ibid.*, 323. Marler to Secretary of State for External Affairs, 19 Dec. 1932

36 External Affairs Archives, file 786-31. Marler to Skelton, 9 Feb. 1933

37 *Ibid.* Bennett to Riddell, 19 Dec. 1932

38 York University Archives, W.A. Riddell Papers. Cahan to Riddell, 23 Dec. 1932

39 Canada, External Affairs, *Documents*, V, 324-7. Skelton to Riddell, 24 Dec. 1932

40 York University Archives, Riddell Papers. Diary entry for 7 Feb. 1933

41 Canada, External Affairs, *Documents*, V, 328. Skelton to Riddell, 7 Jan. 1933

42 University of Manitoba Archives, Dafoe Papers. McGeachy to Dafoe, 31 Jan. 1933

43 Donnelly, *Dafoe of the Free Press*, 146

44 Canada, External Affairs, *Documents*, V, 328. Skelton to Riddell, 7 Jan. 1933

45 Canada, *House of Commons Debates*, 30 Jan. 1933, 1664

46 *Ibid.*

47 Canada, External Affairs, *Documents*, V, 321. Skelton to Herridge, 12 Dec. 1932

48 York University Archives, Riddell Papers. Diary entry for 14 Feb. 1933

49 Canada, External Affairs, *Documents*, V, 332. Skelton to Bennett, 18 Feb. 1933; External Affairs Archives, file 786-31. Skelton to Riddell, 18 Feb. 1933

50 *Ibid.* Memorandum by Robertson, 'Sino-Japanese Dispute,' dated 18 Feb. 1933

51 *Ibid.* Bennett to Riddell, 18 Feb. 1933

52 Canada, External Affairs, *Documents*, V, 333. Bennett to Ferguson, 18 Feb. 1933

53 League of Nations, Special Assembly Records, IV, 21

54 External Affairs Archives, file 786-31. Riddell to Secretary of State for External Affairs, 24 Feb. 1933

55 Canada, *House of Commons Debates*, 24 Feb. 1933, 2431

56 *Interdependence*, March 1933, 1-13

57 Canada, *House of Commons Debates*, 16 May 1933, 5059-67, 5068-9

58 *Ibid.*, 5068

59 *Ibid.*, 5067

60 *Ibid.*, 5067-8

61 *Interdependence*, July 1933, 138

CHAPTER 10

1 PAC, R.J. Manion Papers, vol. 81, file 50. O.D. Skelton to Manion, 1 July 1933, and enclosed memorandum by L.B. Pearson, 'The Problem of Security and Sanctions in the Light of Recent Developments at Geneva'

2 *Interdependence*, Sept.-Dec. 1933 and Mar. 1935

3 *Ibid.*, Sept.-Dec. 1933, 170-71

4 Quoted in Canada, *Senate Debates*, 24 April 1934, 291

5 League of Nations Archives, file 13/19008/4389

6 Canada, *House of Commons Debates*, 15 March 1934, 1534

7 *Ibid.*, 1 April 1935, 2292-4

8 *Ibid.*, 21 March 1934, 1690-3

9 *Ibid.*, 1704-6

10 *Ibid.*, 1706-8

11 Canada, *Senate Debates*, 21 March 1934, 181

12 *Ibid.*, 1 Feb. 1934, 45

13 Canada, *House of Commons Debates*, 27 March 1934, 1856-7

14 Canada, *Senate Debates*, 17 April 1934, 237-44

15 *Ibid.*, 244-51

16 *Ibid.*, 251-3

17 *Ibid.*, 1 May 1934, 326-36

18 *Ibid.*, 29 May 1934, 418-20

19 *Ibid.*, 30 May 1934, 437

20 *Ibid.*, 31 May 1934, 447-50

21 *Ibid.*, 451

22 *Interdependence*, Mar. 1935, 4-8

23 PAC, W.L.M. King Papers, volume D51

24 Canada, *House of Commons Debates*, 1 April 1935, 2307

25 League of Nations Archives, file 50/9965/9965. Undated report by Miss M.C. McGeachy on interview with R.B. Bennett

26 York University Archives, W.A. Riddell Papers. Diary entry for 11 Aug. 1933

27 League of Nations Society in Canada, *Report of Annual Meeting, 1934*

28 Watkins, Ernest. *R.B. Bennett: A Biography*, Toronto 1963, 170

29 Canada, *Senate Debates*, 17 Jan. 1935, 2

30 Canada, *House of Commons Debates*, 12 Feb. 1934, 495-8

31 Canada, Department of External Affairs, *Documents on Canadian External Relations, Volume 5, 1931-1935*, Ottawa 1973, 498. Secretary of State for External Affairs to G.H. Ferguson, 4 Feb. 1934. Hereafter cited as Canada, External Affairs, *Documents*, V

32 League of Nations, *Records of the Fifteenth Ordinary Session of the Assembly, Meetings of the Committees, Minutes of the Sixth Committee*, Annex 1, 97

33 *Ibid.*, 25

34 League of Nations, *Official Journal, Minutes of the Council, Eighty-Fifth (Extraordinary) Session*, 551-2

35 *Ibid.*, 565

36 Riddell, *World Security by Conference*, 90-91

37 Canada, External Affairs, *Documents*, V, 361. Riddell to Secretary of State for External Affairs, 25 April 1935

38 Archives of the Department of External Affairs, file 65-D-1-35. Memorandum, 'Considerations arising out of Riddell's telegram No. 46 of April 17th,' dated 18 April 1935. Hereafter cited as External Affairs Archives

39 York University Archives, Riddell Papers. Diary entry for 5-10 May 1935

40 *Ibid.*

41 Canada, External Affairs, *Documents*, V, 360. Acting Secretary of State for External Affairs to Riddell, 20 April 1935. External Affairs Archives, file 65-D-1-35. Sir George Perley to R.B. Bennett, 27 April 1935

42 Riddell, *World Security by Conference*, 91

43 Canada, External Affairs, *Documents*, V, 364. Riddell to Secretary of State for External Affairs, 18 May 1935

44 League of Nations, *Official Journal*, July 1935, 909

45 League of Nations, *Official Journal, Minutes of the Council, Eighty-Fifth (Extraordinary) Session*, 551

46 York University Archives, Riddell Papers. Diary entry for 16 May 1935. Canada, External Affairs, *Documents*, V, 364. Riddell to Secretary of State for External Affairs, 18 May 1935

47 *Ibid.* Diary entry for 21 May 1935

48 Canada, External Affairs, *Documents*, V, 368-9. Secretary of State for External Affairs to Riddell, 26 May 1935

49 League of Nations Archives, Document cosc/1st Session/ p.v.1.(1)-7(1), 24-6

50 *Ibid.*, 66-71

51 External Affairs Archives, file 65-D-1-35. Riddell to Skelton, 30 May 1935

52 League of Nations Archives, Document cosc/7.(1)

53 External Affairs Archives, file 65-D-1-35. Memorandum, 'Sanctions: Withholding of Key Products from an Aggressor Country,' dated 17 June 1935. Canada, External Affairs, *Documents*, v, 372. Secretary of State for External Affairs to Riddell, 8 July 1935 (initialled by Skelton)

54 Riddell, *World Security by Conference*, 96

55 Canada, External Affairs, *Documents*, v, 371-2. Secretary of State for External Affairs to Riddell, 8 July 1935

56 Riddell, *World Security by Conference*, 96-7

57 External Affairs Archives, file 65-D-1-35. Riddell to Skelton, 19 July 1935

58 League of Nations Archives, Document cosc/7.(1)

59 *Ibid.*, Document cosc/6

60 Canada, External Affairs, *Documents*, v, 374-5. Secretary of State for External Affairs to Riddell, 23 July 1935

61 League of Nations Archives, Document cosc/2nd Session/ p.v.1(1)-6(1), 6

62 *Ibid.*, 8

63 *Ibid.*, 25-6

64 *Ibid.*, 29-30

65 *Ibid.*, 47, 50. League of Nations Archives, file 1/19413/18161

66 External Affairs Archives, file 65-D-1-35. Riddell to Skelton, 5 Aug. 1935

CHAPTER 11

1 Canada, Department of External Affairs, *Documents on Canadian External Relations, Volume 5, 1931-1935*, Ottawa 1973, 380. O.D. Skelton to W.D. Herridge, 23 Aug. 1935. Hereafter cited as Canada, External Affairs, *Documents*, v

2 Eayrs, James, *In Defence of Canada: Appeasement and Rearmament*, 4-5

3 *Winnipeg Free Press*, 16 Aug. 1935

4 Quoted in Eayrs, *In Defence of Canada: Appeasement and Rearmament*, 4

5 *Winnipeg Free Press*, 7 Sept. 1935

6 Canada, External Affairs, *Documents*, v, 382. Secretary of State for External Affairs to Dominions Secretary, 3 Sept. 1935

7 Archives of the Department of External Affairs, file 927-34. W.A. Riddell to Secretary of State for External Affairs, 13 Sept. 1935. Hereafter cited as External Affairs Archives

8 *Ibid.* Secretary of State for External Affairs to Riddell, 13 Sept. 1935

9 *Ibid.* 'Notes by L.C.C. on discussions with Prime Minister Bennett

re Canadian Policy in the Italo-Abyssinian Crisis,' undated

10 Canada, External Affairs, *Documents*, V, 383. Secretary of State for External Affairs to Riddell, 13 Sept. 1935

11 League of Nations, *Records of the Sixteenth Ordinary Session of the Assembly, Plenary Meetings, Text of the Debates*, 14 Sept. 1935, 77-8. Hereafter cited as League of Nations, Sixteenth Assembly Debates

12 Avon, Earl of (Anthony Eden). *The Eden Memoirs: Facing the Dictators*, London 1962, 269

13 Canada, External Affairs, *Documents*, V, 388. Skelton to R.K. Finlayson, 9 Oct. 1935

14 *Ibid.*, 386. R.B. Bennett to Riddell, 9 Oct. 1935

15 External Affairs Archives, file 927-34. G.H. Ferguson to Secretary of State for External Affairs, 9 Oct. 1935

16 Canada, External Affairs, *Documents*, V, 387-9. Skelton to Finlayson, 9 Oct. 1935

17 External Affairs Archives, file 927-34. Memoranda by W.A. Riddell and L.B. Pearson of telephone conversation between G.H. Ferguson and R.B. Bennett, 9 Oct. 1935

18 Canada, External Affairs, *Documents*, V, 391-2. Memorandum by O.D. Skelton of telephone conversation with R.B. Bennett, 10 Oct. 1935

19 League of Nations, Sixteenth Assembly Debates, 10 Oct. 1935, 113-14

20 Canada, External Affairs, *Documents*, V, 390. Acting Secretary of State for External Affairs to Ferguson, 10 Oct. 1935

21 *Ibid.*, 403-4. Skelton to Riddell, 1 Nov. 1935

22 League of Nations, *Co-ordination Committee, Committee of Eighteen and Sub-Committees; Minutes of the First Session*, 30. Hereafter cited as League of Nations, Co-ordination Committee Minutes

23 *Ibid.*, 30-31

24 *Ibid.*, 46, 53-5

25 Scarrow, Howard A., *Canada Votes: A Handbook of Federal and Provincial Election Data*, New Orleans 1962, 90

26 University of Manitoba Archives, J.W. Dafoe Papers. Miss M.C. McGeachy to J.W. Dafoe, 15 Oct. 1935

27 Canada, External Affairs, *Documents*, V, 393. Riddell to Secretary of State for External Affairs, 14 Oct. 1935

28 *Ibid.* Secretary of State for External Affairs to Riddell, 15 Oct. 1935

29 *Ibid.* Riddell to Skelton, 15 Oct. 1935

30 *Ibid.*, 394. Skelton to Riddell, 15 Oct. 1935

31 *Ibid.* Riddell to Skelton, 16 Oct. 1935

32 League of Nations Co-Ordination Committee Minutes, First Session, 93-4, 104

33 *Ibid.*, 80

34 University of Manitoba Archives, J.W. Dafoe Papers. Miss McGeachy to Dafoe, 18 Oct. 1935

35 Canada, Department of External Affairs, *Documents Relating to the Italo-Ethiopian Conflict*, Ottawa 1936, 165-6

36 Riddell, *World Security by Conference*, 114

37 League of Nations Archives, Co-ordination Committee Minutes, Second Session, 56, 58

38 York University Archives, W.A. Riddell Papers. Diary entry for 1 Nov. 1935

39 Canada, *House of Commons Debates*, 11 Feb. 1936, 93

40 Canada, External Affairs, *Documents*, v, 405. Secretary of State for External Affairs to Riddell, 2 Nov. 1935

41 Riddell, *World Security by Conference*, 115

42 Canada, External Affairs, *Documents*, v, 421-2. Riddell to Skelton, 7 Dec. 1935. Riddell, *World Security by Conference*, 121-3

43 Riddell, *World Security by Conference*, 123-4. York University Archives, Riddell Papers. Diary entry for 2 March 1936

44 League of Nations, Co-ordination Committee Minutes, Second Session, 38

45 *Ibid.*, 46-7, 68-9

46 Templewood, Viscount (Sir Samuel Hoare). *Nine Troubled Years*, London 1954, 177

47 York University Archives, Riddell Papers. N.W. Rowell to Riddell, 1 Nov. 1935

48 *Ibid.* Riddell to Rowell, 21 Nov. 1935

49 Riddell, *World Security by Conference*, 124

50 Ghébali, Victor-Yves. 'Les délégations permanentes auprès de la Société des Nations,' Geneva 1969, mimeo., 77-83

51 Canada, *House of Commons Debates*, 11 Feb. 1936, 93

52 Canada, External Affairs, *Documents*, v, 405. Riddell to Secretary of State for External Affairs, 2 Nov. 1935

53 *Ibid.*, 405-6. Secretary of State for External Affairs to Riddell, 4 Nov. 1935

54 *Ibid.*, 406-8. Riddell to Secretary of State for External Affairs, 5 Nov. 1935. Secretary of State for External Affairs to Riddell, 7 Nov. 1935

55 League of Nations Archives, file 1/20612/20441. Riddell to Secretary of Co-ordination Committee, 8 Nov. 1935

56 Public Archives of Canada, W.L. Mackenzie King Papers, vol. 164. 'Press references to oil embargo as a Canadian proposal,' undated

57 External Affairs Archives, file 927-34. Vincent Massey to W.L.M. King, 29 Nov. 1935

58 Canada, External Affairs, *Documents*, v, 410. Skelton to Laurent Beaudry, 26 Nov. 1935

59 *Ibid.*, 412. Beaudry to Skelton, 28 Nov. 1935

60 *Ibid.*, 413. Skelton to Beaudry, 29 Nov. 1935

61 *Ibid.* Acting Secretary of State for External Affairs to Skelton, 29 Nov. 1935

62 *Ibid.*, 414. Skelton to Acting Secretary of State for External Affairs, 29 Nov. 1935

63 Canada, Department of External Affairs, *Documents Relating to the Italo-Ethiopian Conflict*, 172

64 Riddell, *World Security by Conference*, 128-30

65 *Ibid.*

66 York University Archives, Riddell Papers. Diary entry for 7 Dec. 1935

67 PAC, Ernest Lapointe Papers, vol. 33, file 149. 'Press Opinion, A Review of Canadian Editorial Opinion Prepared for The League of Nations Society in Canada,' 9 Dec. 1935

68 External Affairs Archives, file 927-34. 'Summary of expressions of opinion about Canadian statement on oil embargo,' Dec. 1935

69 PAC, R.B. Bennett Papers, vol. 424. Clippings from *Hamilton Spectator*, 2 Dec. 1935, and *Toronto Telegram*, 3 Dec. 1935

70 External Affairs Archives, file 927-34. Chargé d'Affaires, Washington, to Secretary of State for External Affairs, 2 Dec. 1935

71 *Ibid.* 'Summary of expressions,' etc., Dec. 1935

72 PAC, Lapointe Papers, vol. 31, file 139A. Rowell to Lapointe, 2 Dec. 1935

73 External Affairs Archives, file 927-34. Rowell to Lapointe, 2 Dec. 1935

74 York University Archives, Riddell Papers. Rowell to Riddell, 3 Dec. 1935

75 PAC, Lapointe Papers, vol. 31, file 139A. Raoul Dandurand to Lapointe, 4 Dec. 1935

76 *Interdependence*, vol. 12, no. 4, 1935

77 PAC, Lapointe Papers, vol. 31, file 139A. Lapointe to R.B. Inch, 5 Dec. 1935

78 External Affairs Archives, file 927-34. Lapointe to Rowell, 3 Dec. 1935

79 Canada, External Affairs, *Documents*, V, 417. Secretary of State for External Affairs to Riddell, 6 Dec. 1935

80 *Ibid.*, 416-17. Riddell to Secretary of State for External Affairs, 5 Dec. 1935

81 *Ibid.*, 417. Secretary of State for External Affairs to Riddell, 6 Dec. 1935

82 York University Archives, Riddell Papers. Diary entry for 3 Dec. 1935

83 *Ibid.* Diary entry for 7 Dec. 1935

84 External Affairs Archives, file 927-34. Pearson to Skelton, 23 Dec. 1935

85 Canada, External Affairs, *Documents*, V, 425-6. Secretary of State for External Affairs to Pearson, 11 Dec. 1935. Canada, Department of External Affairs, *Documents on Canadian External Relations, Volume 6, 1936-1939*, Ottawa 1972, 876-7. Secretary of State for External Affairs to Riddell, 29 Feb. 1936

86 Canada, External Affairs, *Documents*, V, 426. Secretary of State for External Affairs to Pearson, 11 Dec. 1935

87 Canada, *House of Commons Debates*, 10 Feb. 1936, 40

88 *Ibid.*, 11 Feb. 1936, 97-8

89 *Ibid.*, 126-7

90 *Ibid.*, 2 March 1936, 667

91 *Ibid.*, 675-8

92 York University Archives, Riddell Papers. Diary entry for 6 April 1936

93 Riddell, *World Security by Conference*, 141

94 University of Manitoba Archives, Dafoe Papers. Grant Dexter to Dafoe, 17 Dec. 1935

CHAPTER 12

1 Canada, *House of Commons Debates*, 18 June 1936, 3869-70

2 *Ibid.*, 3871-2

3 *Ibid.*, 3872

4 League of Nations, *Records of the Seventeenth Ordinary Session of the Assembly, Plenary Meetings, Text of the Debates*, 29 Sept. 1936, 68-9. Hereafter cited as League of Nations, Seventeenth Assembly Debates

5 Canada, *House of Commons Debates*, 18 June 1936, 3896

6 *Ibid.*, 3873, 3878

7 *Ibid.*, 25 Jan. 1937, 259-60

8 *Ibid.*, 260

9 *Ibid.*, 27 Jan. 1937, 321

10 *Ibid.*, 4 Feb. 1937, 547

11 *Ibid.*, 19 Feb. 1937, 1063-4

12 Morton, ed., *The Voice of Dafoe*, 94, 96. From *Winnipeg Free Press*, 1 Oct. 1936

13 *Ibid.*, 81. From *Winnipeg Free Press*, 18 June 1937

14 Quoted in Eayrs, *In Defence of Canada: Appeasement and Rearmament*, 37. Diary entry for 21 Sept. 1936

15 *Ibid.*, 40. W.L.M. King to Lord Tweedsmuir, 10 July 1937

16 Quoted in Massey, *What's Past Is Prologue*, 235

17 *Ibid.*, 233

18 *Ibid.*, 233-4. Diary entry for 21 Sept. 1937

19 *Ibid.*, 234

20 Riddell, *World Security by Conference*, 142. Raoul Dandurand to Riddell, 8 May 1936

21 Canada, *House of Commons Debates*, 13 May 1936, 2771

22 Massey, *What's Past Is Prologue*, 237-9. Diary entry for 11 May 1936

23 Canada, *House of Commons Debates*, 18 June 1936, 3867-8

24 *Ibid.*, 3893-4

25 League of Nations, Sixteenth Assembly Debates, Part II, 1 July 1936, 34

26 League of Nations, Seventeenth Assembly Debates, 29 Sept. 1936, 69

27 League of Nations Archives, Document CSP/IIIrd session/P.V.4

28 Canada, *House of Commons Debates*, 24 May 1938, 3182

29 PAC, Collection of Papers from the Office of the Under Secretary of State for External Affairs, vol. 51. Secretary of State for External Affairs to Secretary of State for Dominion Affairs, 18 Aug. 1938. Hereafter cited as PAC, Skelton Papers

30 League of Nations, *Records of the Nineteenth Ordinary Session of the Assembly, Meetings of the Committees, Minutes of the Sixth Committee*, 30

31 Walters, *A History of the League of Nations*, 781

32 League of Nations, *Records of the Nineteenth Ordinary Session of the Assembly, Meetings of the Committees, Minutes of the Sixth Committee*, 61-2. League of Nations, Nineteenth Assembly Debates, 30 Sept. 1938, 99

33 Massey, *What's Past Is Prologue*, 234. Diary entry for 21 Sept. 1937

34 Canada, *House of Commons Debates*, 21 Feb. 1938, 632

35 *Ibid.*, 18 June 1936, 3873-4

36 *Ibid.*, 22 June 1936, 4106

37 League of Nations, Seventeenth Assembly Debates, 29 Sept. 1936, 67-9

38 Canada, *Senate Debates*, 19 Jan. 1937, 12

39 Canada, *House of Commons Debates*, 25 Jan. 1937, 237

40 *Ibid.*, 4 Feb. 1937, 564

41 PAC, Skelton Papers, vol. 51. Secretary of State for External Affairs to H.H. Wrong, 11 Dec. 1939

42 League of Nations, *Records of the Twentieth Ordinary Session of the Assembly, Plenary Meetings*, 14 Dec. 1939, 36

43 League of Nations, *Records of the Twentieth (Conclusion) and Twenty-first Ordinary Sessions of the Assembly, Text of the Debates*, 10 April 1946, 40

APPENDIX A

1 League of Nations, Document C.51(1).M.36.(1).1929.I

APPENDIX B

1 Archives of the Department of External Affairs, file 927-34

Selected bibliography

The following are the more important sources and secondary works which were used in the preparation of this manuscript. Additional references are cited in the footnotes accompanying each chapter.

UNPUBLISHED SOURCES

Governmental documents

Canada
Archives of the Department of External Affairs, Ottawa
Collection of Papers from the Office of the Under Secretary of State for
    External Affairs (O.D. Skelton Papers), Public Archives of Canada, Ottawa

League of Nations
League of Nations Archives, United Nations Library, Geneva

Collections of private papers

BENNETT, R.B. Papers, Public Archives of Canada, Ottawa
DAFOE, J.W. Papers, University of Manitoba Archives, Winnipeg
KING, W.L. MACKENZIE Papers, Public Archives of Canada, Ottawa
LAPOINTE, ERNEST Papers, Public Archives of Canada, Ottawa
MANION, R.J. Papers, Public Archives of Canada, Ottawa
RIDDELL, WALTER A. Papers, York University Archives, Toronto

PUBLISHED SOURCES

Governmental documents

Canada
Documents on Canadian External Relations, vols. 2-6. Ottawa 1919-39
Documents Relating to the Italo-Ethiopian Conflict. Ottawa 1936
House of Commons Debates. Ottawa 1919-39
Report of the Canadian Delegates to the Assembly of the League of Nations.
   Ottawa 1922-39
Senate Debates. Ottawa 1919-39

League of Nations
*Dispute Between Ethiopia and Italy, Co-ordination of Measures under Article 16
   of the Covenant. Co-ordination Committee, Committee of Eighteen and Sub-
   Committees. Minutes.* Geneva 1935-6
Minutes of the Council. Geneva 1920-39
*Records of the Assembly, Plenary Meetings, Text of the Debates. Meetings of the
   Committees, Minutes.* Geneva 1920-46. Title varies
Records of the Conference for the Reduction and Limitation of Armaments.
   Geneva 1932-4

Other published sources
BORDEN, HENRY, ed. *Robert Laird Borden: His Memoirs.* 2 vols. London 1938
CHRISTIE, LORING C. 'Notes on the Development at the Peace Conference of the
   Status of Canada as an International Person' (July 1919). *External Affairs* XVI,
   1964, 163-72
COOK, RAMSAY, ed. *The Dafoe-Sifton Correspondence, 1919-1927.* Manitoba
   Record Society Publications, vol. 2. Altona, Man. 1966
DAFOE, JOHN W. 'A Foreign Policy for Canada.' *Queen's Quarterly* XLII, 1935,
   161-70
– 'Canada, the Empire and the League.' *Foreign Affairs* XIV, 1936, 297-308
– 'Canada's Interest in the World Crisis.' *Dalhousie Review* XV, 1936, 477-84
– 'Canadian Foreign Policy.' *Conference on Canadian-American Affairs.
   Proceedings.* Boston, New York, Montreal, and London 1937, 220-31
DANDURAND, RAOUL *Les Mémoires du Sénateur Raoul Dandurand (1861-1942),*
   ed. Marcel Hamelin. Québec 1967
EASTMAN, S. MACK *Canada at Geneva. An Historical Survey and Its Lessons.*
   Toronto, 1946
Interdependence The official journal of the League of Nations Society in Canada.
   Ottawa 1928-36

MASSEY, VINCENT *What's Past Is Prologue. The Memoirs of the Right Honourable Vincent Massey.* Toronto 1963

MORTON, W.L., ed. *The Voice of Dafoe: A Selection of Editorials on Collective Security, 1931-1944, by John W. Dafoe.* Toronto 1945

PEARSON, LESTER B. *Mike. The Memoirs of the Right Honourable Lester B. Pearson.* Vol. 1, 1897-1948. Toronto 1972

– 'Reflections on Inter-war Canadian Foreign Policy.' *Journal of Canadian Studies* VII, 1972, 36-42

POWER, CHARLES G. *A Party Politician. The Memoirs of Chubby Power*, ed. Norman Ward. Toronto 1966

RIDDELL, WALTER A. *World Security by Conference.* Toronto, Halifax and Vancouver 1947

– ed. *Documents on Canadian Foreign Policy, 1917-1939.* Toronto 1962

WALTERS, F.P. *A History of the League of Nations.* London, New York, and Toronto 1952

UNPUBLISHED SECONDARY WORKS

BOTHWELL, R.S., and J.R. ENGLISH '"Dirty Work at the Crossroads": New Perspectives on the Riddell Incident.' Paper read at the annual meeting of the Canadian Historical Association, 1972

PAGE, DONALD M. 'Canadians and the League of Nations Before the Manchurian Crisis.' PH D thesis, University of Toronto 1972

PUBLISHED SECONDARY WORKS

CARTER, GWENDOLEN M. *The British Commonwealth and International Security: The Role of the Dominions, 1919-1939.* Toronto 1947

COOK, RAMSAY *The Politics of John W. Dafoe and The Free Press.* Toronto 1963

DAWSON, R. MACGREGOR *William Lyon Mackenzie King: A Political Biography, 1874-1923.* Toronto 1958

DONNALLY, MURRAY *Dafoe of the Free Press.* Toronto 1968

EAYRS, JAMES '"A Low Dishonest Decade": Aspects of Canadian External Policy, 1931-1939.' In Hugh L. Keenleyside *et al., The Growth of Canadian Policies in External Affairs.* Durham, NC 1960, 59-80

– *The Art of the Possible: Government and Foreign Policy in Canada.* Toronto 1961

– *In Defence of Canada.* Vol. 1, *From the Great War to the Great Depression.* Toronto 1964. Vol. 2, *Appeasement and Rearmament.* Toronto 1965

GLAZEBROOK, G.P. de T. *A History of Canadian External Relations*, rev. ed. Toronto 1966. Vol. 2, *In the Empire and the World, 1914-1939*

- *Canada at the Paris Peace Conference.* London, Toronto, and New York 1942
GRAHAM, ROGER *Arthur Meighen: A Biography.* 3 vols. Toronto and Vancouver 1960-5
GREATHED, EDWARD D. 'Antecedents and Origins of the Canadian Institute of International Affairs.' *Empire and Nations: Essays in Honour of Frederic H. Soward,* ed. Harvey L. Dyck and H. Peter Krosby. Toronto 1969
KELEN, EMERY *Peace in Their Time: Men Who Led Us In and Out of War, 1914-1945.* New York 1963
MACKAY, R.A., and E.B. ROGERS *Canada Looks Abroad.* London, Toronto, and New York 1938
MACKINTOSH, W.A. 'O.D. Skelton.' *Canada's Past and Present: A Dialogue,* ed. Robert L. McDougall. Toronto 1965, 59-77
MANSERGH, NICHOLAS *Survey of British Commonwealth Affairs: Problems of External Policy, 1931-1939.* London, New York, and Toronto 1952
MCNAUGHT, KENNETH *A Prophet in Politics: A Biography of J.S. Woodsworth.* Toronto 1959
MUNRO, JOHN A. 'The Riddell Affair Reconsidered.' *External Affairs* XXI, 1969, 366-75
- 'Loring Christie and Canadian External Relations, 1935-1939.' *Journal of Canadian Studies* VII, 1972, 28-36
NEATBY, H. BLAIR *William Lyon Mackenzie King: 1924-1932, The Lonely Heights.* Toronto 1963
PICKERSGILL, J.W. *The Mackenzie King Record.* Vol. 1, 1939-44. Toronto 1960
POPE, MAURICE, ed. *The Memoirs of Sir Joseph Pope.* Toronto 1960. For the period after 1907, this is a biographical account written by the editor.
PRANG, MARGARET 'N.W. Rowell and Canada's External Policy, 1917-1921.' *Report of the Annual Meeting of the Canadian Historical Association* 1960, 83-103
SKILLING, H. GORDON *Canadian Representation Abroad: From Agency to Embassy.* Toronto 1945
SOWARD, FREDERIC H. 'Canada and the League of Nations.' *International Conciliation* no. 283, 1932, 359-95
- 'Canada and Foreign Affairs.' *Canadian Historical Review* XVII, 1936, 179-93; XVIII, 1937, 178-98
- *et al. Canada in World Affairs: The Pre-War Years.* London, Toronto, and New York 1941
WADE, MASON *The French Canadians,* rev. ed. Vol. 2, 1911-67. Toronto 1968
WALLACE, W. STEWART *The Memoirs of the Rt. Hon. Sir George Foster.* Toronto 1933. A biographical account based in part on an unfinished autobiography

Index